Joy in the Heart

MYSTICAL PATHS OF THE WORLD'S RELIGIONS

ELIZABETH CLARE PROPHET

SUMMIT UNIVERSITY PRESS®
Gardiner, Montana

JOY IN THE HEART
Mystical Paths of the World's Religions
by Elizabeth Clare Prophet

For information, contact
The Summit Lighthouse, 63 Summit Way, Gardiner, MT 59030 USA
Tel: 1-800-245-5445 or 1 406-848-9500
info@SummitUniversityPress.com
SummitLighthouse.org

Library of Congress Control Number: 2022940280
ISBN: 978-1-60988-418-5 (softbound)
ISBN: 978-1-60988-419-2 (eBook)

SUMMIT UNIVERSITY PRESS®

25 24 23 22 1 2 3 4

CONTENTS

NOTE TO THE READER

The dictations and lectures in this book were first released during the 1992 Freedom Conference, *Joy in the Heart,* held in the Heart of the Inner Retreat, at the Royal Teton Ranch, Park County, Montana, from June 26 to July 5. The first lecture from the conference, "Keys from Judaism: The Kabbalah and the Temple of Man," is published with additional material in the book *Kabbalah: Key to Your Inner Power.* The second lecture, "Roots of Christian Mysticism," is published in the book *Becoming God: The Path of the Christian Mystic.* Another lecture, "The Buddhic Essence," is published in the book with that title.

Two lectures, "The Inner Path of Hinduism" and the first portion of "The Worship of the Goddess: The Path of the Divine Mother," have not yet been published in print. All the dictations and the remaining lectures from the conference were first published in the 1992 *Pearls of Wisdom,* vol. 35, nos. 25–57, and are included in this book. All the lectures and dictations from the conference are available from AscendedMasterLibrary.org.

In the original *Pearls of Wisdom,* bracketed material denoted words unspoken yet implicit in the dictation, added by the Messenger under the Masters' direction for clarity in the written word. For easier reading, the brackets have been omitted from this edition.

CHAPTER 1

El Morya as the Patriarch Abraham

FRIENDSHIP WITH GOD

Take the Leap in Consciousness!

The sons and daughters of God shall inherit the earth! But you must lay claim to the earth and claim it for Almighty God and the God within *you* and the God within the seed of the generations of Lightbearers that yet go forth through my own heart.

I am in the presence and the mantle of Abram and Abraham. And I AM THAT I AM. Know me, then, as father. Know me, then, as the descendant of *Keter.* Know me as *Hokhmah.*

Yes, beloved, the patriarchs and the prophets and the avatars do embody the mighty Tree of Life and do deliver down through the ages even the emphasis on this and another. When you know me as the Ascended Master, you see the full complement and the great harmony, through that living Son of God that I AM, of all of the *sefirot.*

Yes, beloved, I come that you might know a profile of the testing of my soul as warrior and as patriarch, as devotee of God, as one who knew the LORD and to whom the LORD did come. And therefore, the seed of Sanat Kumara, descended through me, is yet to be seen in the fullness of its glory.

I ask you, then, to polish even the "smoking furnace and the burning lamp."[1] Let there be the time, therefore, whereby the vessels of the four lower bodies are strengthened, strengthened in the might of the LORD, that you might understand that the earth is overrun even as Canaan was overrun with those evolutions who took the way of *Din* and rebelled against the mercy of God. And the mercy of God is the Universal Christ. And therefore, it is left unto the sons and daughters of God to call forth not the judgment that is the brand of the judgment and the judging of the fallen ones but the judgment of the LORD that is meted out through the Seven Archangels.

Yes, the Seven Archangels and the eighth and the ninth and the tenth, they do also embody the mighty *sefirot.* And therefore, should you come to know which of the *sefirot* is assigned to each one, you might thereby have a greater access to the Causal Body of those mighty Archangels of the LORD.

I shall not give this teaching unto you this night. For to impart the secrets for the unlocking of the names of God in the hierarchies of Light must come to those who advance in Maitreya's Mystery School and exhibit by years of sacred trust their capacity to keep the honor flame of God and to honor the Light and to honor the garment of the Light and to see that it is not soiled.

Therefore, beloved, I am called Abraham, the Friend of God.[2] I invite you to become friends of God, to cast down your idols, even as I did cast down the idols of Terah, my father.[3] I did dare to challenge anyone who did not place himself under the one God and the one LORD.

Therefore, cast down your idols! I speak to all and every one of you who come from near and afar. The idolatry of the human person and the human self cannot stand in the day of the mighty lamp of God! Know, then, the power of the Light, sacred-fire intensity within the furnace, beloved.

Therefore the sacred fire is available, but it is not accessible to you when you are in a state of idolatry of any human person or any personality, including the personality of an Ascended Master. It is to the Light that you bow and to the Universal Light. Therefore speak not of the greatness of this one or that one, lest you find yourselves outside of this camp.

This, then, is the inner walk with God. Be stripped, then, this night of your self-attachment, self-idolatry! Be stripped and know that the shield of the LORD is your exceeding great reward[4] when you cleave unto the LORD and the LORD only. Know the effacement of self and then know the appearance of the God Self within you.

How can I speak through this vessel except the vessel be emptied and therefore I may enter?

How can I speak through the vessel if the vessel be not stern in the strength of God, fierce and terrible before Evil and uncompromising with friend or loved one or enemy?

For all receive the love of the Sacred Heart of this one [my Messenger], and therefore I can impart that love to you, multiplying the intensity of the heart that my Messenger does embody. I seek to multiply the love of your heart. Therefore, let the fat be consumed by the fire of the lamp, by the fire of the furnace, by the fire of the Mighty I AM Presence!

Oh, be willing to be the chalice of God! If the heart be not perfected, the Son cannot enter.

If *Tiferet,* then, does not enter, how shall the mighty *Keter* and the *Malkut* therefore be one?

The compassionate Christ, the compassionate Buddha, the compassionate Krishna—are not these, then, the friends of God?

I give you a moment of silence that you might contemplate whether or not you consider yourself to be a true friend of God.

[21-second pause]

Friendship with God begins with trust. My trust, then, in the LORD God became the bonding of my soul to God, wherein I put my trust in the LORD and the LORD put his trust in me and entrusted unto me, beloved, the responsibility to give birth to and to nurture your souls forever and forever and forever until you should become the stars, one with your Causal Bodies.

Now you know why I have tarried so long with this stubborn and stiff-necked generation of those who have received so much and yet have taken that "so much" unto a course of self-idolatry while denying others the same freedoms that they demand for themselves. I trust I will not find any of you in this category, yet search your hearts. For you have come to a retreat whereby your soul might enter the path of true mysticism.

I, Abraham, am a mystic of old, always pursuing in my soul that bonding unto the LORD, being willing to leave my country, my father's house, my people to venture forth, and go forth knowing not where I would end up.

The will of God is indeed good. Praise YOD HE VAU HE! Praise God that the will of God is good and that it takes you step by step across the karmic highways of a distant past that must now be fulfilled.

"Trust in the LORD and obey." These are the words of the Psalmist. Make them your own. By faith, *"by faith,"* it is written, "Abraham obeyed God."[5] By faith did the great Lights of old achieve that communion.

Therefore, bind the beast within the temple, the carnal mind and the intellect, which reasons away the directives of conscience: that mighty inner voice of the Son of God—it is unerring. Listen, deliberate that you have listened carefully and truly, and then hasten to act! For each act taken in obedience to the voice of God, whether the voice within or the voice of the LORD God who does stand in the doorway of thy tent speaking to thee—each act in obedience takes you nearer to the place of the homing and the return and the hour when God shall surely give to the seed of Abraham, numberless as the stars,[6] all of the earth itself.

But yet the horror that I witnessed in that deep sleep was the realization of the four hundred years of bondage,[7] that and much more unto the hour of the present, when yet this people do not understand the true meaning of the Inner God and the Inner Son.

I say, let the breach be healed!

And in the sacrifice that I offered, beloved, there was a separation of the parts.[8] And the separation of the parts of the animal sacrifice did signify that there was a separation in this people, a separation between the soul and the I AM THAT I AM. And therefore, there did come down in the very center the angel of the LORD.

And to bring them together and thus to wed the soul to God does necessitate the true internalization of the Son in all of the joy and the beauty of that Universal Christ personified—yes, in the Lord and

Saviour Jesus Christ; personified, yes, in those who will accept that Christ as their own True Self.

So it is, beloved, that the Christ, who has become the chief cornerstone in the temple, is yet a stumbling block to many.[9] "We have no need of him. We are Sons of God also!" I am ashamed of such response to the one whom the LORD God did send into the world that the world through him might have eternal Life.[10]

Yes, there are many Sons of God. But until the Son of God be fully self-realized, that Son is yet a part of the Universal Christ and not individualized because not adored, not internalized, not surrendered to. Thus, beloved, until you determine to imitate that Christ by the mirror image of the soul, you will not be fully bonded to the Holy Christ Self. Therefore, until you pass through that initiation of Sonship and Christhood, you cannot lay claim to Sonship. For Sonship is opportunity, and if opportunity is denied, if opportunity is not taken when it is offered by the one who can impart and initiate that particular initiation, beloved, the cycles without Christhood must turn and they turn again for those who practice the denial of Christ both within and without.

And thus, for the two-thousand-year period of the age of Pisces, I still hear the word "We have no need of Jesus Christ—*We* are Sons of God." And I bow my head before the LORD, who came unto me with so great a promise, and I say:

"How long, O LORD, shall I struggle with this stiff-necked generation who know all things and yet know nothing, for they have not perceived the Son of God, nor in Jesus nor in themselves nor in their contemporaries nor in the little child who shall lead them!"

Therefore, the cleavage between the soul and the I AM THAT I AM remains and shall remain. And how long shall the LORD God extend opportunity unto those who in their spiritual pride deny their need for the Son of God? If they have no need for the Son of God, how can they have need for God himself?

I speak not only of those who are called whether the Hebrews or the Jews. I speak of all peoples who have lived under the dispensation of Jesus Christ in the age of Pisces and that not alone, but also in the golden-age civilization of Atlantis 35,000 years ago.[11] They come again and again and again!

What is this personal quarrel they have with the living Light of the ages?

Had God sent another Son or another, had another been chosen in heaven to be the fullness of the only begotten Son of the Father, full of grace and truth,[12] would they have rejected that one also?

Indeed they would! For the Christed ones have walked the earth. They have come. They have not had the full glory of the Lord Jesus Christ but they have fulfilled the requirements for the bonding to the heart of the Holy Christ Self, hence to the heart of Jesus.

There are not a few, beloved, and they walk the earth this day. But in each and every case where that Christ is raised up in the temple of the sons and daughters of Abraham, so that Christ, and therefore that one, is persecuted and not only persecuted but crucified.

Now I say, in the celebration of the five Sacred Hearts that you have taken up on the first Friday and the first Saturday of the month,[13] you can give the work that is needed to resolve this problem of the rejection of the Son of God in the person of Jesus Christ.

Thus, I have come as Abraham, your father, to plead with you to understand that it is the very force of Antichrist that came out of *Din* that turned judgment to become the destroyer of souls. That very force of Antichrist must be named in your invocations and decrees as the dweller-on-the-threshold of every fallen angel and of those who maintain the antithesis of the Tree of Life and the *sefirot,* those who have created the false, those who have created the substitution and the counterfeit. As you have been told, they live by a borrowed light, for they have no power of their own.

I ask, therefore, my sons and daughters, you whom I have shepherded in all ages and long before we came under my dispensation from Sanat Kumara in ages prior to Genesis—I ask you, then, to dedicate your services to the Sacred Heart of Jesus and the Immaculate Heart of Mary to the slaying of the worldwide force of Antichrist that allows my very own children of my very own loins to yet deny the Son of God within themselves. This does cause the holdup of the entire evolution of the planet and it will make laggards out of many who did begin as true children of the Light.

Yes, beloved, I have seen you again and again tackle the fierceness of the fallen ones arrayed against the Divine Mother in the earth in you and in the Messenger. Therefore, the hour has come when if you do not slay Antichrist that does go after the little ones full of such light who come forth from the womb, that does go after those of all ages and all levels and stations in life, there shall come a turning in the planet not toward Light but Darkness. For it is an hour when the people must choose whether Jesus Christ or Barabbas, whether the thief who has stolen the Light of the Zohar or the one who is the Saviour, who is able to bring together the bodies that have been cleaved.

Now then, beloved, I, in the person of your Guru then and now, fully intend to give you a map and an outline of what must be done systematically to deal with this force. It is a force deep in the core of the dweller-on-the-threshold. (Most of you here yet have the dweller-on-the-threshold, which does not completely dissolve until the hour of your ascension unless you have a specific attainment or have had specific intercession from me.)

Thus I say to you that at the core of the dweller-on-the-threshold within yourself is that point and it is the dot of the original beginning of the not-self. It is not the dot that produced the creation of you, the Christed being, but the dot that was the force, anti-Being.

That point, beloved, is what causes you to espouse Evil, to fall into the hands of the tempter, to deny the voice of the Inner Christ, to deny the giving of love and compassion in words of comfort when you could easily give them rather than remain silent. Therefore, each one must root out of himself that which is a force of division and separation whereby *Malkut, Tiferet* and *Keter* are not able to be as one.

It is a division in your members, which is dangerous. And all who have not come to resolution with the Son of God in heaven and the Son of God in the earth, as God has sent many, many servant-Sons through the ages, will have this point of the cleavage within, of the separation of their souls from God, and the profound angst, even that "angst" that is spoken of.

Yes, beloved, it is a deep nonresolution that will never come to resolution until you have made your peace with Jesus the Christ. You cannot make peace with the Son until you have made peace with the Father, and the reverse is the case. You cannot have peace with the Son unless you have made peace with the Mother and peace with the Holy Spirit.

Thus, the four personalities of the Godhead—the Father, Son, Holy Spirit and the Mother—must be raised up in you. This means you must come to a resolution within and without, at the level of the human consciousness and the divine consciousness, with this identity in all other persons in your life.

Do you understand what I speak of, beloved? ["Yes."]

The foundations of psychology that have been laid and taught to you under the guidance of the Ascended Master Kuthumi will take you to the place of understanding—yes, understanding. But that is where psychology stops. Psychology cannot give you the full power of that lamp and that furnace, the full sacred fire and the very smoking that does take place when there is intense, deep transmutation.

Yes, the LORD God initiated me that night that I might receive in trust the commission and go forth and never waver, even unto the present hour, in my responsibility to the seed of Light of Sanat Kumara.

Yes, beloved, there must be peace within your members. And some of you have stubbornly refused to examine the components of selfhood, have stubbornly avoided the altar, and therefore the fire could not leap to greet you!

For where were you when I came? There was an empty place at the rail, a space that you did not fill.

How can I impart the fire when you so remove yourselves?

I am with you every day!

Shall I tell you how many times I have simply withdrawn because I could not get your attention from outer focusing on the outer things of this world?

Well, I tell you, the events and personalities of the world will pass. And you will pass also. The question is: Will you come to the gates of Darjeeling full of the knowledge of this world and yet empty of the spiritual fire?

Try me. Try me! *Try me, I say!* Call for my fire if you desire a new self, for *purge you I will!* And if you dare to remain a dolt at the same level for the rest of your life, I, Abraham, will shun you. For how can you neglect so great a salvation?[14]

Salvation is the elevation of the soul through the ten *sefirot,* through the steps and stages. Acquaint now yourselves with Holy Justinius and the seraphim of God and know God as he sends his living flames of the *sefirot,* guarded and borne by the bearers, the seraphim themselves.

Every day is opportunity to receive of my fire!

How can you leave me and expect that I will follow you?

Shall I follow you to the ends of the earth?

Maybe. But, beloved, there is a timetable in your chart, and I speak of the chart of the Keeper of the Scrolls. There is a timetable. Therefore, read. Read of the wise one. So it is written: There is a time to sow and a time to reap, a time to be born and a time to die.[15] Yes, there is a time to face Morya squarely, to get straight your life, to love the will of God more than wealth and material things and indulgences and sensuality that does but waste the precious fire I give you. Come into alignment with me in this conference—ten days, ten *sefirot,* ten steps of consciousness.

I AM Abraham always and I nurture my own. But many a parent will tell you that for all the nurturing, the children did not quite make it. Thus, there must be a resiliency, a receptive chord. Do not become pillars of stone, therefore set in the gaze, the mien and the stance of the proud who think they have come far enough on the spiritual path and now can be above all others. Beloved ones, you are in your infancy, but you can quickly accelerate to be wise men and women, wise children of the Light.

And who are the wise ones?

The wise ones are those who pursue the bonding to *Tiferet, Tiferet,* the Son of God—yes, the bonding to the very center of cosmos, the very nucleus of the atom, the compassion, the fires of compassion.

I place my Electronic Presence over you so that you can feel in this very moment what it is like to surrender to God and walk with God and be happy in the greatest happiness you have ever known until joy spills from your faces as sunbeams come from your very auras and you are a sun center.

Do not fear to give up those attachments, for the will of God will lead you by the shortest distance to the very goal that you desire. Do not shun me or the will of God. Sanat Kumara has sent me to *you* personally. I have accompanied you to this *FREEDOM 1992.* I have come here. I have come to greet my own and I desire to do so from the very heart of Father.

Some of you have not known a father or have not had a good relationship with a father in this life or another life. The child within is keenly disappointed and does suffer for want of this true and so necessary association. Beloved ones, we understand these things. But unless we demand more than an understanding of our psychology, we shall remain in that rut.

You cannot lift yourself up by your bootstraps, but I, Morya, will take you on my magic carpet. (We have used them long centuries. It is not a myth.) And I will take you to new heights of consciousness. I will show you how you can be in thirty years—if this night you determine to make your resolution with the Father, with your own father in heaven and on earth and in me—that you might make your peace with the Son. You cannot love the Son in yourself if you do not love the Father who did bring you forth.

Therefore I ask you, do you love me as your father? ["Yes!"]

I come to you with the deepest love of my heart for healing, but you must know how to erase with the violet flame, how to encircle with Astrea's sword and circle of blue flame, how to bind the very record of that dweller-on-the-threshold, how to purge yourself of the patterns and even the misuse of the Light that sometimes well-meaning and sometimes not so well-meaning parents have put upon you.

I say this day, I am freeing you from this bondage and I am freeing you by sacred fire! And those of you who have studied the causes within and studied the books recommended whereby you might become masters of your own soul's psychology will find even a greater resolution for my coming and your coming.

Let us move forward together! Let us go hand in hand! I place my

Electronic Presence with each one of you as your father. I am exclusively and uniquely your own. It is a one-on-one relationship. You can have all of me to yourself, each one of you. For I AM that Son whose point of origin is the Great Central Sun, and therefore the Light that passes through me to you is the replication again and again and again of beloved Alpha. Thus, beloved, know this relationship and accept it as sufficient.

If you yet yearn for the human relationship that can never be because the father is no longer here, not accessible or available or does not have the capacity to be father, then what will you do? Will you mourn forever?

I want the very roots of the sorrow of the deepest self to be consumed, and I am coming to you nearer and nearer with the fire of the lamp and of the furnace of God. I am coming, beloved, for you have willingly placed yourselves in my presence. Therefore, I shall do with you what I will, yet you may yet reject my offering.

I wish to pick you up and put you in another place on the other side of the world, you see! I wish to take you out of that circle of your karma and your human creation and your becoming set in your ways as the years move on. But, of course, this is almost not possible without your cooperation.

As someone once told the Messenger regarding a loved one, you cannot simply transplant a little flower, for it will not grow in another soil. So, you see, beloved, if I should pick you up and place you now in the true Shamballa of the East, you might be happy there for an hour or a day or three days. But pretty soon you would say, "Take me back to the scene of the familiar, the scene of my karma, the people I know, the people I need and those who need me." So you see, beloved, for this acceleration, greater than that which is usual, there must come about in you a *leap* in consciousness.

I show you the outline of my life. And I took the leap in consciousness. Each time I felt the contact of God, knew the presence of the LORD, I took the opportunity for a giant leap and I skipped the steps in between.

Did I suffer a loss?

Was I lonely?

Well, a bit, I must admit, for the human consciousness itself is slow to adjust to abrupt changes. But, beloved, I brought up the rear of that human consciousness and I beat it into submission and I said, "We go this day! We march! We go into battle for the slaughter of the Nephilim kings." That victorious battle enabled me to bring the fruits of my victory as a mighty tithe to the beloved Melchizedek, king of Salem and priest of the Most High God.[16]

Yes, beloved, on and on and on we went, Sarah and I. And on and on and on we go this day. We would take you with us, but I announce to you that cycles do come to an end and you are nearing the day when you must enter and come up to the level of the Father and the fatherhood of earth's children that I have borne. For the cycles will turn. Some will move on. Some will remain. But you must step into the shoes of your God Parents, even as you take over the functions of your human parents when you reach adulthood.

It is an hour, then, when I reach the greatest proximity to your souls. May you know that I love you. May you know that there is a palace of Light where we meet and there is a retreat in Darjeeling.

As the cycles have turned this summer solstice, I am the closest that I shall ever be to my chelas. I offer you my Diamond Heart, beloved, and all that I am.

Will you have me and have all of me? ["Yes!"]

I bid you enter the next step and pursue oneness with God daily.

June 26, 1992

CHAPTER 2

Saint Joseph

"I AM NOT DONE WITH PISCES!"

Turn Back the Adversary in Defense of the Child!

I come to you out of the heart of God—thy God and my God—for there is but one. I come to you containing in my Causal Body long ages of preparation for the age of Pisces.

From the hour of the Lord Jesus' reign 35,000 years ago on Atlantis unto the hour of the betrayal of his reign by the dark forces, through the aeons that have descended, the preparation of the age of Pisces and the coming of that Son of God was ongoing.

The challenge to the hierarchy of Light was how to lead those rebellious ones back to the heart of the Sun. Thus, all parties to that civilization and to the succeeding civilizations of India and throughout the earth have reincarnated again and again and again, all being led (sometimes pulled by the very nose) to the heart of the Christic experience within their very own heart: their heart one with the Heart of God.

Oh, it has been a hard, hard generation who have resisted the coming of my Son, Immanuel! Therefore, I did reincarnate again and again. And you are not aware of my many incarnations as high priest, as scientist, alchemist, originator of dispensations of the Seventh Ray in every age to the very limit that that age could endure and that would be provided for by dispensations of the Solar Logoi.

Notably, my embodiment as the prophet Samuel did bring me to the place of the anointing of the young son, David, son of Jesse.[1] Yes, there was the one who must be king and who should descend from his own Christhood unto the hour of his being embodied as the Lamb of God to hold that office of the Lamb of God, who has been, who was and is slain from the very foundation of the lower worlds. Since these lower worlds have been created and sustained in measure by fallen angels and in far greater measure by the LORD God, who would not see his evolutions lost, so that Lamb has embodied and has been slain.

Your Holy Christ Self is indeed the Lamb of God. And as you allow this Christ to be "formed and re-formed in you"[2] in the likeness of the Holy One of God, so you shall know the experience of the slaying of the Lamb and the attempt of the fallen angels to pierce to the very soul of your being in order to snuff out the candle of the living Christ in the earth.

Now I have many sons and daughters, but they began with the One. Remember there was a moment before the creation when creation was not, but only *Ein Sof.* And remember how the Light went forth and did expand and the *sefirot* came forth on a descending scale.

I speak, then, of the moment of the appearing of *Tiferet,* the Son of Righteousness, the only begotten of that God. Therefore, the hour of that coming was the hour of the descent of the living Christ midpoint on the Tree of Life. And therefore that Christ Presence did seek to woo the soul by the lesser *sefirot* [below *Tiferet*] to the level of the middle figure [the Son] of the Chart of your I AM Presence. This Jesus came to do in not one but many incarnations throughout the ages.

And so I was chosen to father the Son of God in his final incarnation and in so doing to father the Piscean age, as I said, by long preparation beforehand. All the players in that scene of the family and all whom we met and worked with, aye, John the Baptist and great adepts of the East and those with whom we were in contact whose names are not recorded—all those players to the scene, including disciples and the multitudes, descended knowing that they would act out the greatest pageant of all history. And in acting it out, I say to you, beloved, they were counseled and trained to play their role of individual Christhood and to play it to its fullest.

Thus, beloved, you are also counted in this mandala of Lightbearers—the beauteous, wondrous pattern of souls coming together, each one having a precious jewel to contribute to the Piscean dispensation. For reason of the dark powers that have been unchecked, that should have been checked and could have been checked had the powers and the forces of God been directed to that end, I tell you, the Piscean age has been an age of darkness when it could have been an age of great light, even a golden age.

Thus, *you* have come of age! Thus, you have understood profoundly that God has placed in your hands the work of binding the force of Evil, which has no power except the power that the mass consciousness does give to it. Therefore, in every place where you raise up that Christ, where the individual son or daughter of God or child of God does give glory to that Christ and raise it up, so there is that point of challenge, that point of saying to the hosts of Darkness: "Thus far and no farther! Go back into your lair. You shall not spot the footprints of my Lord!"

Blessed ones, to take your stand with the will of the mind, the fire of the heart, the devotion of the soul, the power of the indwelling Spirit and the power of the YOD HE VAU HE: this is your calling! And I tell you, a new empowering is coming upon you in this conference. Therefore, to receive it and seal it, I say, be purged, be rejuvenated, be restored, be illuminated, beloved ones!

For the day must dawn, must it not?

Yes, the day must dawn when you find yourself as the mirror image of your own beloved Holy Christ Self. And therefore, the separation will be slight and as that rapprochement occurs wherein the soul no longer fears to enter into complete union, no longer fears the wedding day or the wedding garment, I say, beloved, you shall walk the earth again as Christed ones as you did in that ancient golden-age civilization on Atlantis when you had balanced 51 percent of your karma. And many did ascend who went on to balance 100 percent of their karma in that time and dispensation, while others, some among you included, did lose ground and therefore did lose the 51 percent they had gained.

And therefore, you have traversed long embodiments and a certain amount of the drudgery of dealing with returning karma as it has accelerated in this many-thousand-year cycle* that is upon you again. Yes, beloved, hours and cycles turn and you have come back to the very point of beginning. In the Beginning, the point of Light and then the midpoint, the moment when, though you had garnered Light, you lost it.

How did you lose it, beloved?

I can tell you the fallen angels known as serpents are more than cunning. They have perverted the signs and the signals of the Kabbalah and therefore used it to imprison souls of Light. Not by mere enticement or the pride of the eye or the glitter of the body did they draw you away but by the very black magic that is the misuse of the set of the *sefirot.* The counterfeit set of the ten *sefirot* had been created by the one *Din* in the intensity of the judgment itself, the judgment that the fallen ones meted out upon the children of God. And thus, Evil did gain hold in the manner described to you by the Messenger according to the teachings of the Zohar.

Now understand, beloved, as you have the knowledge of the I AM THAT I AM and as you have called upon that power, so you have called upon *Keter.* And therefore you have had that point of contact with the first of the ten *sefirot.* So make the point of contact with each of the *sefirot* and understand that by so placing your heart and soul and mind and will and dynamic decree in these chalices, by setting yourself at a like vibration with them, you can now turn around the evil works of *Din* and those who carry the *Din* consciousness and demand the judgment of the forces of Antichrist and therefore work the work of God on earth, which is the ultimate binding of the evil force. Yes, beloved, the "other side" must be tackled, as the beloved Abraham has told you.

And therefore we come, fathers both, who have nurtured you. And we come with the blessed Mother Mary. We come with other Mothers ascended and the one unascended,† that you might know that there is

*The 25,800-year cycle of returning karma has come full circle with the conclusion of the age of Pisces.

†The embodied Messenger Elizabeth Clare Prophet bears the mantle of the World Mother. In that office she, with other devotees of the World Mother, makes continual intercessory prayer on behalf of the world's children.

a nurturing spirit in the heart of the earth to nurture you to the place where you can stand face-to-face, eyeball-to-eyeball, as they say, with the adversary who did betray you at Maitreya's Mystery School, known as the Garden of Eden.

And now in this hour and in this day, with increased self-knowledge and confidence in the absolute protection of the Spirit of the living God in your I AM Presence and Archangel Michael, you can indeed challenge, turn back and bind the Adversary that he go not out again to tempt the little ones, to violate their souls, to abuse their bodies and their minds.

Beloved ones, there are the filthy ones in the earth who are engaged in the violation of the sacred chakras of life in little children. You must demand their judgment and their binding before the altar of the LORD God! Come forward, then, in defense of the child! Come forward in defense of the Mother, the Cosmic Virgin, and all of the fathers in the world, who must come now and stand by their wives and by the mothers of their children!

Let the Holy Family be restored! This is the work, beloved. It does take your giving the judgment calls dictated by my Son Jesus and the call for the binding of the dweller-on-the-threshold (as you have been told) of the Antichrist in the earth and the seed of Antichrist planted in you long ago, which must be exorcised and excised by you.

Yes, I AM Saint Joseph, and I walk in the full mantle of my office as protector of Mary and of every mother and every woman and of every child in the earth. And I tell you, beloved, that I play that role. As many in the earth call to me as Saint Joseph, so I respond to that name.

Knowing who I am, therefore, I can be called by any name, any key of any name of any past incarnation. Thus, I have rolled them into one and determined to be called by you merely "Holy Brother," *Saint Germain.*

I, beloved, come to you with a heart full of love and hope and determination. I come to you in the realism of that which must be bound first in yourself before it can be bound by you, in the name of God, in others. I say, submit yourselves to the altar of God and trust my mouthpiece, for I can work with you and deal with you if you recognize that the Messenger is a personal Messenger to each one of you when you need that Messenger.

I say, beloved, it is too late, too late and far too late—if you count from the hours of 35,000 years ago (and we have returned to that cycle now in this day) when you walked away from the Son of God—to continue your dalliance in the doings of your ego. It is not a time to assert the human ego. It is not a time for argumentation and squabbling and a need for personal glory.

Beloved, all these things must be set aside in the perspective that has been given to you many times before, and it is this:

Whatever you think you might gain from another round in the world, whether it be the intellectual world, the psychological world, the world of art and theater, the world of music and science, beloved, you have seen it all, you have done it all before. It is in your Causal Body. You have satisfied your soul's need to do these things again and again!

But I tell you, all of your efforts in all of the fields that are open to you will come to naught if you do not put first things first, in this case the binding of the evil force at work at this level of the worlds. Understand this. Civilizations will crumble. Wars shall come to pass. Plagues shall be upon the earth, and earth changes. Yes, unless you bind the evil force, all these things will effectively wipe out the years of your efforts in this or that discipline.

But I tell you, if you make your first and foremost holy calling the binding of that Evil, which means, beloved, to become day by day the fullness of the embodiment of your Christhood so that you are indeed empowered to bind that Evil, then all these other things will fall in line. And what you put into a work of your calling and your profession will endure and it will be sealed by the violet flame. And no tempter or fallen angel will be able to come into your playroom and knock down the towers you have builded with your blocks.

Yes, beloved, civilization will stand or fall. It will stand only if you determine to bind the force of Antichrist that was in the heart of Herod whereby he sent out his henchmen to slaughter the male babies in order to be sure to destroy the living Christ Jesus. And therefore, the angels of the Seventh Ray led us in the flight into Egypt[3] and it was indeed a flight from the terror of the powers-that-be of the time.

And do not think that it was not a challenge for me and for Mary.

Yes, it was indeed! For we were in the form that you are in this day, we were in the times and we knew exactly what could happen if we did not play our role.

Care for your children! Care even more for your souls and their souls! Care, beloved, and guard the sacred citadels. For Christed ones have been lost in the earth for want of parents who had the teaching and the understanding of maintaining the I-AM-the-Guard consciousness.

Trust no one with your children except those who are tried-and-true devotees, beloved. Take care. For the Devil does yet wander about seeking whom he may devour,[4] and he would devour the very souls of your children before they may come of age for the realization of their Christhood.

I say, this place is indeed the cradle of a new civilization of Lightbearers! And I, Saint Joseph, am on hand as always to inaugurate cycles and dispensations by the power of the Seventh Ray.

Therefore, I come to you in the great glory of God and I tell you that the mission of Jesus Christ was an absolute God-success for those who did receive it and who did, therefore, by the power of his mouth-to-mouth, heart-to-heart resuscitation come into their own victory in the Light. But very quickly the fallen angels, the wolves in sheep's clothing, did come along, did distort the doctrine, did destroy the works of Origen and others. And therefore the perversion of the teachings of my Son are in the earth today, entrenched in doctrine and dogma and inciting fear in the many hearts of Light who should have gathered in this tent for this convocation upon the coming of Alpha and Omega—blessed be the holy names of our Father-Mother God.

Yes, beloved, they ought to be here! And because the forces of Antichrist attacking them through the media, through the anti-cult movement have not been bound, therefore there is that wall that does stand between them and this altar. I say, tear down the wall by the fiat of the LORD! Tear down the wall, beloved!

For many, many can drink at this fount. And in the twinkling of an eye, as it were, even in a ten-day cycle or a period at Summit University, they can see through all of the false teachings and see through the false teachers and know who they are and know them by their fruits,[5] or should we say by their "nonfruits"? For they produce nothing of worth from their tree of life but only turn back the children of the Sun from their Sunward flight. They are the gray ones, and they are becoming grayer and blacker by the hour as their karma descends.

Beloved ones, this is truly the hour of which my Son did speak. Lo, the harvest is white, yet the laborers are few.[6]

Who shall be the harvester of souls in my name?

I come to you to place my mantle and Presence of Saint Joseph over you so that you may go and do the work and be our hands and feet, our hearts and our chakras in the earth.

Blessed ones, if you will spend your life and time and hours in this endeavor, I assure you that to have my Presence over you will ultimately manifest in you as the regaining of your strength, your health, your youth.

Beloved, if I may work through you, I will raise you up. But you must give attention to me. Remember me as I walked by the child Jesus, as I walked with Mary and as I guided them until the hour of my transition. Remember, then, how Jesus did go alone, joining the caravan to the East.[7] Yes, beloved, the Son of God was overshadowed by angels and by the hierarchy of the dispensation of the Piscean age and by myself when I was no longer in embodiment.

Yes, beloved, we have work to do! We have some unfinished business with the fallen ones who have moved against my Son and against you as my sons and daughters in every age, lifetime after lifetime.

This is the day and the hour to say to them:

> Thus far and no farther! We have the Word! We have the name! We have the understanding! We shall invoke the power of God and it shall not fail us. And your day is *done!* You have no power! Your day is done and you will not seduce our souls nor our children's souls nor our children's children's souls!
>
> We shall send forth a mighty ripple of Light that is the ribbon of our own crystal cord. And we shall send it into the future that all evolutions and Lightbearers shall know! They shall know your name, ye fallen ones, ye extraterrestrials who

> have come to manipulate the genetic code of the evolutions of God! *We shall see you bound!* For we know your name and we pronounce it and we say: Your judgment descends in the name of God now! [49-second standing ovation]

Now I say to you, beloved, the fallen ones have been working overtime on you and many others of your companions who are not here for one reason or another. And they have sought to move you this way and that way. They have worked hard to insert into your mind thoughts that are not your own, interpretations of life, inserting desires in the mind and in the desire body.

Yes, beloved, you must take care and be on guard and protect your aura and forcefield and give the fiats, as the Messenger has demonstrated them, with the full power of the Word, the fervor of the heart chakra, the power of that mighty threefold flame that is the very same flame that does burn in the heart of Alpha and Omega. There is no difference, beloved, except in size, intensity and balance.

Therefore, you are the issue of God: Beware, for those who are not the issue of God who wander about, as I have said, seeking whom they may devour, have played with you and with some of you they have had a heyday. You have been moved this way and that way. You have been seized with an idea that they have planted. You have followed it and it has burst as a bubble, taking with it your supply and your very lifeblood.

And then you have gone another way and a-this-way and a-that-way instead of first seating yourself in the place of the Holy of holies of your heart chakra with your Holy Christ Self and simply saying:

> *Be still and know that I AM God and that the I AM THAT I AM within me is that God! And I will not be moved from my course of service to my God.*

Any distraction will do, any stray thought, just to get you away from your own interior castle, your own inner altar and the altar of the Most High God.

I want you to know that the angels of the LORD have so moved in on planet earth that they are just waiting almost breathless for someone of any religion or walk of life but especially for you, beloved, since you understand the science of the spoken Word, to utter the call for the binding of this and that fallen one. These fallen ones are ready to be picked off, beloved ones! And the angels of the LORD are ready to do your bidding. Won't you take this conference, then, as an opportunity to take your stand in defense of the work of my Son Jesus Christ, which is the work of Him that sent him?[8]

Yes, beloved, do that work for the binding of that Antichrist and see how the world will change because you have walked in this world, you have worked in this world, you have placed the imprint of the soles of your feet and the soul of your temple in the very planet itself.

And I tell you, one day it shall be said: "Blessed are these feet and the imprints they have left that we may walk in them—the footprints of the saints of God who saw the oncoming Darkness and reversed it by the power of the judgment of God to defeat the judgment of the fallen angels."

Now I, Saint Joseph, give you your very first assignment and it is this: As you lay your head to rest this night, make the call to be taken to the Royal Teton Retreat at the Grand Teton. You have done the work magnificently, and the multiplication of your Ashram rituals as you come together in such numbers is a beauty to behold as the whole planet glistens with an *antahkarana* that you are establishing and strengthening every hour and day of your presence here, multiplied by the chalice of Elohim[9] in the Heart of the Inner Retreat and multiplied by the Western Shamballa and the heart of Lord Gautama Buddha, blessed be his name.

Therefore, from the heart of the Royal Teton Retreat you shall be escorted, then, to Yugoslavia, and you shall be accompanied by many legions of angels of the Seven Archangels and of the mighty God Surya. And you shall place your bodies in the midst of the people and you shall call at inner levels for the binding of the serpents and the fallen ones who are creating this slaughter.[10]

Remember, beloved ones, after the flood of Noah the decree went forth that human government must be established for the defense of human life. When the nations and the governments of the earth cease to use their powers to defend life anywhere and everywhere upon this planet, I say the reason for being of both the nations and their governments has come to an end.

Now you have seen the great powers, and what have they done to stop this slaughter? Who has interceded?

All have turned their backs with silly sanctions and mealymouthed words and no action. And again and again and again the slaughter in the nation continues night and day until even you are sick of seeing it on the television.

Well, beloved, there are Lightbearers everywhere and there are Lightbearers in Yugoslavia. If this slaughter is allowed to continue, I tell you, it shall open such a depth of the bowels of hell (as it already has and which opening you must call for the cosmic reinforcements to seal) that this action of the slaughter of the people will then spread. It will be repeated in your own cities, even as you have seen the upheaval in Los Angeles.[11] Beloved ones, these two situations are related.

Where the slaughter of the good and the evil, where the slaughter of people of any kind is allowed to continue and to go unchecked, there is a rending of the veils of the entire planet and an opening of the pits and of the astral plane. Therefore, beloved, this is a most urgent matter.

Let us seal the place where Evil dwells in Yugoslavia and elsewhere. Let us make the call to Astrea for the binding of the evil ones on the astral plane and in physical embodiment. And let us pray for the saving of the souls of Light.

Blessed hearts, war has been on this planet as long as there have not been Christed ones, such as yourselves and such as you are becoming, to stand up against that sinister force. War must end! Call therefore to Lord Krishna, to Karttikeya, to all the mighty ones of God who lead those armies of heaven, including the God Surya, that war may end upon this planet—and the warring within the members of the people and the warring in their souls.

Yes, beloved, you live in an age when you can triumph and triumph ultimately. And remember that you did not turn your back on Saint Germain and Portia, on Jesus Christ or Mary, his Mother, but you decided to confront that force directly, come what may, and to trust

God to be your mighty shield, your buckler, your defense and your armour.

I AM Saint Joseph. And though I come as the Hierarch of Aquarius, I am not done with Pisces! For I am determined to see a victory out of it all and, through you and this Messenger, the publishing abroad of the true teachings of Jesus Christ. For they are the foundation of Aquarius *and Aquarius cannot rise without the self-knowledge of every man, woman and child upon this planet of his own Holy Christ Self and of the Son of God and of the I AM Presence and of the violet flame!*

See to it, then, ye warriors of the Spirit and of the earth! See to it, ye saints of God in the flesh! Now make your life count as it has never counted before in all past ages and graduate with glory in your ascension in the Light!

Leave, then, your children to move on in your footsteps. Do not spare the rod. I did not spare the rod with my son Jesus and therefore he grew up the disciplined one. Whether you think you have an avatar or not, recognize that the four lower bodies must be disciplined and the soul itself.

Yes, beloved, I AM Saint Joseph and I shall not relinquish my role either in the Catholic Church or anywhere where I am called. And where you call to my beloved wife, Mary, I AM there. Therefore when you sing the *Sanctissima* songs, know that I am a part of the answer and the resounding flame from the heart of the Blessed, the most blessed Cosmic Virgin, who embodied to give birth to your Saviour and my Saviour, your Lord and my Lord. [43-second standing ovation]

June 27, 1992

CHAPTER 3

Lord Lanto

TURN THE WORLD AROUND!

A Replica of the Great Causal Body

Welcome to my Heart! I come from the mountain of the LORD and I come to you as your tutor, beloved hearts. I will tutor your souls this night that you might receive Alpha and Omega having the maximum light focused in the crown chakra.

Therefore, the legions of the Second Ray and all who are the Buddhas and the Bodhisattvas are beginning to stream to this very Heart of the Inner Retreat, cleansed now and being cleansed by the rain for the clearing of some ancient records that must be removed. And a little at a time they are being removed, beloved, year upon year, as the light you invoke does penetrate and as elemental life do cooperate.

It is the consideration of the Council of the Royal Teton and the Darjeeling Council that it is necessary for you to prepare more adequately to receive the Light* of Alpha and Omega and of Helios and Vesta. Therefore, we request that you concentrate on the decrees of the Second Ray and weave them in a braid with the violet flame, supporting this matrix with your judgment calls and pillars of blue flame from the heart of Hercules and Astrea, Archangel Michael and Surya.

*Christ consciousness and God consciousness

Blessed ones, this preparation shall allow you to take and hold more Light—Light for the illumination of a world! For a new day has dawned and that new day, beloved, is the coming of age of many souls of Light, who will reach the point of the crown chakra as you raise up the sacred fire yourselves and hold that focus for the opening of the crown.

Jophiel and Christine contribute mightily to the dispensation of illumination. And I think, beloved ones, that you do not give them enough attention even in the singing of the hymn to Jophiel and Christine. For they do come and they do tarry, beloved, and they will saturate you in yellow fire! They will do much more if you will reconsider and reread their dictations. You will discover that they have mentioned the clearing of the planet of many conditions of ignorance and all manner of burden upon the people, but they must have your dedication to their activity.

We have therefore had your Messenger place on the cassette of the Archangel Michael songs[1] our songs to the beings of the yellow ray. Let them ring in your hearts and in your headsets so that you may have streams and ribbons of yellow fire coming down, imparting hope to the nations, hope to your own beating heart!

We of the Council of the Royal Teton are aware of the opening of mighty vortices of Light from the Central Sun and the opening of hearts and minds. Yet how the brains of the people of this planet need a scrubbing! How the sacred fire of the Mother must be focused and employed by you for this distillation, for this cleansing, beloved!

The yellow flame is a purifying fire. We desire to see the Christ Mind congruent with the lower mind, yet vessels must be emptied. And not only must there be a fasting from food but there must be a fasting from the entertainment of the world and the continual bombardment of the mind by the rhythms that are not rhythms at all but are arhythmic.

So, beloved, in order that we may use the minds of the people constructively, we call upon you and all elemental life, and especially the body elementals of the people, to engage in that decree work whereby many may come into a true illumination of their own consciousness, their own being, their own lifestream, their own tie to God.

How can the people perceive the kingdom of God within them if that kingdom is so cluttered with the debris of the centuries?

Beloved ones, you may know this and you may have heard this before but I speak in the context of a world in transition, and unless the minds of the Lightbearers and of the children be quickened, where shall we find the planetary home?

You can see through the schemes of the politicians and those who represent you in the offices of government. This nation is in a crisis of confidence and many do not even dare to run for office again, so convinced are they that their constituents will not elect them.

Truly it is the hour of the raising up of the Feminine Ray. And may the woman who does come forth to represent the people be blessed, and let the man who does come forth be blessed. And let them both raise up the Light of the Feminine Ray, for only thereby will the true God-solution to the world's problems be found, beloved, and be known.

We come for the education of the heart as well as the mind. We come with gladness that so many students desire to study at Summit University and have answered the call of Kuan Yin to come to learn how to teach the children. Surely it is an hour when wisdom is exploding everywhere and the hunger for the knowledge of God is everywhere. And where shall they go for that water which they may drink which will give to them everlasting Life?[2]

Tell them! Tell them, I say to you! Tell them of the Christ that lives in the heart. Tell them of the soul that must rise. Tell them of the kingdom of God and of the world in transition and of the hour and the day when the mountains shall shake and the trembling of the earth shall come and there shall be the melting of the elements with a mighty fervent heat[3] and the alchemy of a world shall come about.

Let that alchemy and that quaking and shaking begin where you are! Let it begin, therefore, for the settling and the leveling and the leavening of consciousness. Let there be the repolarization of every lifestream upon this planet to the Great Central Sun Magnet! Come forth, O legions of Light!

Now behold with your inner eye how rings upon rings of angels of the yellow flame do congregate. And so the legions of Holy Justinius, Captain of Seraphic Bands, do come with their rings upon rings of white fire. And therefore we are building in this place, beloved ones, a replica of the Great Causal Body and we begin with the white fire core of the seraphim of God, who establish their fount of Light in the Great Central Sun. And the legions of the yellow ray come.

And therefore the first two spheres of the Causal Body are being established over this place and these two spheres, beloved, relate to certain evolutions, certain key lifestreams, who must make their ascension through the victory of those spheres and those worlds and those preparations that they long ago received in those quadrants of the Great Causal Body of God in the Great Central Sun.

Therefore, as we lay down this replica of the Great Central Sun Magnet during this conference, you will find that there will be an awakening within your soul of your experiences in the heart of the Great Central Sun with your twin flame in the Beginning. And therefore you will remember why you have come, what you were sent to do, what was the point of your origin and destiny. See, then, how, nestled in the white fire core of Alpha and Omega, you were born sons and daughters of God, mated to go forth to bring the full complement of the Father-Mother to the evolutions whom you would reach.

It is time to go back to that point of origin, to begin the whole round all over again and to retrace it, almost as with a computer of the Mind of God—to go through light-years of the descent of the soul finally to these octaves, to trace your footsteps and then to engage in the reverse and to return, step by karmic step, all the way back to that point of origin.

Thus, in going to the center, in coming out from the center and going unto it again, you are weaving the mighty cosmic daisy and you are seeing the increase and the adding unto your Being, unto the I AM THAT I AM, of these mighty rings of Light. They are vast, beloved! The rings of Light incorporate the entire cosmos, and yet you can relate to that individualized Causal Body as a mighty sphere above you.

Is not this the wondrous activity of our God, beloved?

Is it not the action whereby the living Christ does reach out to save that which is lost?

Thus, out of the fiery purity of your original blueprint, go forth into the golden yellow sphere and reactivate the Mind of God within you and allow the fat upon the brain to be removed and dissolved until the brain itself glistens like crystal and is able to coalesce the white fire of God of your Holy Christ Self.

What a worthy goal! What a joyous goal to empty the pockets of the cells of every organ of the body and every atom of those organs. What a joy, beloved, to find yourself being restored to the Adam Kadmon, yes, beloved ones, to the original matrix of perfect man and perfect womb-man.

To return to that point, beloved, will allow you to bring forth again original root races and lifestreams who also go back to that etheric blueprint and have been denied it and therefore have not entered into embodiment. I speak also of the seventh root race.

Now then, for the turning around of worlds, let the physical bodies be prepared, let the desire bodies be prepared, let the etheric body be prepared, let the mental body be prepared!

Beloved souls of Light, hear my call in this hour! Hear my awakening, even as I take hold of the giant sheet that does traverse a cosmos. And I shake it, beloved! And the waves go forth, the waves of illumination, the waves of white-fire purity, preceded, then, by legions of the violet flame and of the blue lightning and of the Ruby Ray, who are clearing the cosmos for the descent of the sons and daughters of God.

There are so very many who desire to descend to this level for the rescue mission of the Christs and the Bodhisattvas. They are in place, beloved. Now we come to see that you are in place and that you understand how to seek the refinement of the Spirit.

I AM Lanto, Chohan of the Second Ray. I come on behalf of the Royal Teton Council and I come on behalf of Alpha and Omega. I plead with you: Let not this nation go down in ignorance for a failure to educate the children in the true things of the Spirit and to set the geometry of the material universe in right programs of education so that the children we send forth might be vessels for a greater science, a greater sound of music and discoveries and dispensations that may be channeled through them because, beloved, you have laid the foundation and given them the proper teaching as well as the education of the heart.

Let there be the turning around, beloved! For you know there does come a time in the downward spiral of degeneration, whether of a body or an organ, when it simply fulfills itself in the death spiral. *There is a time to turn a world around and there is a time when it is no longer possible.*

I say, you have come to the point on this day and date wherein it is possible to turn the world around! And yet I say to you: Insert a mighty momentum of fervent prayer into the earth in this place to start that spiral, to make yourselves congruent with Elohim! For unless you do, beloved, there may not come another opportunity.

How long, how long can Elohim, therefore, hold back the avalanche of the descent of civilizations worldwide?

You are seeing it everywhere. Do not become ho-hum about what you see, for what you see is truly the most dangerous aspect of a world in transition. And instead of seeing a world going up, you are seeing a world going into the spirals of self-disintegration. Look all around you and see the bodies and minds that are disintegrating.

Know whereof I speak! And know that it is the angels of the Second Ray that must come in your name and by your call for the mighty quickening of the people! For their ears, their minds, their hearts, their eyes have waxed dull and they no longer see cause related to effect and effect related to cause.

I cry out for enlightenment and for the enlightened ones to decree for that enlightenment unto all who can potentially carry it, namely, the Christ-bearers, the children of the Light and all who will come into our camp and determine once and for all to be servants of God.

I have made a plea to you, beloved, perhaps not as great as I would have liked to. But I must speak, as I speak from my heart, and I must tell you that to burden you anymore or to burden the councils of the Brotherhood anymore would perpetuate my delivery too long.

Therefore, I cast out a flame of hope! I cast out cloven tongues of yellow fire! And they sit upon you, one and all, on the crown chakra as though it were the day of Pentecost, and yet it is not. It is the day of the coming of the Lords of the Second Ray. It is the day of the coming of the Buddhas and the Bodhisattvas. It is the day of the coming, beloved ones, of a commitment and a promise that must be on both sides.

I ask you to give attention to the yellow ray and see what you can do to *awaken* America!

I AM Lanto, always very near to you in the quietness of Wisdom's flame.

June 28, 1992

CHAPTER 4

Mighty Victory with Justina

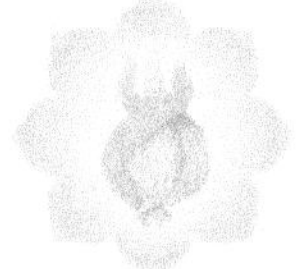

BREAK THE SPELL OF NON-VICTORY!

A Moment when All Could Be Won and All Could Be Lost

Ho, legions of the Great Central Sun!

Ho, legions of the Great Central Sun!

I AM Victory! And I AM *here* to break the spell of non-Victory in the lives of the Lightbearers of earth! [47-second standing ovation]

Ho, I AM come! And I am here to put down these fallen ones who have determined to pervert the very life-force, the lifeblood and the beings of the servants of God.

I AM here, beloved ones, for the spirals of Victory descend!

I respond to Alpha and Omega. I respond to all the legions of the Second Ray. I am responding to and representing the mighty Bodhisattvas who dwell on the inner planes of the etheric octave and desire to take embodiment. I come to you brimming with a joy that we can meet together the expectations and even the demands of Lord Lanto and all who serve with him, who read as we do the handwriting on the wall.

Therefore, beloved sons and daughters, be drenched in the flame of Victory! Be drenched in the flame of Justina! And know that we are one and that we add the momentum of our twin flames to those cloven tongues of golden fire that descend upon your crown chakras now. And they are meeting a certain amount of density and therefore we feed them our fire as the Light does penetrate through the etheric sheath, through the mental, through the desire, through the physical.

O beloved ones, help us with right diet. Help us with pure thought. Help us with meditation. Help us with doing your *pranayama.* Yes, beloved, we will remake you in the image and likeness of God if you will cooperate. *Therefore, will you cooperate?* ["Yes!" (22-second standing ovation)]

I speak quickly and with a mighty fire, that I might inject in you the sense of acceleration. You have been on other worlds and systems of worlds and in higher octaves where you would think more easily and more quickly, your motions would be more direct and mercurial and you would accomplish so much more of the penetration of the Mind of God and the drawing forth even of the engineering and the design and the architecture of the golden cities of Light in the etheric octave.

Yes, you have lived in those levels, you have known a greater communication and now, I say, the forces of anti-Victory, the forces of non-Victory have heaped upon you a momentum and a burden and a weight, beloved ones. *And you must listen to me!* You must know that it must be challenged by you and you alone!

And the fire of you is the fire of God in you, for you are God-Victory in manifestation! And I see you as manifestations of ourselves, of Victory and Justina, in the God Flame of Victory. And I see you in your mighty golden robes and golden winged sandals of Victory. And you are that Victory and I affirm it now!

And therefore I say: Take the fire of Victory in your souls! Take the fire of God-Victory that is the God-Victory of your own Mighty I AM Presence and *jump* out of those snakeskins, *jump* out of that density and go forward enjoying the vastness of the universe. For your own mind can tap it because you have chosen to develop your heart and meditate in your heart, and therefore the rings of fire grow—and therefore the Bodhisattvas may come to you, they may touch you, they may quicken you!

Beloved ones, come into balance. Come into balance, I say! And cherish nothing in this world more than your own individual equilibrium—your equilibrium in your own Tree of Life, in your own Mighty I AM Presence.

Let us say that everything that detracts from that equilibrium south, north, east, west, beloved ones, does detract from your mighty Victory. And I say, a mighty Victory you must have! And you should not make it merely by the skin of your teeth in the hour when your name is called at roll call at Luxor. Yes, beloved, you should graduate with flying colors and the highest honors! You should be ready for your ascension *tomorrow,* if necessary, or the next tomorrow or the next year or the next five. Yes, beloved, be ready now, and then walk the earth as that example that others may see and follow.

This *is* an hour of cycles turning. Whether we can turn them around depends on the response of every Lightbearer on this planet to my message given this day! And therefore I ask you to communicate your response through prayer, through decree, through the dissemination of information, through giving to individuals the *Pearl of Wisdom* that shall be printed of my dictation and telling them of the work and of the calls of the legions of the Second Ray.

It is a moment, beloved, when all could be won and all could be lost. Do not discount your Godhood! One individual who is God, and knows it, is the pillar of fire, the rod in the earth that shall be the focus of the Great Central Sun Magnet. And many coming together in this place, even once a year, beloved, does produce that concentration of fire whereby we may penetrate and probe in the earth and place our probes, allowing the Light you invoke to penetrate more deeply and more deeply.

Therefore I say, prepare for coming here again next year, starting the day that the conference has concluded. Make your plans, determine to have the funds and the means and decree for the absolute God-Victory of souls.

Now I will tell you what we did with these earthquakes this day.[1] We have taken the opportunity of your holding the balance for the earth in this place to allow these earthquakes to happen (as they would have inevitably happened) but with the least amount of loss of life and damage because *you* have kept the Flame, because you have tarried these days, because you determined to go and you did go to the Royal Teton Retreat last night.

And therefore you did journey with legions of Light and you did perform a mighty spiritual work over Yugoslavia.[2] And it did come to pass that you established a coordinate in that nation and other coordinates upon the planet with other servants of God whereby these earthquakes might be for a mitigation of world karma, a balancing of planetary forces and a release of pent-up misqualified energies in the earth.

Therefore, understand how much we can do when we have a body of Lightbearers who can remain at the same place for a period of ten days or even more, but for any amount of time we are grateful—even if you determine to do a twenty-four-hour marathon in your Study Groups and Teaching Centers, where you can hold the flame of harmony and make of that flame one of God-illumination with the violet flame and all the calls that you give.

I will tell you, beloved, the volcanic release in Alaska[3] has the same portents. And some of you who are "old-timers" have seen earthquakes of this dimension (yet not of this magnitude) happen from time to time during conferences and it has always been because the student body has been able to hold the balance for a release. And without that holding of the balance, there could have been far greater calamity and destruction to life.

You know that earth changes are in the planetary plan, but how and where they shall manifest and what degree of burden or loss of life shall be upon the people surely rests upon the individual decision that shall be made each and every day by the servants of God on earth.

I say, become fiery electrodes! Love the wisdom teachings, pursue the path of the mystics, be together in the Light and therefore convey a spiritual teaching and a spiritual consciousness. Read the books and the foundations of these mystical paths of the world's religions and thereby understand all people. And when you give your Ashram rituals, beloved, you will be able to contact in a deeper way so many souls of Light because now you will understand their path. And when you understand their path you understand their vibration.

(Therefore, be comfortable by being seated.)

Beloved ones, in order for me to speak to you I must have a

dispensation from the Lords of Karma, from the Four and Twenty Elders and beyond that the Solar Logoi. Therefore, I deem it a great privilege to be with you in this hour.

It has been weighed time and again preceding conferences and it has been decided that I should not speak. For the power of Victory is great and the power of Victory can unleash such tremendous enthusiasm and fire of purpose that when it does descend on the unenlightened evolutions of a planet it can stir up the urge to go out and do those things that are not the will of God.

Therefore we have created a trusted chalice, as you are that chalice and as you have placed your trust in God and made yourselves available to Lord Krishna and the hosts of the LORD. I desire, then, to continue to release this night the Power, the Wisdom, the Love of Victory! And to do so I need your cooperation in harmony. I need it, beloved, because if the Light I release is so easily misqualified by those who are among the most advanced in the outer world today, then, you see, I will make that karma and I will again be limited in coming.

Consider, then, all those areas of your life in which you desire to be victorious. You would do well after this session or in the morning to write down each point of your personal lifestream and activities where you desire *victory.* You can chart it on a map, beloved, a map of your life, and you can put those golden ribbons at that place where you are determined to have your victory—*victory* over self and every condition, *victory* in this Church, *victory* in the dissemination of the Teachings, *victory* in the nations, *victory* in the governments, *victory* in education, *victory* in every area of life!

Beloved ones, look all around you in this hour, and what do you see? You see *defeat,* beloved hearts. Everywhere people are being defeated by their own ignorance, by their own absence of the fiery coil of the Divine Mother, of the sacred fire rising up within them. They are being defeated on every hand—in the economy and in business and in life. There is a world depression that is not as apparent as it might be. For if the world could know the state of world depression that is upon the people, perhaps they would determine to do something about it.

Well, I will tell you, your violet flame marathons in this conference, sprinkled with the intensity of the yellow fire, will awaken and quicken some. They will awake as from a deep slumber and they will begin the quest and they will search.

And when they search, *who* will they find?

They will find *you* as myself and Justina, and we will be there with you and we will be there to bring home the Victory!

Let America awake! Let Americans awake! And let the fire of the entire Spirit of the Great White Brotherhood go forth from your hearts.

I, Victory, with my beloved consort, greet you in this hour! And we are transferring to you increment by increment that which you can spiritually assimilate of Victory. Therefore continue your calls and affirmations to me this night and see what we will do together!

There are other events in the planet in store during this conference. We desire to see a mighty action for the right, for the feeding of the hungry and the liberation of souls and the exposure of the dark forces that are yet intent upon global warfare. These must be bound on the astral plane, and those in embodiment must be bound as well, by legions of Victory, legions of Jophiel and Christine!

We come in anticipation of Alpha and Omega. Now, precious hearts of Light, so rise to that mighty occasion.

June 28, 1992

CHAPTER 5

Holy Justinius

SEE WHAT YOU CAN DO!

For the Acceleration of Earth without the Destruction of Earth

Ho, Legions of seraphim from the Great Central Sun! March, then, to the Heart of the Inner Retreat! March, then, and establish now with legions of the Second Ray that platform for the coming of our beloved Alpha and Omega!

So the legions come, beloved, and I salute you in their name. I salute you in the name of the God Flame in your hearts! Visualize now the seraphim who form the concentric rings round the Central Sun making their way to this place to assist you in holding the balance in the earth for the coming of Alpha and Omega. [21-second standing ovation]

These seraphim are your very best friends and probably the friends you ignore the most. I shall remind you, therefore, that they are of the order of Serapis, that they attend your ascension and that they have attended the degrees of your ascension in every embodiment since you have left the Great Central Sun.

When they place their mighty wings upon you, these four-winged creatures therefore superimpose themselves upon your bodies. And with one command from you, made by the authority of the Christ in your heart, you can watch how the seraphim bring you into alignment—how they bring all the functions of all of the levels of your being into alignment. Miracles, *seeming* miracles, take place in the very auras of the seraphim of God!

Do not neglect, fathers and mothers, health-care practitioners, physicians, healers, *do not neglect* the call to the seraphim of God when you are dealing with even the slightest out-of-alignment state. For the seraphim are the greatest physicians of all. They are the greatest healers, ranking with the highest legions of Raphael and Mother Mary.

And therefore, because they have in their auras the mighty power of the Central Sun and the white fire core of being and do always carry the vibration of your Father-Mother God (who have given you life and divine plan and matrix and their attention to every detail of your life), the seraphim can restore you by the energies of the Great Central Sun. And there is no greater restorative power than that of the Great Central Sun as it is transmitted and stepped down by and through the seraphim of God.

I say, one and all, reread the *Dossier on the Ascension.*[1] And now enter into the highest conception of the point of the Beginning beyond the Beginning, the point of *Ein Sof.* This you can achieve through the mind of the seraphim as in no other way.

Why, to look upon you and your neglect of the seraphim, one would almost think that you really want to be sick and have your ailments! For if you really did want to get rid of them, beloved ones, would you not call upon the seraphim, I say? ["Yes!"]

Well, then, as they say on this planet, examine your psychology and determine why you want to enter into a codependency between yourself and your ailments!

Beloved ones, it is time to have done with those ailments. It is time for the resurrection. It is time for the ascension flame! Now be drenched in these fires as they are tempered to your present condition and know that some of you have truly not prepared for our coming, but you may do so even in these few days by way of preparing yourselves to contain more Light.

It is a wondrous occasion when the Solar Logoi will authorize so many legions of seraphim to come to earth. Now, beloved ones, consider this, for you are wise ones. Consider that since with the coming of Alpha and Omega so many hosts of Light come in attendance, there shall ultimately be in this conference an extraordinary gathering of the hosts of the LORD for those dictations.

Therefore say to yourself: "With so many in such proximity, why should we not request some labors from our beloved El Morya? Why should we not go to work, when we have such reinforcement of one another, to go after that force of Antichrist in the world?" And see and prove here, now, if the LORD God himself and if we will not defeat that force through you, and how mighty numbers and even the number of the 666[2] will go down!

See what you can do, beloved! And be impressed with the fact that your journeying in the inner octaves and your presence here has already, even in the third day of this conference, allowed earth changes to take place without further calamity.

Blessed ones, it is a delicate matter for elemental life and the attending angels, who must tend a planet in transition, a planet which must be saved, a planet which must be healed, a planet which must be purged all at once—*this is a delicate operation.* And some of you know that this is directed from the retreat of Cuzco and by the mighty power of Surya as he maintains his focus in the God Star, Sirius.

Therefore, I assure you that thousands upon thousands of Ascended Masters who are experts in the sciences of geology at all levels of the earth are working now at a very intense level. And they request your support. And they are Ascended Masters, beloved! You simply do not realize the conditions of the earth and the horrendous weight of untransmuted karma that weighs down the earth and elemental life, not to mention the pollutions and the toxins that weigh down the bodies of the people themselves.

This earth has been raped, as you know, by extraterrestrials. It has been abused. And yet you have found a pristine place, fairly untouched, to consecrate the work of the Great White Brotherhood. And that place, as you know, has been dedicated long, long time for its connection to the Grand Teton.

So, beloved, when I tell you that Ascended Masters and Archangels and Elohim are working very hard to produce the acceleration of earth without the destruction of earth, I know whereof I speak! And you can think of the individual on the operating table whose life hangs in the balance. And if such and such a procedure is tried, perhaps the patient will not recover and therefore the decision must be made by physicians and surgeons: "Shall we try it or not?"

Blessed hearts, earth is a sick planet and many divine physicians are attending. We bid you join us. Join the seraphim of God! Join the legions of the Fifth Ray! And make this experience in the very mountains of the LORD one that counts for all evolutions of the planet!

I AM Justinius, Captain of Seraphic Bands! And I announce to you the day and the hour when the opportunity shall be open to you to take your ascension *if* you prepare for it from this moment on. Yes, beloved, it is only an opportunity if you exercise it. It is only an open door if you will walk through it and if you will have the courage to take every step that is necessary to make it. Then you will know how it feels to walk the earth as an Ascended Master moving among those who are the Lightbearers, quickening them! You will know what it is to place your Electronic Presence everywhere over the Lightbearers.

Therefore, take care that you leave in embodiment many fine souls and well-trained ones so that the continuity of the spiritual life of the true mystics of all ages may survive on planet earth and that thereby the earth herself may survive!

Into your hands I give you the planet, beloved ones. It belongs to *you.* This is your day and your hour. See what you can do to bring her Home, with her evolutions cut free!

I AM your servant, Justinius. [31-second standing ovation]

June 28, 1992

CHAPTER 6

Elizabeth Clare Prophet

BECOME SHIVA!

Tonight we are going to do whatever it takes to get you to become Shiva! And since nobody was even moved to leap up in the presence of Shiva while we were singing to him,* we've got a little work to do. I'm going to give you some background on Shiva now so we can get on with the bhajans until you become "jumping Shivas."

Shiva is very personal to me, a very personal friend, a very personal being who defies being circumscribed by any concept of him. Yet he is always there.

Shiva means "auspicious" or "kindly." He is indeed both. He is known as the Destroyer, and we welcome the Destroyer because we want everything that is not like God where we are to be transmuted by the all-consuming sacred fire. As the Third Person of the Hindu Trinity, he destroys the universe at the end of each world age so that it can be created all over again.

The Hindu Trinity is defined in the Hindu scriptures, the Puranas, as consisting of Brahma (the Creator), Vishnu (the Preserver) and Shiva (the Destroyer and Regenerator). All three are manifestations of Brahman.

---

*The Messenger and congregation sang the bhajan "Śiva Śambhu" (number 654) prior to this lecture.

Brahman is God in the Beginning—God in the Beginning with the Word. And by the Word did Brahman create and without the Word was nothing made that was made.[1] Do not confuse Brahma with Brahman. Brahma is Father; Vishnu, Son; Shiva, Holy Spirit—the Trinity who serve under Brahman and the Word.

As I mentioned in my lecture "The Inner Path of Hinduism," devotion to the Trinity is not widespread among the Hindu people, but I teach that the Hindu Trinity is parallel to the Christian Trinity. Shiva represents the stripping action of the Holy Spirit, whose love consumes the forces of ignorance and anti-Love. Shiva is not only the destroyer of the universe: he is the destroyer of evil, hatred, disease, worldliness, evildoers and demons. And, as Anjani Srivastava writes, Shiva is also "a nourisher who bestows long life."[2] But he will not give that nourishment until he has cleansed the vessel.

When you call to Shiva, you must be prepared for a purging by the holy fire of Love. And if you desire to receive that purging, when it comes you will be filled with such Light and God-Power as to not know where to turn to direct your service to life.

Shiva is known as Shambhu (benign), Shankara (beneficent), and Pashupati, which means "lord of cattle." Actually, it means the lord of souls in the sense of the shepherd who tends the sheep. He is also known as Mahadeva (great god).

Shiva is associated with death. He dances on battlefields and cremation grounds, and what he is doing is extracting the light that was once held in the cells of the body. He is withdrawing it and sending it back to the Godhead, back to the Great Central Sun.

He is first and foremost the destroyer of the human ego. He destroys the ties that bind us to human existence. You may think you do not want him to destroy those bonds and yet, I tell you, when he does you will find that you have a much stronger binding to God. You will have bonds that come from God and the whole universe that bind you to the soul and the heart of all people in the world, that bind you more tightly to loved ones, to children, to those in your immediate family. When the selfish, self-centered human bonds are not there, the God bonds become much stronger.

We are in a period of transition where we fear to let go of what is really not worth hanging on to, because we don't understand the unknown. The unknown is what is real. What we have today is unreality. Reality is more rich, more intense in color, in vibration, in thought, in feeling.

Everything you experience today that is ephemeral will pass away. Nothing lasts in the human condition. You can experience the same things at a higher level and they will never pass away. Love never passes away. Wisdom doesn't pass away. Caring doesn't pass away. The true love of soul to soul becomes immortalized through Shiva—it becomes immortalized through Vishnu and through Brahma.

Hindu scholar Margaret Stutley writes that Shiva "is also the death of Death, the bestower of immortality on his devotees."[3]

If you are not willing to have your mortality destroyed, then Shiva cannot give to you your immortality.

There is somewhat of an attachment to that human skeleton and that human body. Even the highest yogis have had moments of great burden and sorrow in leaving their body in their final *samadhi,* when the soul passes on and does not return. This is called the *mahasamadhi.*[4]

Stutley says Shiva is "the embodiment of yogic power that destroys the bonds binding the individual spirit to the world and so gives liberation."[5] What I have been telling you in this conference is that you can have God and the whole universe and yet not lose the levels of human experience that are necessary to your evolution and to your working through your psychology. It's not as if suddenly you were to embrace God as a totality and as your total being, and as a result you wouldn't know yourself and no one else would know you.

I can tell you, the people who count will know you. The people who don't count and shouldn't be your companions in the first place will somehow not be around anymore. You have to expect to make new friends and to make the Ascended Masters, the angelic hosts and the Archangels your friends. And when you do, you'll meet millions of people upon earth who also move in those circles.

After all, there are some things that are worth making a transition for. There are some things that are worth going up the steps for and leaving behind some of the old landmarks. If you really love your friends and companions, even though they may have led you astray here and there, and you really feel for their souls, the only way you can ever help them is to go up a couple of stairs. Then you can step down and reach out that powerful arm you will have acquired through your devotion to Archangel Michael and pull them up and transfer to them the Light you have gained.

And that doesn't come overnight. You can't be a student and a teacher all at once. You need to be working on that path until you come into a true strength where you can help those whom you never could help when you were on an equal footing with them at a lower level of consciousness.

Shiva often appears as a yogi with snow-white face and matted hair, dressed in a tiger skin. He is the friend of yogis who helps them to attain their goal of God-realization.

You are yogis whether or not you practice any kind of physical yoga. You need to remember that. You may be a bhakti yogi, you may be a jnana yogi, a karma yogi or a raja yogi.

So we are all yogis because we are taking upon us the yoke of Jesus Christ, which is Light and which is easy. "Come unto me, all ye that labor and are heavy laden, and I will give you rest. Take my yoke upon you and learn of me, for I am meek and lowly in heart and ye shall find rest unto your souls. For my yoke is easy and my burden is Light."[6] We are yogis under the Ascended Masters. We are yogis as we perfect the science of the spoken Word.

So Shiva, dressed up as a yogi, is a true friend of all yogis. We see him in this role in the Vedic myth of the winning of the waters. In the myth, the Vedic god Indra slays the serpentine monster Vritra, thereby releasing the waters to flow to the sea. As I mentioned in my lecture on Hinduism, this myth is symbolic of the practice of yoga. Indra represents the Self and the waters represent the light released from the chakras to flow upward to the crown.

In one version of the story, Indra cannot succeed without Shiva. Shiva lends him the strength he needs to conquer Vritra. This tells us that it is Shiva who will give us the strength we need to overcome the serpent of the not-self so that we can attain enlightenment.

Shiva is also known as the distributor of the seven holy rivers. This means that he is the one who distributes the light to our chakras and will help us control the light in our chakras and balance the light at each of the levels.

You will notice that I have a statue of the wonderful dancing Shiva in front of me on the altar. I have carried this Shiva with me all over the world in my Stumps and wherever I speak. Shiva stands between me and the dweller-on-the-threshold of anyone in the audience or anyone in the world or any force on the astral plane that would attack the delivery of the Word from the altar.

If you would like to have a Shiva of this size and presence and strength, please let us know and we'll see if we can get one for you. I think it's one of the most important statues of our Church and Shiva works through it for you in an absolutely fantastic way.

Shiva's consort, or Shakti, appears in three primary forms. *Shakti* means "power." It is the Feminine Principle of the Godhead, the Divine Mother who went forth out of the Divine Whole. Shiva's main Shaktis are Parvati, daughter of the god Himalaya, a benevolent goddess and devoted wife; Durga, "the unfathomable one," known as the destroyer of demons; and Kali, "the power of time." Kali is a symbol of destruction, who appears with black skin wearing a necklace of skulls. Yet she bestows blessings upon those who seek knowledge of God and is revered by her devotees as the Divine Mother. As you know, she was the chosen deity of Ramakrishna.

Lord Shiva lives on the summit of the sacred Mount Kailasa in Tibet. He is pictured there both as a solitary ascetic and with his Shakti, Parvati. John Snelling, in his book *The Sacred Mountain,* recounts how Parvati contributed to the origin of Shiva's third eye:

> Legend describes [Parvati] playfully covering her Lord's eyes as he sat in meditation on a peak of Himalaya. Instantly all light and life were extinguished in the universe until, out of compassion for all beings, the god opened his third eye, which blazed like a new sun. So intense was its blazing that it scorched the mountains and forests of [the Himalayas] to oblivion. Only

> when he saw that the daughter of the mountain was properly contrite did he relent and restore her father [who is the mountain] to his former estate.[7]

This legend shows Shiva as the Destroyer. The opening of his third eye represents the opening of the eye of knowledge that destroys ignorance. Swami Karapatri explains: "The frontal eye, the eye of fire, is the eye of higher perception. It looks mainly inward. When directed outward, it burns all that appears before it. It is from a glance of this third eye that . . . the gods and all created beings are destroyed at each of the periodical destructions of the universe."[8]

Shiva is also known as the Lord of the Dance, Nataraja. His dance destroys the fetters that bind the soul. He dances triumphantly on the demon who personifies ignorance and illusion.

As scholar Veronica Ions writes, "When dancing, Shiva represents cosmic truth."[9] In his upper right hand, Shiva holds a drum, which represents the sound from which the universe was created. His upper left hand holds a tongue of flame. His left foot is raised, telling us that we can raise ourselves and attain salvation.

Ananda Coomaraswamy writes, "[The] deepest significance [of Shiva's dance] is felt when it is realized that it takes place within the heart and the self. Everywhere is God: that Everywhere is the heart."[10]

Shiva is the great Guru who comes to save us from ignorance, from forgetfulness and our human ego. His kindly love is a fierce love that strips us of all that separates us from oneness with him. Shaivites repeat the mantra *Om Namah Shivaya*—"I bow down to thee, Lord Shiva"—in order to attain union with Shiva. Let's give it together now:

Om Namah Shivaya (given 69 times, clapping)

Ommmmmmmmmmmmmmmmmmmmmm

We're going to give some other Shiva mantras so I would like you to visualize Shiva all around you. See his Electronic Presence larger than life, larger than you, and you inside of him. (This is if you desire, if you have the will to do so.) And as you give the mantra, bow to Shiva before you.

You can follow the exercise linearly by seeing him first before you as you give your adoration to him through the bhajan. Then, as he comes toward you, feel the union of the Divine One with your soul—the Divine Lover of your soul with your soul. And finally, see Shiva superimposed over you and you inside of him.

Now, I would like you to give these bhajans in great devotion to the Holy Spirit—if you feel comfortable doing so. If you don't feel comfortable with Shiva, that is your right. But if you do and you do the meditation, I ask you to notice when you spontaneously feel that presence of Shiva around you to such an extent that you can no longer remain in your seat but must literally stand up. Then notice when you can no longer stand up without jumping in the air by the very power and force of the Shakti of Shiva, of the sacred fire of his being. And just let yourself do it!

So all who wish to participate in this may do so.*

Messenger's Invocation:

O infinite Light sealed in our hearts, we adore by thy Holy Spirit, *Shiva!* By the infinite Light of God, so manifest thy rings upon rings of Light in this place. *Shiva!* ["Shiva!"]

O mighty one of God, come forth! Dispeller of Darkness, destroyer of Death and Hell, *descend, descend* to the depths of planet earth. Come now! Multiply your Presence a billion times. Stand in the aura. Dance in the aura! Sit in the heart of every lifestream upon earth. *Shiva!* ["Shiva!"]

O living Light, penetrate now! Penetrate now, Mahadeva. Penetrate now! Let us be drawn up in the fire of the Ruby Ray, in the planes of the Dhyani Buddhas and the planes of the Bodhisattvas and the planes of the Buddha of the Ruby Ray.

Lord Gautama, Sanat Kumara, Seven Holy Kumaras, Lord Maitreya, Jesus Christ, all hosts of the LORD's Spirit of the Great White Brotherhood, invoke now *Shiva!* ["Shiva!"]

O living Light, draw the line now. Draw the line now! *Draw the*

*At this juncture, the Messenger and congregation sang the bhajans "He Śiva Śaṅkara" (number 658) and "Mānasa Bhajore" (number 660), followed by the mantra *Tat Tvam Asi.*

line now! As thou didst assist Indra, so release and free now our geothermal waters! Release and free now our geothermal waters!

[Congregation affirms with the Messenger:]

Release and free now our geothermal waters!

Shiva! ["Shiva!"]

Come forth, O Divine Mother! Come forth, Parvati. Come forth, Durga. Come forth, Great Kali. O thou Divine Mother, secure the earth unto the very core of the earth. Secure the Grand Teton and the Royal Teton Ranch. Secure the earth for the Lightbearers all!

I call unto the Lord Shiva in this hour for the binding of Death and Hell. All hosts of Shiva, all manifestations of Shiva, mighty Electronic Presence of Shiva, be everywhere in the earth this night, in every bush and flower, in every heart of every deer, every elk, all that roam these lands. O God in all levels of creation, let there be now, we pray, the liberating power of *Shiva!* ["Shiva!"]

I call forth the Light. I call forth the living presence, Brahman. *Brahman, Brahman, Brahman,* come forth! Release through thy Word the glory of creation, the victory of the Great White Brotherhood in the earth, the victory of all Ascended Masters and their chelas. Blaze the power of the Godhead now, O Lord!

Come forth, Brahma, Vishnu, Shiva! Come forth, Vak, Divine Mother! We greet thee in our hearts, in our temples. Within, without, thou art *Shiva!* ["Shiva!"]*

June 30, 1992

*Following the invocation and in preparation for the dictation of Lord Shiva, the Messenger and congregation sang the bhajan "Hara Mahādeva" (number 657).

CHAPTER 7

Lord Shiva

ONLY MAKE THE CALL, "SHIVA!"

Ho! *Shiva* is come—come to you, each one!

I AM come. I AM here. I intensify the fire: Shiva!

I intensify it first and foremost in your heart. Open your heart now to receive the infinite God that I AM, that you are, that we are. For I, Shiva, desire to enter.

Open your heart! I knock at the door.

Will you receive me, my loves? ["Yes!"]

Thus, I come. I come as the great regulator of life and the flow of life—oh, the mighty flow of life in your being! I come to cleanse and purify your heart from the physical level to the very heart of the Inner Atman unto the Inner God—not that the Atman requires purification but that your perception of the Atman requires purification.

O my beloved ones, won't you be this night my Parvati, my Durga, my Kali and be seated as brides, one and all?

With great anticipation mighty yogis of the East have seen me fly to this place and they are joyous as they hear with the inner ear the devotions to Shiva.

Shiva I AM. Shiva you are. Will you not be now the negative polarity of my being forever and forever and forever so that we may purge the earth of Death and Hell so that earth may go through her purgation and the souls of the earth and the dead, and the deader than dead, might be consumed by the power of Divine Love?

Lo, I AM that Shiva! Lo, I AM intensifying that fire! Now I send forth my Light through all the arteries and the veins and the capillaries. I send my Light now!

Take a mighty inbreath with me. Now over the mighty breath that you inbreathe, which is my own breath, I am sending Light and re-invigoration and eternal youth and regeneration.

Lo, I AM THAT I AM. *Lo, I AM THAT I AM!* And I may be seated in your physical body! I may be seated in your desire body! I may be seated in your mental body! I may be seated in your etheric body! Now then, if you will invite me, I will do so promptly.

[Congregation gives forth fiats and clapping Shivas for 39 seconds.]

I enter for a solemn purpose, beloved. I enter because I desire to give myself this night to the mighty warriors of Light, whom you are, to the blessed devotees, to the blessed mothers and sisters and daughters and knights and heroes all over the world. I desire to give you a boost! I desire to give you that much of myself which the law of your being allows.

Each day the law of your being is read to you by your Holy Christ Self. The law changes almost like the readings on the stock market, beloved, for there is the coming and the going and the rising and the falling as you make negative karma, as you balance the negative by the positive and as you continue and continue and continue.

Now then, beloved ones, I am desiring to give you more Light for prolonged incarnation. I can give this to you, beloved, today but the one sure way for you to sustain it and maintain it is to recite or sing one of these bhajans to me daily.

In the power of the sound you have generated and will generate again and again, may you have a recording of this assembly in this place in the Heart, in this place that is purged physically and at inner levels by the mighty rain of Alpha, by the mighty rain of Omega. (The clearing of the earth is one of the points on the agenda of this conference for the Darjeeling Council and for others of our bands.)

So, beloved, if you will take the recording of the sound that is echoed in this tabernacle of the congregation, resounding amongst the hills and the mountains, you will know that I will surely *jump* inside of you again each day for the giving of one, a single one, of these bhajans.

I look to your longevity, *for I look for pillars of fire in the earth!* I look for those who shall walk with the walking stick of Shiva, who will walk with my flame and in the honor of God and who will be a focus of that white fire, dispersing Death and Hell where'er they walk.

Yes, beloved ones, I look for Western Shaivites who will follow me, who will be myself that I might be their self—and that is the key! If you will allow me to be yourself for moments of the day, *I will repolarize you.*

Take care, then, that you observe the rules of the Great White Brotherhood, that you let not the sun go down upon your wrath,[1] that you resolve all things by the fire of *Shiva,* by the fire of the violet flame, by the blessed heart of the great avatar Saint Germain.

Yes, beloved ones, we rejoice that the Western yogis and yoginis are pursuing the path of the violet flame. It is an action ray which, when coupled with the ruby fire that I bear and the white light, will bring immense change in the earth!

Now, change needs to come quickly, yet not so quickly as to be a scorching fire that destroys in the process of the change. The violet flame will bring it about gently.

It is worth all lifetimes and many lifetimes to stay at the Heart of the Inner Retreat, to stay near the Royal Teton Ranch where you can have some livelihood for yourselves and your families. It is worth it just to be able to come together in such numbers at least one day a week that is set aside for this mighty action of the sacred fire's invocation. It will not take much more for the hierarchies of the Himalayas and the Great White Brotherhood to do much for the earth.

I can tell you, in these days deep changes are taking place gently by transmutation. Oh, thank you for the violet flame you have invoked this day! All elemental life blesses you, honors you and bows before the Light of God within you.

You need these servants of God and man in nature, beloved ones. And when they see your auras blazing and your dedication in their behalf, there is a ripple of mighty hope going forth through the mountains, the forests, the hills of all the hemispheres!

And they desire to see this entire body of students transported here and there over the earth! So we shall accommodate them, shall we not? ["Yes!"] Therefore we shall go this night.

You have made your certain connection with the Great White Brotherhood. Make the call and seal yourself in that Sacred Ritual for Transport and Holy Work.[2] So do it, beloved, without the necessity of going through again all of the words; but accept and affirm in your inner being before you retire that you shall therefore journey with Shiva.

You will journey to the places in the earth where earth is violated, elemental life is violated, the resources are violated and the toxins and the poisons are violating the bodies of all people but most especially those of the Lightbearers.

Let there be a cleansing in the earth without major cataclysm! *This is our goal.* To this we call you!

Saint Germain has called you in the past and many of you have responded, giving day after day your calls to the violet flame. I ask you to consider again, as the cycles are turning in this decade, how you will]multiply the mantras of the violet flame by the Ruby Ray, and the Ruby Ray by the power of the mantras to Shiva, to Lord Krishna, and see what you can do to *clear* the minds, *clear* the opposition, *clear* those conditions that you hear about in the media.

Beloved ones, I ask you to be seated as my brides. If you will remain seated and be still in the posture of your preference, you will find that I am able now to build along the spinal altar a certain conductor of light and a certain action of the healing of your central nervous system and brain. This is essential, beloved ones. You are hearts to be cherished and I indeed cherish you!

Blessed ones, there are many actions being taken in the earth, none more diabolical in this moment than the decree by the justices of the Supreme Court of the United States of America, five in number, who have agreed to uphold *Roe v. Wade* and the right, which is now called a "constitutional" right of woman, to abort her own Life becoming Life, her own child in the womb, her own *God* in the making, for that is *God* that is being aborted![3]

It is the abortion of the Atman! It is the abortion of a mission! And therefore it becomes, in some respect, *the abortion of an age* each time an individual is denied entrance into this world!

Can you believe, beloved ones, as I have seen with my own eye, that abortion actually being shown on television last night? Blessed ones, how can there be such low, low levels of descending into the Darkness and dragging woman and her child to that level?

O beloved ones, these members of this Court are examples of those who followed the way of *Din* in the betrayal of the LORD God's judgment and therefore took upon themselves the right to judge life, the right to condemn life, the right to criticize life, the right to purge and destroy life.

Yes, beloved ones, they shall come to naught. The living Christ Jesus under Sanat Kumara has given to you the individual judgment calls and the judgment call for the binding of the dweller-on-the-threshold.

These individuals who have upheld a law that should never have been made a law, these individuals who have neglected the Holy Child now find upon their own heads the ultimate burden of karma for every child who is aborted hence, following their decision.

Beloved ones, this is an hour of great, great Darkness in the land, for we had hoped that there would be one individual who could be moved. Well, I AM *Shiva* and I tell you, I went to each one of them at inner levels and I attempted to move them. And they did defy and reject me and they would not be moved from their position to guarantee the right to kill the child who is God in the womb. *For shame! for shame! for shame* upon this civilization!

Therefore, I say, what shall we do?

We shall call the judgment upon those who know what they do! And these five *know* what they do. And all those who have led woman astray, those who know what they do and pronounce their judgment upon the unborn and provide the milieu for abortion and the abortion tools and the abortion clinics and the abortion doctors—all those who know what they do, *they* shall receive unmitigated judgment from my heart!

For I AM the destroyer of Death and they are Death incarnate, and they are seeking to lead the children of the Light into their death camp and to take them from embodiment.

Oh, shame! oh, shame! oh, shame! beloved, that that very abortion you saw on television was the abortion of a mighty Lightbearer!

I enlist those who fear me not, who know that there are few resources directly available to them through which the spiritual fire can be directed. Blessed ones, remember the scorching power of my third eye, remember the whirling of my being and my aura as I dance in the heart of the sun—and my own aura of the sun-manifestation.

Therefore, you see that an Ascended Master, an Archangel, a God or Goddess may go to those in embodiment and attempt to move them, attempt to convince them, even show them the akashic records of where they will end up by the folly of their decision. But, beloved ones, we do not interfere with free will. This is the law of all those who are beyond this level of embodiment.

You have free will in the earth. These justices represent you. Therefore, you can call to God and through your call, through your presence and through your life the judgment may descend upon them for their actions, for their deeds and even for their rejection of Shiva! Understand, therefore, what lies in your hand.

All you needed to understand was the mighty power of the *Ein Sof* and of the *sefirot* and then you could see the mighty Tree of Life superimposed upon you as the Mighty I AM Presence. You could see the powers of God waiting to be invoked—*waiting, waiting!*

When you say, "How long, O Lord, how long, O Lord, wilt thou allow such suffering in the earth and the murder of the child?" the LORD God says back to you, "How long, O ye sons and daughters, how long, O ye brides of Shiva, will you wait to make the call and call for the judgment and the binding of the dweller-on-the-threshold of the entire consciousness, *the diabolical consciousness of abortion* that comes directly out of the pit of Death and Hell?"

How can you stand it any longer when you have the tools, the sponsorship and you must only say the word to see the turning of the cycles and the turning of the Darkness and the dark ones until they shall no longer be able to inhabit the earth?

For the vibration of earth shall accelerate through your call! And as it accelerates, beloved ones, therefore it will *spin off* those who are not of the Light, who will refuse to rise in vibration. And they must go to another place that they created long ago.

And these very ones who complain, these "environmentalists" who complain about the pollutions of the earth, they will go to the very place that they themselves have polluted in the past and they will truly have to deal with an environment that they themselves did destroy!

And I speak not only of the physical environment, I speak of the astral plane and the mental belt. And the mental belt is highly polluted. So is the etheric octave!

And therefore, beloved ones, when *you* increase in Light, when *you,* the sons and daughters of God, understand that the earth is the LORD's and you are the LORD's and you are his caretakers here below, you are going to go forth to keep the flame for planet earth.

And when you keep the Light in your body and you keep the Light in the temple, then *you* will dominate the Darkness and the dark ones by the Light: *you,* the Lightbearers, will be the dominant power, as the fallen ones are now the dominant power.

Therefore, we are able to help the individual, but how can we help the multitudes, beloved ones, when they are beset by and do embody the mass consciousness that is perpetrated upon them by the Nephilim gods and the fallen ones?

But I say to you, *you* have the power in your Mighty I AM Presence! *You* have the power in God and *not* in your human self, *not* in your carnal mind, *not* in the dweller-on-the-threshold but in God and God alone, who lives in you, to call for the binding of the destroyers in the earth—*not* the destroyer who is Shiva: rather call to Shiva, who will destroy the destroyers! For I AM *Shiva!*

[*"Shiva!"* (22-second standing ovation)]

Only make the call, *"Shiva!"* Only make the call, *"Shiva!"*
Only make the call, *"Shiva!"* Only make the call, *"Shiva!"*
[Congregation gives Shiva's fiat, clapping:]
Only make the call, "Shiva!" Only make the call, "Shiva!"
Only make the call, "Shiva!" Only make the call, "Shiva!"
Only make the call, "Shiva!" Only make the call, "Shiva!"
Only make the call, "Shiva!" Only make the call, "Shiva!"
Only make the call, "Shiva!" Only make the call, "Shiva!"
Only make the call, "Shiva!" Only make the call, "Shiva!"
Only make the call, "Shiva!" Only make the call, "Shiva!"

I have given you this mantra. I have burned it into the cells of your being and into your very bones lest you forget to only make the call, *"Shiva!"* [Congregation joins Shiva, clapping:]

to only make the call, "Shiva!" to only make the call, "Shiva!"
to only make the call, "Shiva!" to only make the call, "Shiva!"
to only make the call, "Shiva!" to only make the call, "Shiva!"

Beloved ones, I have stood and stood through a certain adept, who shall not be unveiled to you this night. I have stood through and around and in a certain adept and I have pierced my eye through the eye of that adept in physical embodiment and I have shown that one that a certain individual in a certain place, a total stranger standing there, was an immediate manifestation in physical embodiment of an alien from a UFO. And that individual was there and was identified. And I did put through the eye of the adept the power of my own eye, and that individual quickly moved from that place and, out of the sight of the adept, was bound and was removed.

Blessed ones, I say to you: Work for your adeptship! *Work* for it and cherish it. Cherish it as though your adeptship were the very necessity for you to be the presence in the earth that must be there for the denying of abortion, for the sparing of those souls who must enter. Think of it as working for your knighthood or your ladyhood.

Yes, beloved ones, think of the necessity to rise to the degrees of self-mastery because in that self-mastery I can work through you and know that you—as I knew with that one—will not in any level or degree misqualify the Light or the manifestation of my presence, for you, like that one, will have proven yourself trustworthy many, many times.

I will take no chances. I will not make karma for your indiscretions, for your misuses of the Light. Therefore, *see* who I will work through, who has the inner peace and the balance of the four lower bodies, who has followed the Messenger in using the diet of the Eastern adepts as a means to that God-control of all the physical levels of the body and then the emotions and then the mind and then the memory.

Beloved ones, the discipline is total, but look at what is before you! If suddenly this place were removed and all of a sudden you were in a large arena and in that arena were men of war, men of largeness, and they were slaughtering thousands and thousands of babies, you would leap to the center, you would bind them, you would rescue those whom you could rescue.

The situation of abortion is out of sight, out of mind. You are heroes and heroines every day of your lives as you serve, but *do not blind yourselves* to these events taking place daily—the murder of the child. Do not close your ears to the screams of the child, for they are heard across the planet. And these screams coming from every state and nation are reverberating such a sound, such a sound, beloved ones!

What Lightbearers could possibly be attracted to embody here when the very sounds of the earth rise up, whether as the agony of the child aborted or as the anger of the fallen ones as they go through the horrors of untimely death by all of the plagues coming upon the race?

Yes, there is great pain in the earth, but there is no pain so great to my heart, to your heart or to the heart of the Divine Mother as that pain of a soul that is dying, the soul that is being lost, the soul that is fading away, whether from weakness or from the anger and rebellion against God that in turn has also become a passivity.

The death of the soul, beloved, even far exceeds the pain of the abortion of a child. For a child may come again and be born again if parents can be found but when there is the death of the soul, the potential to realize God is permanently removed from that particular individuality in God that had opportunity to make that individuality permanent.

I think you agree with me that the infamy of planet earth has reached a high watermark. ["Yes."] And I think you know in the depth of your souls and in the marrow of your bones that things cannot get much worse without some reaction from the Great Tao, from the Great *Ein Sof,* from the Great God, the unmanifest God who chooses to manifest himself through us.

Yes, beloved, it is an hour of such opportunity for the binding of the forces of Antichrist. I solemnly speak to you. *May you not forget my word and my message.* May you fulfill all things necessary, and I say *necessary,* in your life. But may you not heap, and stack upon heap, obligations and activities that are actually not necessary to your livelihood, to your divine plan, to your good karma of caring for those in your care and for doing to others as you know God would have you do unto them, whoever is at the door.

There are things you must do in life, but won't you all admit once and for all there are many things you do that are not a necessity at all, whether to your health, to your ongoing edification or even to the opening of the flower of love of the heart.

I ask you, please, please make a list of those things that you can put aside and say, "I have done these things long enough, for many lifetimes. I can set them aside. For God in every child on planet earth is crying out to me and I cannot deafen my ears to those cries. I must help the little children. For once I was a little child, too, and I was helpless. And I took the hand of my mother and I took the hand of my father and others in whose care I was, and I went where they took me. I had no power of my own to do this or that. And I waited the long years till I came to that point of maturity when I could say, 'I am an adult. I am free at last! I am my own person. I shall do what I must do.'"

Blessed ones, being a child in the earth of whatever age is truly an unenviable position today, for child abuse is on the rise and there are the toxic chemicals in the body, in the water, in the food, in the substances they partake of, in the toys they play with.

What is fed to the child mind through the television is nothing but Death and Hell itself! I place my image over the television—between it and children—but, beloved ones, they and their parents have free will and I can only screen out so much.

Remember, you were once a child and helpless. And remember, when you are in your final days you may also be helpless. But *today* you have the strength and the vigor of life for all that you would acquire by following the right formulas for existence on earth. You have my offer of my presence.

I believe that deep down in your heart there is not one of you who is present at this conference who cannot say, because you are true chelas of the Light, that you are not satisfied with your present condition of spirituality and that you are here because you are *compelled* by your inner soul and your Inner Atman to rise another level and then another level and then another level!

You have reached a certain plateau in certain areas and you have finally said, *"I cannot rest here!* I am not breathing enough of the breath of eternal Life! I am not imbibing enough of the Light of the Eternal God and I am not doing enough for my people. I will find out how! I will *do something* and I will see change in my life, that I might give a better self to my Lord Brahman."

Blessed ones, in the flame, I AM Shiva. *Shiva,* yes. ["Shiva!"] *Shiva*, yes. ["Shiva!"] *Shiva,* yes! ["Shiva, yes!"]

I AM that flame. I AM that Shiva where you are. I want you to feel this with a great God-Reality. I AM here now as the slayer of illusion! And for this very moment I take the mighty sword and *I slay illusion all around you!* And I ask you to take the remainder of this class to see just how much more you can see for the illusions that I will now take. [Shiva does his sword work through the Messenger.]

As you might say, "You could cut it with a sword!" The illusions are as thick as the densest cheese you would find. Can you imagine living with such illusions? Yet you do, beloved ones. But the sacred fire raised up and the violet flame will clear them.

My beloved brides, I take you to my chamber, the chamber of my heart, this night. We shall go and minister to elemental life from the gathering place of the Royal Teton Retreat, where millions of other Lightbearers who are receiving this instruction at inner levels will be happy to join you. Our final stop will be, once again, Yugoslavia.[4]

You have made profound progress at deep inner levels. Let us keep it up [journeying to Yugoslavia] for thirty-three days, beginning from the moment of our going forth and then our return.

In the name of the Divine Mother, in whose body I serve, Above and below, I AM Shiva!

And who are you? ["Shiva! Shiva! Shiva! . . . "]

[Congregation gives forth clapping *Shivas* for 45 seconds.]

June 30, 1992

CHAPTER 8

Omega

DO NOT DOUBT GOD!

Love God and Love One Another

Our Most Beloved Sons and Daughters:

We come surrounded by legions of angels whose acquaintance you have met in ages past. Be at home, then, for we place over this place, so consecrated by your hearts and the heart of Lord Gautama Buddha, even the replica of our Home, your Home in the Great Central Sun. So long, so long—as time is reckoned and as cycles of coming and going are reckoned—has been your absence from our Home.

Now you have said the Om. You have sounded it from within. Now experience it in this moment that will be for you, we trust, a springboard to a new thrust for your Victory and for the ultimate Victory of the Lightbearers of the earth. Therefore, be at rest.

Our gratitude to servants of the Light, helpers, angels, elementals, all who have come to prepare this place. In a single year you have made it once again our cradle—the cradle where we do give birth to souls of Light annually.

Oh, it is a coming together! Oh, it is a sun center, this very place! And thus, beloved, a planetary and a personal purging is ongoing. Welcome, then, the rain, for it is a special rain of our beloved Alpha.

I, then, Omega, greet you, and I greet you in the love of such tender understanding of your innermost thoughts and needs and desires and questionings and doubts.

It is not easy to be in this octave, beloved. But I would remind you that the divine spark within, which is called by a number of names by the various ones who have experienced the divine spark, even the Atman itself, truly does have a name and that name is Alpha/Omega. We are the Divine Presence in your heart. Brahman is the Divine Presence. The Universal Christ is that Presence.

Therefore, as we can understand even the dilemma of living in this octave, so will you not understand that there is also the very present possibility for you to live in that holy aura, truly that universe of Light that is the secret chamber of the heart?

This place of our Home of Alpha and Omega with which we surround you in this hour is available to you, each one, as you will retire to the secret chamber of your heart each day.

Beloved, just as all of Death and Hell move against your going in consciousness to the Great Central Sun, so do not underestimate the opposition to your soul each and every day of your life—that opposition which would deny the soul her entering in, as the great ritual of the conclusion of the day, entering in to the secret chamber of the heart.

This you do in the name of your Mighty I AM Presence and Holy Christ Self, in the name of Archangel Michael. For you do understand that there are boulders and mountains of karma that stand between you, as the soul seated in the seat-of-the-soul chakra, and that secret chamber that is the replica of our Home and of all universes within and without.

Therefore, under the old dispensation, you could not have lawfully risen to such a holy place without having balanced that karma, but in this day and hour the Archangel Michael does place his Presence over you. And therefore, in the presence of that God-free, wondrous manifestation of I AM THAT I AM, your soul may rise to that level (as she has not done in many centuries) and be tutored, beloved ones.

Is this not the mighty grace of the Lord, who weeps for you, who loves you, who desires you not to be absent but with him, with him in the very heart of Brahman?

Therefore, grace and mercy abound—and the grace of the Word, the Shekinah, beloved ones, the mighty power of Mother Flame and of Shakti of God. By that grace and mercy, then, you are able to come to the secret place of your God and to do so regularly and daily. To so do will strike in you a new tenderness, a tenderness so rare, whereby you can hardly find a harsh feeling or a harsh word thereafter—so wondrous, so loving is the Presence and so much love do you find in that secret place where the threefold flame does burn.

Let the rituals of the heart not take hours, beloved. There is no time and space in this. There is being the caretaker of your thoughts and feelings, the body, the heart and the mind, so that by a thought at the end of the day you can give the fiat to Archangel Michael, you can call to us as Father-Mother and you can mount the spiral staircase from the seat-of-the-soul chakra to the secret chamber of the heart and be one.

And then when day breaks and you must go and pick up your karma again after you have journeyed through the night to the etheric octaves, you return through that point of the secret chamber of the heart to your lawful place in the seat-of-the-soul chakra and you work the works of God. And you have such love that you pour into each work! And you retain the memory of the exercises of the guarding of the throat chakra, of the silence of the bliss of God that you can maintain no matter what is the requirement of the hour.

You, then, compress the fire of being and concentrate it, using it not for many, many idle words but saving it for the peace-commanding presence, raising it up to the point of the third eye, whereby you may see and know and make, without error, your decisions and take your steps and live in the cycles of the hours as though you were living, and indeed you are, in the spheres of the Great Causal Body of your I AM Presence.

I AM your Divine Mother, beloved ones, and I desire to make you comfortable in the earth. (Yes, I know there are many who attempt to take from you that comfort.) Comfort comes first from the twin flames of the Holy Spirit, Alpha and Omega. It comes also as these flames may manifest the basic necessities of life and that which does establish the circle of hearth and home and family and community of brothers and sisters who are keeping the Flame with seraphim at the altar of God day and night.

Yes, beloved, I understand the burdens that are upon you and I understand, all too well, those who place them upon you.

Receive from my heart, O Mother of the Flame, in this hour the empowerment to call on behalf of the sons and daughters of God for the binding of the oppressor and the oppression. Receive it now, O Mother, and exercise it in behalf of thine own, whom thou doest love so profoundly!

O beloved hearts, in your Holy Christ Flame is the intensity of Light which can be multiplied by you to accomplish so much more than you accomplish *for your nonbelief.* Yes, beloved, it is a matter of believing.

Those who believe in God and in the God-identification of one and another and another in embodiment, beloved, may therefore have that tie of God-identification established through that One to the Great Central Sun and know many miracles. Those of nonbelief can receive nothing—I say *nothing*—whether from Alpha and Omega or from our Messenger.

Therefore, go after with the vengeance of Kali the very momentum of nonbelief, unbelief, doubt, self-doubt and doubt of God which torments you and causes you to doubt anyone and everyone whom you may meet!

Blessed hearts, self-doubt is self-denial and it is the denial of God. It is a most dangerous state of consciousness. You must wage war against it! For unless you remove it, how shall we enter in and how shall you enter in?

You see, doubt breaks the cord of Light you build with your decrees. Each cutting doubt is a cutting of the rope you have built and raised unto the sky as a yogi with yogic powers.

Yes, beloved, do not doubt the Law! Do not doubt God! Recognize God in yourself and do not doubt his Spirit in you as the Atman. This is the most precious advice I could give you for a lifetime and many lifetimes.

When you are sure of the self that is God within you (and there is absolutely no reason why you should not be, because God is faithful unto you even when you have been faithless), when you are absolutely faithful to that God and trust that God, beloved, there is therefore established a tie that cannot be broken, neither by yourself nor by Death and Hell—except you yourself by free will should once again entertain doubt and break it.

This, then, is the portion that you must give to God. If you will but give faith and trust and build upon it wisdom and illumination, wisdom and understanding, and build upon it a true and profound knowledge of the will of God, then you will find through your study not one or five or ten but many, many reasons why you ought to have faith and not doubt.

O beloved, if the Lord Jesus Christ when he journeyed into the cities "did not many mighty works there for their unbelief,"[1] do you think the father and the mother of Jesus Christ or the son, the daughter of God in the earth who is the bearer of the mantle may do any more?

I tell you no! And therefore, we witness to the work of the Messenger unto those who believe and have faith and see beyond the veil the shining of the God Presence that is able to reach out to them and raise them. Thus, they are raised. Thus, they are healed.

We see that that work cannot manifest in those who have inner conflict, inner compromise, who violate the laws of Alpha and Omega, do not confess, atone, receive penance, do not determine to work upright in the face of their God or even, God forbid, have in their conversations the criticism of the Messenger or our servants.

Beloved ones, what we offer you today is a very direct and living contact to us through the Messenger and through the mantle of Guru that is upon her solidly and sealed. Thus, know it. Understand it. The Path and the relationship are open to *you* as long as you will maintain the single foundational quality, which is love.

Love contains all others! Love balances all others! Love consumes all others! In the center of God's love and your love for him, you may approach such a close nestling to the heart of myself, your Divine Mother.

I will tell you that the Messenger will never pursue you, beloved.

You yourselves must make the request to be a known and counted and sponsored direct chela of the Messenger and, through the Messenger, to be a chela of the heart of El Morya and the entire hierarchy of Light unto our hearts.

Yes, beloved, let the ties become tighter! Let them not become bondage but let them become a mighty soul liberation unto all who are a part of the great *antahkarana* of Life!

I, Omega, bring you the greetings of untold billions of points of Light and angels and sons and daughters—points of Light, who after all are simply the One.

Their love be upon you this day and forever. May you receive it this day and forever because you vow to yourself and your God Self never to leave off loving God and loving God in one another.

How can you go wrong with this formula?

I myself do not know.

July 1, 1992

CHAPTER 9

Alpha

THE FOURTH WOE

"I Will Become the Example!"

Hail, O Alpha's Sons and Daughters!

I AM come. I AM Alpha here and in you. And I deliver unto you this day *my Love, my Love, my Love!* [43-second standing ovation]

Again the heathen rage and the people imagine a vain thing. But I, the Lord, do hold them in derision. Therefore, let us laugh today, let us laugh tomorrow and let us laugh again![1]

For though they seek to take from you the geothermal waters of the Divine Mother in the earth, I tell you, they shall never take from you the waters of everlasting Life, which I bring this day and which my angelic hosts now offer you as the cup of cold water in Christ's name, and more—as the elixir that you might quaff and know that I am urging on the points of light and cells in your body to move toward the ascension in the Light! [27-second standing ovation]

Now stand very still and receive the beloved seraph who loves you, who knows you, who attended your birth in the Great Central Sun. Can you imagine that there is such a seraph who has known you since first you opened your eyes and saw the Beloved and saw your God?

So that one, that precious one, now hands to you each one this cup of the elixir. Drink, then, beloved ones. It is sparkling and ready.

[22-second pause] Every Lightbearer in embodiment upon earth who has raised himself or herself to a certain level, with or without this Teaching, shall also be served this drink during the hours of rest. Now then, beloved, be seated for the assimilation of the elixir and my word.

There are some things that are to be endured in the earth and there are some things that cannot be tolerated, nor by God nor by his sons and daughters. Therefore I am grateful that you are in the earth in this hour. I have placed you here, beloved, but that which I could never do is to force your free will or your hand to become devotees and disciples of Alpha and Omega in this life.

You were surely God-taught. You were surely received before our altars in the retreats of the Great White Brotherhood. You were shown the possibilities and the karmas and the pitfalls and your weaknesses and your strengths and the actions of past lives that did take you apart from the way, the straight and narrow way, and how you would confront them again and that]you would be tested, you would be initiated.

Now then, the angel of the Keeper of the Scrolls[2] stands before you. And in a moment and in a flash you can already review this life and see how you came upon or, I should say, *how there came upon you* fallen angels, cunning. And they have purveyed their drugs and all manner of illusory experiences, drawing you into the byways of the misuse of the light of your seven chakras.

That which they most desired to pervert in you, beloved, was and *is* the chakra of the Divine Mother. For it is the fount of life on earth and the fount of eternal Life that rises from the base-of-the-spine chakra to the crown and is activated and crystallized and sealed by the descending Light of your I AM Presence.

Because, therefore, you call to your Mighty I AM Presence daily and hourly, and some of you even awaken realizing you have been making the call in your dreams—beloved ones, because of this, we have not stressed to you Kundalini yoga. For you are accomplishing the goal by the merging of the Light of the descending action of your Mighty I AM Presence and the rising action of the Omega flame within you. And by the force of the descent of the Alpha flame in you, the Alpha flame does magnetize and draw up the Omega. And therefore, you find that there is a regulating and there is a balancing, there is a strengthening of the chakras.

And if you follow the diet of the Messenger, which is the diet of the Eastern adepts, adapted to your needs and life-style, beloved ones, you will know the strengthening of the corresponding organs and you will know that I, Alpha, with Omega, will place more and more of our flame in each part of the body and especially those parts that have the greatest strength.

Therefore know your strengths always, beloved. They are a chalice for our coming. And I speak not only of physical strengths but character strengths—the strengths of the mind, the will and the heart. And also know your weaknesses and determine what is your greatest weakness, beloved. Then go after it and remember that it will also be related to the weakest of your organs.

Thus, you must bring up the whole manifestation of the four lower bodies. This we seek. Each one must become his own pyramid of Life. Each one must raise up that coil of the ascension flame depicted in the book of Djwal Kul.[3]

Yes, beloved, come now and understand where you have faced the fallen ones and where they outdid you because your teachers were not in embodiment and at your side from your earliest birth and from your childhood. And then again, when you have had teachers, you have chosen to ignore them at a certain stage of your life and you would learn your lessons by experimentation and experience.

Beloved ones, it is understandable that there are some things that must be learned by experience. Otherwise, we should all be placed in a box. We should place *you* in a box and open it up when you are twenty-one years old!

Well, beloved, that experiment of Skinner never did work, never would work, but the fallen ones attempted it as one more means to drive the children of the Light crazy. Yes, beloved ones.

Therefore, I tell you, you have chosen the world to be your guru. And I ask you: How many here this day are through with having the world as your guru? ["I am!"]

Well, it is a wise choice, beloved ones, for you have seen the world long enough and in long embodiments. But even in this one a certain amount of pain has been necessary to wean you from the temporary pleasures of the world. And, of course, you have had to be weaned from placing your trust in other individuals, who would suddenly abandon you, taking with them the members of your family, your children, your belongings, and never be seen again! And you in dismay have said, "How can this be?"

Well, it is because you have trusted in the flesh and you have not first trusted in God. Had you trusted in God, beloved ones, things might have turned out better. And that is the lesson you should have learned.

There are some karmas that you must balance personally and that cannot be balanced in any other way. If you come upon such a karma, go for it, *drive into it.* Use your mighty sword! Be diligent, give it your all! If necessary, lay down your life and take it again. Give all of your strength each day. Be restrengthened in the night and go for it again and again until you hear the mighty holy angel of God: "Blessed one, you have accomplished this karma. It is fulfilled. It is concluded. You may now step out of this situation and move on with your life, if it is your choice."

So, beloved, we recruit you where you are and we say, if you truly desire to receive the training of the Gurus of Maitreya's Mystery School, we shall give it to you as never before. You must understand that neither the Masters nor the Messenger shall interfere with your life one iota unless you request it, unless you implore us and determine that you would like the direct contact and the direct disciplining and the direct love whereby you can be quickly delivered of certain elements of your lifestream that perhaps you are not even aware of yourself.

Therefore, beloved, if you will address your letters in writing in the physical octave to me and to my beloved Omega and to the Messenger, stating what level of chelaship you would desire wherever you might live on earth, or whether you enter this Community as a chela, so, then, we shall begin our course. Whether at inner levels or on the outer simply depends on how much the Messenger is able to give on a one-to-one basis.

You can understand this, beloved, for there are thousands upon thousands upon earth who are yearning for this relationship. And we, Alpha and Omega, bring you the message this day that in consideration of the Messenger and of yourselves, we shall place ourselves in position through the Messenger that she might tend to the many, not necessarily physically, personally, but by a mighty action of the heart and the mind and by a certain soul tutoring at inner levels. For, beloved ones, there are certain elements of karma/psychology in everyone that must be dealt with. And therefore, you can do this as tens of thousands of chelas and come up another step. Thus, there are gradations and grades for all.

Beloved ones, you may have wondered why the Messenger has not spoken to you directly about many things. It is because you have not made that commitment in physical writing that you desire that Guru-chela relationship. Therefore, I can tell you, when you desire to have this, the Messenger will not spare the rod *or* the love to bring you to that very centeredness in the heart of your own God Presence.

One thing I will tell you: the Messenger has no desire whatsoever to possess you but to bring your soul to us. Therefore, you may accept my word and place your trust in me that *you can rely on your Messenger to assist you all the way Home!* [39-second standing ovation]

Please be seated.

Beloved ones, I address you now on matters of global concern, matters that must be dealt with by the hierarchy of Light and by yourselves. Your success in dealing with these matters does depend on the Guru-chela relationship that you keep. And, of course, you know that the beloved El Morya, the beloved Lanello are the ones closest to you in this octave through the Messenger.

Therefore, I speak of my coming on the occasion when I pronounced the three woes—*Woe! Woe! Woe!*—and I told you, beloved, that these are the woes of karma and that these woes that descended are the woes of the violation of the Light of the Father and of the Son and of the Holy Spirit. And I did state to you, beloved, that one day, *one day* (and that day known only to me) I would release the fourth woe.[4]

And the fourth woe, beloved, is the woe of the descent of the karma of the misuse of the Light of the Divine Mother and her seed. The hour has come, therefore, for those violators of the body of woman and of her children to receive their judgment.

Blessed hearts, all have had opportunity abundant to come to the defense of woman, to come to the defense of *soul—soul* who is the feminine principle and the potential to realize the fullness of God. Yes, this opportunity of ministering unto the souls of male and female and child, of son and daughter of God and every level of evolution upon the planet has been given. And I say, beloved, of all things in the earth, that which is most neglected by all is the individual soul.

Then there is the persecution of the child, the abuse of the very Christ in the body of the child and therefore the defilement, or attempted defilement, of that Christ being formed and descending into that temple.

I speak, then, of this portent of the fourth woe, but I would first speak to you now of certain things in the earth that have changed.

You have seen the receding of World Communism. Blessed ones, the trees of World Communism have been topped. But the trunk of the tree and the root of the tree has not changed, has not lost its vitality. Therefore beware, for your representatives in the West desire to believe all lies of the Liar and even to accept all murderings of the Murderer.

Be it known, then, that though the outer colorations may change, the beast of World Communism is far from dead in the earth. It is a mentality. It is a vibration and a state of consciousness that has been long on the earth, far antedating its present manifestation in this century. Thus, though Lenin unfurled it and though Stalin intensified it, yet there are those, many in embodiment today, who at heart still maintain that focus of World Communism.

There has been major change in the earth. Do not think that it has not been by the action of the invocation of the Light, for it has! And since my prior coming, you have accomplished many labors by long hours of giving of decrees here and in your Teaching Centers and, therefore, much has been cleared in the earth of the fallen ones.

Yet, on the other hand, those in positions of power who enjoy that power, who know that their day is through have not in any way responded to the Light nor to the Seven Archangels nor to the message proclaimed to them by the Seven Archangels of the consequences of their deeds.

Neither the president of the United States nor the Congress has seen fit to put in place the necessary defense of this nation. And therefore, beloved, there is a vulnerability that continues, and it continues for the breaking down of defense itself and the continuing trust on the part of the people of those who are not yet Christ-identified and far from it.

The byword of the brothers and sisters in white, beloved, is "Trust no man, trust no woman." Therefore, whom do you trust?

You trust the divine spark and *the God within each one.* And to that God you bow and with that God you make contact, beloved. When you come upon individuals who have long ago snuffed out the divine spark, who have long ago squandered the Light, who have denied the soul potential to be and therefore draw their energies from the masses of the people whom they control, what is there to trust in them?

I speak of the leadership of East and West and of every nation! And I speak of those in the leadership at all echelons and compartments of society. There is no nation that has a corner on these Nephilim gods, beloved ones.

And you see in this hour the great mistrust of the Congress of the United States by the people. Well, beloved ones, when the new recruits come in, as they will be elected, I remind you: Trust no man, trust no woman, but trust in God *and invoke that God!*

And if you want to see real God-action through your representatives in every nation upon earth, then I say, do not fail to exercise the decree for the binding of the dweller-on-the-threshold. For that carnal mind, that not-self, must be bound that the Great Tao may act through them, that the *sefirot* may act through them, that the I AM THAT I AM may act through them, that the Lord Christ, the Lord Krishna and the Inner Buddha might act through them!

There is no assurance of the Light acting through anyone who is not a devotee or through anyone who is. It is not guaranteed unless either that one who knows of the decree gives the decree or others give that decree for him or her. The binding of the not-self provides the greatest freedom of choice to the soul, to the heart and to the very goodwill of many servants of God in government.

One day they promise this and the next day they take it away, and that is because of the influence of the lower levels of being. Therefore, this call for the binding of the dweller-on-the-threshold accomplished by yourself on yourself and loved ones and all Lightbearers of the earth is the single greatest, most effective call you can make for world change and for the putting of the brake on the downward course of civilization. Therefore, I tell it to you.

And I say to you, you must know who your representatives are on every issue. You must know *who* will be making decisions for you and *when.* It then becomes your spiritual responsibility in this octave, in our name and in the name of the Seven Archangels, to call for the binding of all forces of Darkness that would interfere with your representatives in their bringing about the manifestation of the will of God.

It is not that you wish to interfere with their free will, beloved. It is that you desire to liberate their mind and heart and soul to receive the will of God and to act upon it.

Let not your prayers, then, be prayers of malintent, of manipulation—not that they are, for you are dispassionate and objective in your calls—but understand that where the individual representative of the people is, through ignorance, not free to affirm the rightness of the law of God and man and how it is to be interpreted, that individual is subject to making karma.

You as angels in embodiment, and many of you are, and you as sons and daughters of God must stand in the defense of life and attempt to uphold those individuals who could be making good karma, who have a good soul and a good fire within them yet do not have the sure and certain understanding of what they must do, nor the vision nor the inner knowledge. Therefore, knowledge above all, as you have been told, is *the key* to the saving of a planet.

Now therefore, beloved ones, it is indeed a time of great transition. It is a time when, more than ever, people cannot find leaders. They have no confidence in those whom they see. They take the one that is the least evil, not finding one who is God-good.

I understand this, beloved hearts, and I tell you, if you cannot find that person whom you seek, then you must become that person yourself! Is not that what the whole world is telling you in this hour? So you must say to yourself:

"There are no examples. Therefore I will not look here or there. *I* will become the example by the grace of God and in true humility of Alpha. *I will become the example!*"

Blessed ones, there are not sufficient role models. Become them! I urge you to consider that calling and to remember, though you think no one sees your good deeds or your bad, when you are a soul tied to the Great White Brotherhood your soul is seen by every other individual on planet earth and everyone on planet earth does take his step and his stride from your step and stride.

All the earth watches the devotees of Light. So do the forces of Death and Hell. You are indeed seen, beloved! And where you are a Light that lightens your home and your town, people know it, even though they may not know you or see you. They sense your presence and know that in your town there is a soul putting on her Christhood. And therefore, they sleep easier at night because you are there.

I say, beloved, and I implore you as your Father: *Do not let the people down.* Do not let the people of earth down and do not let us, your parents, down. For you can make the difference! Yes, beloved, *you can make the difference but you must do it!* It is not enough that I tell you you can. You must do it!

And doing it somehow becomes a fuzzy proposition and you allow the forces to stop the physical actions, to stop the conclusion of projects that have come forth as a gift from my mind to your own. And you see the project, and perhaps you start it, but you do not bring it to completion; and therefore it is aborted, it is stillborn.

Blessed hearts, if it is a right idea, then see it through and give your decrees and, come what may, do not give up! The key here is to determine that it is a right idea. And this you must do by your meditation and decrees to the Great Divine Director, to Cyclopea, to El Morya, to the entire Spirit of the Great White Brotherhood.

Angels of God, take your positions now at all points in the earth! Cosmic reinforcements, rings of seraphim, legions who have come, you have surveyed the earth. You have received unto your bodies of light the photographs, the recordings on film and sound tape of all that is taking place where you stand. We, therefore, have for our archives in the sun of Helios and Vesta and in the Great Central Sun recordings of all that is taking place on planet earth at all levels.

This is a necessary reading taken by us when we are, as you would say, physically present in the earth. We take our readings also from the higher spheres. But this is a specific reading, beloved, where we shall be able to view, as you would view in your motion picture theaters, the sound, the aura, the intent, the mind and the record of all that has been recorded.

Blessed ones, understand that when such a thorough review of a planetary home and system is taken, cycles are indeed turning, and in this hour we are seeking what is the greatest mitigation that can come and what is the judgment that will not be turned back. Therefore, beloved ones, I ask you to stand. Please keep silent.

Urrrrrrrrrrrrrrrrrrrrrrrrrrrrrrrrrrrrr

Urrrrrrrrrrrrrrrrrrrrrrrrrrrrrrrrrrrrr

Ehmmmmmmmmmmmmmmm

Powers of the octaves, *powers of the octaves,* powers of the octaves, release now the fourth *woe!*

Woe! Woe! Woe! Woe!

Therefore, there is the descent into the earth in this hour of the judgment of the persecutors of the Divine Mother and her seed and of the souls of Light and of the children of the Light—the persecutors of the Divine One in every temple on earth, the persecutors of Atman and of the living Christ and of the Inner Buddha.

Therefore, you who have embodied this persecution of the Divine Mother, I declare to you as I place my Electronic Presence before every one of you on planet earth—on the astral plane, the etheric plane and in the mental belt—I declare before you:

> *Your judgment has descended! It is sealed in your four lower bodies. It is sealed in your record. It is descending now and in this hour as I speak. Mark and note it well!*

Therefore, the judgment has descended. And you who have again given liberty to woman to murder her child, you who represent millions upon earth who agree with you—you stand guilty before mankind and all aborted souls on the etheric plane. You, therefore, shall come to judgment, for *you* have committed the murder of God and *it shall not stand!*

Therefore, it is done. And I, Alpha, seal this judgment. And you will not remove it! You will not dodge it! You will not displace it! You will not in any way extricate yourself from the hold of Alpha's judgment!

Woe! Woe! Woe! Woe!

In the four quadrants of the earth, I release the Light of the Dhyani Buddhas for the fixing of the judgment:

Woe! Woe! Woe! Woe! Woe!

Therefore know, beloved, that when the buildings fall all around you and the avalanches descend and the continents shake, *you* must stand fast in the very pillar of your God! And as I said in my former address, when the fourth woe descends it is time to get thee up into the mountain of God.[5]

I AM Alpha. Those who bear my Light are sealed, protected, nurtured, tutored. There is *no* ongoing dispensation for those who are not servants of Light. But unto those who become servants of Light there is the grace complete, necessary to their victory in this life or a succeeding life, where their karma does not allow it in this one.

This is the pledge of Alpha. Do not doubt it but take advantage of it. For I AM here. I AM Brahman. I AM the Atman. As Above, so below, *I AM your Self.*

July 1, 1992

CHAPTER 10

Elizabeth Clare Prophet

THE LIGHT OF PERSIA— MYSTICAL EXPERIENCES WITH ZARATHUSTRA

In the name of my Mighty I AM Presence
I bow to the Light of the Ascended Master Zarathustra.

The teachings of one man have influenced Judaism, Christianity, Islam, Taoism, Mahayana Buddhism, Christian and Jewish Gnosticism, Pythagoras, Plato, the Essenes and all of us who are gathered here. Yet very little is known about him.

His name was Zarathustra, he was the founder of Zoroastrianism, and he started a revolution of Light against Darkness that is ongoing today. And *we* are a part of that revolution!

Mary Boyce, Emeritus Professor of Iranian Studies at the University of London, points out: "Zoroastrianism is the oldest of the revealed world-religions, and it has probably had more influence on mankind, directly and indirectly, than any other single faith."[1]

Who was Zarathustra?

According to R. C. Zaehner, former Spalding Professor of Eastern Religions and Ethics at Oxford University, Zarathustra was "one of the greatest religious geniuses of all time. . . . [He] was a prophet, or at least conceived himself to be such; he spoke to his God face to face. . . . [Yet] about the Prophet himself we know almost nothing that is authentic."[2]

Zarathustra lived in a nonliterate society, whose people did not keep records. His teachings were passed down by oral tradition, and much of what was later written down about his life and teachings has been lost or destroyed.

What scholars have been able to piece together about him comes from three sources—the study of the historical milieu prior to and during the time Zarathustra is believed to have lived, tradition, and seventeen sacred hymns called Gathas. Scholars concur that Zarathustra composed these hymns. The Gathas are recorded in the Avesta, the sacred scriptures of Zoroastrianism.

It is not clear where or when Zarathustra was born. It is believed he was born in what is now east central Iran, but that is not certain. Zarathustra's date of birth is even more difficult to establish. Scholars place it sometime between 1700 B.C. and 600 B.C. The consensus is that he lived around 1000 B.C. or earlier.

The Gathas are the key to determining Zarathustra's approximate year of birth. They are linguistically similar to the Rigveda, one of the sacred texts of the Hindus. According to Boyce:

> The language of the Gathas is archaic, and close to that of the Rigveda (whose composition has been assigned to about 1700 B.C. onwards); and the picture of the world to be gained from [the Gathas] is correspondingly ancient, that of a Stone Age society. . . . It is only possible therefore to hazard a reasoned conjecture that [Zarathustra] lived some time between 1700 and 1500 B.C.[3]

Other scholars working with the same evidence place his birth between 1400 and 1200 B.C.

The Gathas say that Zarathustra was of the Spitama family, a family of knights. One school of thought says the name Zarathustra means "owner of old camels." Well, if that is the real meaning, Zarathustra, we are your camels!

Dr. H. Michael Simmons of the Center for Zoroastrian Research says this meaning comes from *Zarath,* meaning "old," and *Ushtra,* meaning "camel." But the Greek name for Zarathustra is Zoroaster, which Simmons says means "Golden Star," or "Golden Light."[4] So, happily we are saved!

Zarathustra, will you have us as your golden stars?

Let's look at Zarathustra's life before he received his calling. In the Gathas, Zarathustra referred to himself as a priest. There were different categories of priests. The specific group Zarathustra belonged to wrote elaborate religious poetry.[5]

Zarathustra also referred to himself as a *manthran.* Can anybody guess what that is? A *manthran* is one who is able to formulate mantras. You just about got that, didn't you?

Zarathustra was also an initiate. According to Boyce, "He . . . describes himself [in the Gathas] as a 'vaedemna' or 'one who knows,' an initiate possessed of divinely inspired wisdom."[6] But first and foremost, Zarathustra was a prophet, and *he is* a prophet and he lives today among us as an Ascended Master.

The Gathas depict him as talking to God. They say, "He is 'the Prophet who raises his voice in veneration, the friend of Truth,' God's friend, a 'true enemy to the followers of the Lie and a powerful support to the followers of the Truth.'"[7]

Zarathustra was an outspoken enemy of the followers of the Lie. I like that kind of a guy, don't you? [7second applause] All of us count ourselves, I think, as true enemies of liars, but how many of us often go up to them and tell them about it? That's what's special about Zarathustra.

Tradition holds that at the age of twenty Zarathustra left his father, mother and wife to wander in search of Truth. Ten years later he had the first of many visions. See how long God tries your soul. So keep on allowing him to try you.

Boyce writes: "According to tradition Zoroaster was thirty, the time of ripe wisdom, when revelation finally came to him. This great happening is alluded to in one of the Gathas and is tersely described in a Pahlavi [Middle Persian] work. Here it is said that Zoroaster, being at a gathering [called] to celebrate a spring festival, went at dawn to a river to fetch water."[8]

Now, at dawn tomorrow be sure you're at the Mol Heron Creek! Wait till you hear what happened to Zarathustra:

> He waded in to draw [the water] from midstream; and when he returned to the bank . . . he had a vision. He saw on the bank a shining Being, who revealed himself as Vohu Manah 'Good [Mind]'; and this Being led Zoroaster into the presence of Ahura Mazda and five other radiant figures, before whom 'he did not see his own shadow upon the earth, owing to their great light'. And it was then, from this great heptad [or group of seven beings], that he received his revelation.[9]

We can conjecture that the seven beings of this great heptad were none other than the Seven Holy Kumaras.

Ahura Mazda means "Wise Lord." Zarathustra recognized Ahura Mazda as the one true God, the creator of the universe. The significance of this cannot be overstated. Zarathustra may have been the first monotheist in recorded history. Zaehner points out, "The great achievement of the Iranian Prophet [was] that he eliminated all the ancient gods of the Iranian pantheon, leaving only Ahura Mazdah, the 'Wise Lord', as the One True God."[10]

Some scholars assert that Zarathustra was not a strict monotheist but a henotheist, that is, one who worships one God but does not deny the existence of others. This is a technical distinction. As David Bradley, author of *A Guide to the World's Religions*, notes, "[Zarathustra] was a practicing monotheist in the same way that Moses was."[11] Bradley thinks that Moses knew of the existence of lesser gods but insisted on the necessity of siding with the true God against all other gods.[12]

Shortly after his first vision, Zarathustra became a spokesman for Ahura Mazda and began to proclaim his message. According to Simmons, Zarathustra instituted a religious reform that was more far-reaching and more radical than Martin Luther's challenge of the Roman Catholic Church.[13]

Zarathustra's reform had a number of facets. His main objective was to stamp out Evil. He began to condemn the religious doctrines of his countrymen.

The old religion, as best we can tell, had two classes of deities—the *ahuras,* or "lords," and the *daevas,* or "demons." According to Zaehner:

> It is . . . the *daevas* specifically whom Zoroaster attacks, not the *ahuras* whom he prefers to ignore. . . . In all probability he considered them to be God's creatures and as fighters on his side. In any case he concentrated the full weight of his attack on the *daevas* and their worshippers who practised a gory sacrificial ritual and were the enemies of the settled pastoral community to which the Prophet himself belonged.[14]

At first Zarathustra had little success in spreading his message. Zaehner observes, "It is obvious from the *Gathas* that Zoroaster met with very stiff opposition from the civil and ecclesiastical authorities when once he had proclaimed his mission."[15] He was persecuted by the priests and followers of the *daevas.* According to tradition, they tried to kill him a number of times.

It took ten years for Zarathustra to make his first convert, his cousin. (That's what you get for attacking everybody else's gods!) He was then divinely led to the court of King Vishtaspa and Queen Hutaosa.

Vishtaspa was an honest, simple monarch but was surrounded by the *Karpans,* a group of self-seeking, manipulative priests. They convened a council to challenge the revelations of the new prophet and successfully conspired to have him thrown in jail. As the story goes, Zarathustra won his freedom by miraculously curing the king's favorite black horse.

Vishtaspa granted him permission to teach the new faith to his consort, Queen Hutaosa. The beautiful Hutaosa became one of Zarathustra's greatest supporters and assisted him in converting Vishtaspa.

After two long years, the monarch was finally converted. But Vishtaspa required one final sign before he would totally embrace the faith. He asked to be shown what role he would play in the heaven-world.

In response, Ahura Mazda sent three Archangels to the court of Vishtaspa and Hutaosa. They appeared as effulgent knights in full armour, riding on horseback. According to one text, they arrived in such glory that "their radiance in that lofty residence seemed . . . a heaven of complete light, owing to their great power and triumph; . . . when he thus looked upon [them], the exalted king Vishtaspa trembled, all his courtiers trembled, all his chieftains were confused."[16]

Radiating a blinding light and the sound of thunder, they announced that they had come on behalf of Ahura Mazda in order that the king might receive the fullness of the message of Zarathustra. They promised Vishtaspa a life span of 150 years and that he and Hutaosa would have an immortal son. The Archangels warned, however, that if Vishtaspa should decide not to take up the religion, his end would not be far away. The king embraced the faith and the entire court followed suit. The scriptures record that the Archangels then took up their abode with Vishtaspa.

In a dictation given January 1, 1981, the Ascended Master Zarathustra spoke of King Vishtaspa and Queen Hutaosa, and this is what he said:

> I AM come to deliver the sacred fire of the Sun behind the sun to raise you up and to establish in you the original teaching of Ahura Mazda, Sanat Kumara, delivered long ago in the land of ancient Persia unto me and unto the king and queen who received the conversion of Archangels and of the sacred fire and of holy angels by the descent of Light. Thus, by their lifestreams' acceptance of my prophecy, there came to pass the multiplication of the bread of Life from the heart of Sanat Kumara, whose messenger I was, whose messenger I remain. . . .
>
> The teaching of the hosts of the Lord and the coming of the great avatar of Light, the teaching of betrayal and the consequent warfare of his hosts against the evil ones, was understood and propagated. The law of karma, the law of reincarnation, and even the vision of the last days when Evil and the Evil One would be vanquished—all of this went forth by the conversion of the king and the queen and the reaching out of the faith to all of the subjects of the land.
>
> Thus, the tests were given by the Archangels through my office unto these two chosen ones. Thereby passing the tests, they became blessed as secondary emissaries of Sanat Kumara. And therefore, I the prophet and they holding the balance in the earth manifested a trinity of Light and the figure-eight flow.

> Realize the necessary ingredients for the propagation of the faith throughout the earth.
>
> The Archangels send their Messenger with a gift of prophecy that is the Word of Sanat Kumara to every culture and in every age. Thus, the prophet comes forth with the vision, with the anointing and with the sacred fire. But unless the prophet find the fertile field of hearts aflame and receptive, the authority of the Word does not pass unto the people.[17]

Thus, we hear that Ahura Mazda is none other than Sanat Kumara.

Let's take a closer look at Zarathustra's teaching. Zarathustra recognized Ahura Mazda, the Wise Lord, as the creator of all, but he did not see him as a solitary figure. In Zoroastrianism, Ahura Mazda is the father of Spenta Mainyu, the Holy Spirit. *Spenta* means "holy" or "bountiful." *Mainyu* means "spirit" or "mentality." The Holy Spirit is one with, yet distinct from, Ahura Mazda. Ahura Mazda expresses his will through Spenta Mainyu.

Boyce explains: "For Zarathushtra God was Ahura Mazda, who . . . had created the world and all that is good in it through his Holy Spirit, Spenta Mainyu, who is both his active agent and yet one with him, indivisible and yet distinct."[18] Simply put, the Spirit is always the Spirit of the Lord. When we speak of the Holy Spirit, it is the Spirit of God.

Ahura Mazda is also the father of the Amesha Spentas, or six "Holy" or "Bountiful Immortals." Boyce says that the term *spenta* is one of the most important in Zarathustra's theology. To him, it meant "possessing power." When used in connection with the beneficent deities, it meant "possessing power to aid" and hence "furthering, supporting, benefiting."[19]

Zarathustra taught that Ahura Mazda created the world in seven stages. He did so with the help of the six great Holy Immortals and his Holy Spirit. The term *Amesha Spenta* can refer to any one of the divinities created by Ahura Mazda but refers especially to the six who helped create the world.[20] According to Boyce:

> These divinities formed a heptad with Ahura Mazda himself. . . . Ahura Mazda is said either to be their 'father', or to have 'mingled' himself with them, and in one . . . text his creation of

> them is compared with the lighting of torches from a torch.
>
> The six great Beings then in their turn, Zoroaster taught, evoked other beneficent divinities, who are in fact the beneficent gods of the pagan Iranian pantheon. . . . All these divine beings, who are . . . either directly or indirectly the emanations of Ahura Mazda, strive under him, according to their various appointed tasks, to further good and to defeat evil.[21]

The six Holy or Bountiful Immortals also represent attributes of Ahura Mazda. The Holy Immortals are as follows:

Vohu Manah, whose name means "Good Mind," "Good Thought" or "Good Purpose." According to Boyce, "For every individual, as for the prophet himself," Vohu Manah is "the Immortal who leads the way to all the rest." Asha Vahishta, whose name means "Best Righteousness," "Truth" or "Order," is the closest confederate of Vohu Manah.[22]

Spenta Armaiti, "Right-mindedness" or "Holy Devotion," Boyce says, embodies the dedication to what is good and just. Khshathra Vairya, "Desirable Dominion," represents the power that each person should exert for righteousness as well as the power and the kingdom of God.[23]

The final two are a pair. They are Haurvatat, whose name means "Wholeness" or "Health," and Ameretat, whose name means "Long Life" or "Immortality." Boyce says these two enhance earthly existence and confer eternal well-being and life, which may be obtained by the righteous in the presence of Ahura Mazda.[24]

"The doctrine of the Heptad," she says, "is at the heart of Zoroastrian theology. Together with [the concept of Good and Evil] it provides the basis for Zoroastrian spirituality and ethics, and shapes the characteristic Zoroastrian attitude of responsible stewardship for this world."[25] In later tradition, the six Holy Immortals were considered to be Archangels.

When it came to Good and Evil, Zarathustra tended to see things in terms of black and white. According to Zaehner, "The Prophet knew no spirit of compromise."[26]

There is no prophet who ever knows any spirit of compromise. I will tell you why. The prophet of God embodies the Mighty I AM Presence.

He is not the mediator. He is the one who embodies God as Law and Lawgiver. And so he walks the earth with a great intensity of fire, seeking to separate people from their relativities that suck them into the maya and glamour of the illusionary existence.

So this was true of the prophets of Israel. They had such an intensity of oneness with the Mighty I AM Presence and they delivered that intensity. That "stuff" of the Mighty I AM Presence is the stuff that prophets are made of.

Zaehner says: "On the one hand stood Asha—Truth and Righteousness—[and] on the other the Druj—the Lie, Wickedness, and Disorder. This was not a matter on which compromise was possible [as far as Zarathustra was concerned]. . . . The Prophet [forbade] his followers to have any contact with the 'followers of the Lie'."[27]

The origin of the conflict between Truth and the Lie is described in the Gathas. It is presented as a myth about two Spirits, called twins, who must make a choice between Good and Evil at the beginning of time. One of the two is the Holy Spirit, the son of Ahura Mazda. The other is the Evil Mind or the Evil Spirit, Angra Mainyu.

Zarathustra introduced the myth with the following words, which underscore the all-important concept of free will and that every man must choose the Truth or the Lie: "Hear with your ears, behold with mind all clear the two choices between which you must decide, each man [deciding] for his own self, [each man] knowing how it will appear to us at the [time of] great crisis."[28] Then he proceeded to recount the myth:

> In the beginning those two Spirits who are the well-endowed twins were known as the one good and the other evil, in thought, word, and deed. Between them the wise chose rightly, not so the fools. And when these Spirits met they established in the beginning life and death that in the end the followers of the Lie should meet with the worst existence, but the followers of Truth with the Best Mind.
>
> Of these two Spirits he who was of the Lie chose to do the worst things; but the Most Holy Spirit, clothed in rugged heaven, [chose] Truth as did [all] who sought with zeal to do the pleasure of the Wise Lord by [doing] good works.

Clothed in rugged heaven, he came! Isn't that an apt description of the character of the Holy Spirit as he appears to us?

> Between the two the *daevas* [the demons] did not choose rightly; for, as they deliberated, delusion overcame them so that they chose the most Evil Mind. Then did they, with one accord, rush headlong unto Fury that they might thereby extinguish the existence of mortal men.[29]

The Holy Spirit and the Evil Spirit are, as Zaehner puts it, "irreconcilably opposed to each other."[30] Zarathustra said, "I will speak out concerning the two Spirits of whom, at the beginning of existence, the Holier thus spoke to him who is Evil: 'Neither our thoughts, nor our teachings, nor our wills, nor our choices, nor our words, nor our deeds, nor our consciences, nor yet our souls agree.'"[31]

Zaehner notes that this state of conflict affected every sphere of activity human or divine. In the social sphere, the conflict took place between the pastoral communities of peaceful cattle breeders, who were "followers of Truth or Righteousness," and the bands of predatory nomads, who raided the cattle breeders. Zarathustra called these predatory nomads the "followers of the Lie."[32]

On the religious plane, the conflict took place between Zarathustra and his followers and those who were followers of the traditional Iranian religion and worshiped the *daevas.* The adherents of this ancient religion said it was founded by Yima, the child of the Sun. Zarathustra attacked Yima and the ritual of animal sacrifice he had introduced.[33]

He also condemned the rite associated with drinking *haoma,* the fermented juice of a plant that caused "filthy drunkenness."[34] Scholars are not sure what *haoma* was, but they conclude from the description of the effects it had on those who drank it that it probably contained a hallucinogen. Zaehner writes: "For Zoroaster the whole cult with its bloody sacrifice and ritual drunkenness is anathema—a rite offered to false gods and therefore a 'lie'."[35]

Zarathustra said "the followers of the Lie" destroyed life and strove to "sever the followers of Truth from the Good Mind."[36] The followers of the Lie knew who Zarathustra was, recognized the danger he represented and did everything they could to destroy him. To this end, they continued to sacrifice bulls and participate in the *haoma* rite.

According to Zaehner, "There would seem to be little doubt that an actual state of war existed between the two parties, Zoroaster and his patron Vishtaspa standing on the one side and the so-called followers of the Lie, many of whom he mentions by name, on the other."[37]

Finally, the battle went on right within man. John Noss, author of *Man's Religions,* observes that "it was perhaps Zoroaster's cardinal moral principle, that each man's soul is the seat of a war between good and evil."[38]

One of the principal weapons used to attack demons and evil men was the prayer written by Zarathustra, the Ahuna Vairya. This short prayer is the most sacred of Zoroastrian prayers. I will read it to you:

> As the Master, so is the Judge to be chosen in accord with Truth. Establish the power of acts arising from a life lived with good purpose, for Mazda and for the lord whom they made pastor for the poor.[39]

The lord in the last line of this prayer is thought to be Zarathustra himself. The prayer is ancient. It is written in the style of the Rigveda. According to Simmons, this prayer is a mantra. Simmons says that Zoroastrians believe that "pronouncing words in Zoroastrian ritual has an effect on the external world." They believe that if a particular mantra is pronounced correctly, it will affect outer circumstances.[40]

A mantra is always effective when properly recited, whether it is given in the form of our decrees or as Hindu mantras or other legitimate mantras handed down to us from the heirs of Sanat Kumara. All true living Gurus on this planet have descended from Sanat Kumara. He is the Great Guru and the one who sponsors the earth and the Great White Brotherhood in the earth. He is the one who has released the mantras through them. Descending from his lineage are the Buddhas, the Bodhisattvas, Jesus Christ, and so forth—all of the great Lights that have come down.

When we give their mantras and give them correctly, the entire four lower bodies of the earth and her people are affected. And that means that we ourselves must be a chalice for the mantra and hold the balance for the mantra as it penetrates the sheaths of the earth.

Zaehner sums up:

> For Zoroaster there is only one God, Creator of heaven and earth and of all things. In his relations with the world God acts through his main "faculties" which are sometimes spoken of as being engendered by him—his Holy Spirit, [his] Righteousness, [his] Good Mind, and Rightmindedness. Further he is master of the Kingdom, Wholeness, and Immortality, which also form aspects of himself.
>
> Righteousness or Truth is the objective standard of right behaviour which God chooses. . . . Wickedness or disorder . . . is the objective standard of all that strives against God, the standard which the Evil Spirit chooses at the beginning of existence. Evil imitates the good creation: and so we find the Evil Spirit operating against the Holy Spirit, the Evil Mind against the Good Mind, the Lie or wickedness against Truth or Righteousness, and Pride against Right-mindedness.
>
> Evil derives from the wrong choice of a free being who must in some sense derive from God, but for whose wickedness God cannot be held responsible. Angra Mainyu or Ahriman, [names for] the Devil, is not yet coeternal with God as he was to become in the later system: he is the Adversary of the Holy Spirit only, not of God himself.[41]

But in the end, according to Zoroastrian doctrine, Good will triumph over Evil.

These concepts about the birth of Evil very closely parallel the concept of the birth of Evil that we studied in the Kabbalah. It would be well for you to compare the two when you are able to study both of these lectures or do your own research on the subject.

Another important point we have here is that Evil imitates the Good. In order to win good souls to its cause, it must appear to be good.

This is where we find that disciples on the Path under the Ascended Masters are most often fooled. They look at people and, without the discernment of the Holy Spirit, they think that because people are parroting good they must be good. They go through the footsteps and the motions of good, they are outwardly personable, they appear to be good human beings. But when you study the parrots, you will see that at subtle levels they often do have evil motives and so they put a patine of good over an evil core. That is why the scriptures say that we must "try the spirits" to see whether they be of God.[42] And, "By their fruits ye shall know them."[43]

Remember, Evil has nothing original of its own. It's a copycat. Everything it does and everything it has it has to first copy from God and then slightly distort—introducing an inharmonious chord, a sour note, a kind of a downward spiral that is interesting, enticing, enjoyable, pleasurable, et cetera, but very subtly it takes you down by degrees.

The force works on souls not for a day or a decade but for centuries. Century upon century upon century the Lightbearer, the potential Lightbearer, the potential Christ, will be worked on by evil forces presenting themselves as good.

How many evil people have you ever met who said to you, "Hi! I'm evil and I want you to know it"? Even a black magician will not reveal himself to you until he has, as Mark Prophet always used to say, "chewed you up and spat you out."

So beware. Beware and test the spirits and don't make hasty judgments or hasty alliances—or hasty decisions to part with your money. This is one of the biggest problems we see. People part with their money because within themselves they have a desire to multiply that money, to invest it, to gain by it. And so they will trust almost anyone who comes along and will, without even examining or thinking or scrutinizing, enter into some business deal that is ludicrous on the surface.

So please understand that people are not willfully evil unless they are tied to Absolute Evil. But they may have taken on themselves, through many lifetimes, the ways of the Evil One. They may have compromised Truth, compromised their speech, compromised their actions, all the while actually believing that they are very good people. And deep down inside, they probably *are* very good people, but at the moment they are in a position to influence you on the downward spiral.

So, this is about the old story of the rabbi who sits his son on the wall and tells his son to jump off the wall. And he says, "I'll catch you." So his son jumps off the high wall, but the rabbi doesn't catch him and he falls and hurts himself. So he says, "Dad, why didn't you catch me?" And his dad says, "Because I don't want you to ever trust anybody."

Trust God and wait and see. Pray about things and sleep on them and be careful where you commit your life and your energy.

Now here are a few final concepts from Zarathustra's teaching. His concept of morality can be summed up with the words "good thoughts, good words, good deeds."[44] This is the threefold ethic of Zorastrianism. Boyce writes:

> All Zoroastrians, men and women alike, wear [a] cord as a girdle, passed three times round the waist and knotted at back and front. Initiation took place at the age of fifteen; and thereafter, every day for the rest of his life, the believer must himself untie and retie the cord repeatedly when praying. The symbolism of the girdle (called in Persian the 'kusti') was elaborated down the centuries; but it is likely that from the beginning the three coils were intended to symbolize the threefold ethic of Zoroastrianism, and so to concentrate the wearer's thoughts on the practice of his faith.
>
> Further, the kusti is tied over an inner shirt of pure white, the 'sudra,' which has a little purse sewn into the throat; and this is to remind the believer that he should be continually filling its emptiness with the merit of good thoughts, words and deeds, and so be laying up treasure for himself in heaven.[45]

Fire, of course, also plays a central role in Zarathustra's religion. Fire was a symbol of Ahura Mazda. It was also a symbol of Truth because of its power to destroy darkness.[46] Bernard Springett writes in his book *Zoroaster, the Great Teacher:*

> Fire, the great object of reverence of Zoroaster's disciples, . . . has ever been looked upon as a symbol of Spirit, and of Deity, representing the ever-living and ever-active light—essence of the Supreme Being. The perpetual preservation of fire is the first of

> the five things consecrated by Zoroaster. . . . The perpetual preservation of fire typifies the essential truth that every man should in like manner make it his constant object to preserve the divine principle in himself which it symbolises.[47]

According to tradition, when Zarathustra was seventy-seven he was assassinated by a priest of the old Iranian religion. Springett writes that "fabulous accounts of Zoroaster's death are given by the Greek and Latin patristic writers, who assert that he perished by lightning, or a flame from heaven."[48]

Much of what happened after Zarathustra's death is shrouded in mystery. Scholars say that his successors reintroduced the old gods that he had dethroned back into his system. They also condoned the *haoma* ritual. (Today Zoroastrians use a nonhallucinogenic substance in this ritual.)

By the time the Medes came to power in the seventh century B.C., Zoroastrianism was a major force in Persia. But when Alexander the Great conquered Persia in 331 B.C., he killed the priests and burned down the royal palace, destroying whatever may have been recorded of Zoroastrian tradition.

As Boyce describes it, "The Zoroastrians sustained irreparable loss through the death of so many of their priests. In those days, when all religious works were handed down orally, the priests were the living books of the faith, and with mass slaughters many ancient works (the tradition holds) were lost, or only haltingly preserved."[49]

About A.D. 225, Zoroastrianism reemerged in Persia and was the state religion until around 651, when the Moslems conquered Persia. Although Zoroastrianism was officially tolerated, the Arab conquerors encouraged conversion to Islam through societal pressures, economic incentives or force. Many Zoroastrians converted or went into exile. Loyal Zoroastrians who remained in Persia were taxed for the privilege of practicing their faith. In later centuries, persecution of Zoroastrians escalated. As of 1976, there were only 129,000 Zoroastrians in the world.[50]

According to Zaehner:

> Zoroastrianism has practically vanished from the world today, but much of what the Iranian Prophet taught lives on in

> no less than three great religions—Judaism, Christianity and Islam. It seems fairly certain that the main teachings of Zoroaster were known to the Jews in the Babylonian captivity, and so it was that in those vital but obscure centuries that preceded the coming of Jesus Christ Judaism had absorbed into its bloodstream more of the Iranian Prophet's teaching than it could well admit.
>
> It seems probable that it was from him and from his immediate followers that the Jews derived the idea of the immortality of the soul, of the resurrection of the body, of a Devil who works not as a servant of God but as his Adversary, and perhaps too of an eschatological Saviour who was to appear at the end of time. All these ideas, in one form or another, have passed into both Christianity and Islam.[51]

Some modern-day Zoroastrians say that Zarathustra taught a path of mystical union with God. Dr. Farhang Mehr, a founder of the World Zoroastrian Organization, says that the Zoroastrian mystic seeks union with God but retains his identity. In his book *The Zoroastrian Tradition,* he writes: "In uniting with God, man does not vanish as a drop in the ocean."[52]

Mehr says that Zarathustra was "the greatest mystic" and that the path of mysticism is rooted in the Gathas. According to Mehr, the path of mysticism in Zoroastrianism is called the path of Asha, or the path of Truth or Righteousness.[53]

Mehr delineates six stages in this path, which he correlates to the attributes of the six Holy Immortals. In the first stage the mystic strengthens the good mind and discards the evil mind. In the second stage he embodies righteousness. In the third he acquires divine courage and power. This enables him to selflessly serve his fellowman.

In the fourth stage the mystic acquires universal love. This allows him to replace self-love with a universal love—God's love for all. In the fifth stage he achieves perfection, which is synonymous with self-realization. And in the sixth and final stage, he achieves immortality, communion (or union) with God.[54]

Now let us take another look at Ahura Mazda. We have seen that Ahura Mazda is none other than Sanat Kumara, the Ancient of Days spoken of in the Book of Daniel. Sanat Kumara is the hierarch of Venus and Great Guru of the seed of Christ. The name Sanat Kumara comes from the Sanskrit, meaning "always a youth."

Aeons ago all Light had gone out in the evolutions of earth. So great was their departure from cosmic law that the Cosmic Council decreed the dissolution of the planet. Sanat Kumara volunteered to come to earth to keep the threefold flame of Life on behalf of her people. The Solar Lords granted him a dispensation to do so. One hundred and forty-four thousand souls from Venus volunteered to come with him to support his mission. They vowed to keep the Flame with him until the children of God would once again serve their Mighty I AM Presence.

Many of you were among that 144,000, also spoken of in the Book of Revelation.[55] You volunteered to come here with Sanat Kumara, and you knew that you would remain until the people you were responsible for had the teaching of the Mighty I AM Presence and once again had found the way back to God.

That day is dawning in this age, and thereby we know that finally we do have an opportunity to take our leave of planet earth, if we so choose, in the ritual of the ascension. And so the twentieth century has been a wondrous century, and it is a wondrous century of opportunity that is coming upon us as the fulfillment of the ancient teachings is made known publicly in the marts of the world.

So, Sanat Kumara established his retreat called Shamballa on an island in the Gobi Sea, now the Gobi Desert. Four hundred, who formed the avant-garde, preceded Sanat Kumara to earth and built this most beautiful palace of Light and retreat on that spot.

The first to respond to his flame was Gautama Buddha, followed by Lord Maitreya and Jesus Christ. Sanat Kumara held the position of Lord of the World until his disciple Gautama Buddha reached sufficient attainment to hold that office. On January 1, 1956, Gautama Buddha was crowned Lord of the World. Sanat Kumara retained the title Regent Lord of the World and returned to Venus and to his twin flame, the Lady Master Venus.

What we learn from the records and the history of Zarathustra is nothing compared to what we learn when we stand in his aura. Being in the presence of Zarathustra is like being in the presence of the physical sun itself. The mastery that he has of spiritual fire and physical fire is, if not the highest, among the highest of any adept ascended from this planet.

If you want to keep the flame of Zarathustra, you must visualize him keeping the flame, the divine spark, in your own heart. He is the greatest "fire-tender" of them all, if you will.

And when you call to him, remember that when you are engaged in the battle of Light and Darkness and you give our call for the binding of the forces of Antichrist, there is no greater devourer of the dark forces than Zarathustra himself. And he does it with his ten thousand flames. And to think of him having had this zeal for thousands upon thousands of years (and, who knows, perhaps as far back as Atlantis and Lemuria) as he came again in the dawn of history to Persia to bring the knowledge of the religion of fire—it is truly awesome.

This is why Zoroastrianism and Mighty Zarathustra are placed on the Eighth Ray chakra, the secret chamber of the heart. It is the Eighth Ray chakra and the eight-petaled chakra. In order to enter there, you must first be able to stand in the twelve-petaled heart chakra. The threefold flame burns on the altar of the secret chamber of the heart. Your high priest, who is your Holy Christ Self, retires to that secret chamber to keep that flame. Zarathustra and other Ascended Masters can and do visit you there and they tutor your soul.

Since we are Keepers of the Flame, we are fire-tenders. We are surely initiates of Zarathustra if we desire to be and, more than that, initiates of the priesthood of Melchizedek.

It is very important that we are acquainted with this religious tradition of Persia and that we have and feel in our hearts this tremendous zeal of this Zarathustra, who is alive and more alive than ever today! Just remember, Ascended Masters are never static. They increase and add rings upon rings to their Tree of Life. And in Zarathustra's case, he is most certainly adding rings upon rings of fire to his aura and Causal Body.

I will say, if you dare, call him to stand where you are tonight and feel what it feels like to have that substance melted that is hard as rock, as rock can be—substance that has been in your subconscious and your unconscious for aeons. That is the experience we anticipate as we prepare now for the dictation of the Mighty Zarathustra. Thank you.

[21-second standing ovation]

Messenger's Invocation before the Lecture:

Light descending from Ahura Mazda, penetrate all elements of being. Let Light be reflected in Light.

O Thou Fiery One, Mighty Zarathustra, we welcome you to the chamber of our heart! O Thou Great Master of the Eighth Ray chakra, burn brightly tonight! Burn brightly thy flame on the altar of our hearts.

O Holy One of God, thou who hast shown us the way of the sacred fire consuming all Evil, evil ones and the energy veil, mighty pioneer in the separating of Light from Darkness, enter this company of souls who love you, who adore the sacred fire that you are. Take us, then, tier upon tier, to the planes of heaven. Part the way by sacred fire!

We gladly submit to thy flame, O Blessed One, whilst thou dost hold for us the mighty balance for all substance not of the Light, all sticky substance of the human consciousness.

Blaze, O fire! *Blaze,* O fire! *Blaze,* O fire of Zarathustra!

In the name Ahura Mazda, in the name of the Father, the Son, the Holy Spirit and the Divine Mother, Amen.

July 1, 1992

CHAPTER 11

Zarathustra

THOU PURGING FIRE!

Do Not Quench the Flame

Lo! Lo! Lo! Let the full fire of your Mighty I AM Presence descend. *Descend* now! O come forth, thou purging fire! After the purging rain, so let there be the purging fire and the purging wind for the purging of the mind and the soul and the heart!

Wherefore did you come to the mount of Zarathustra if you did not reckon to receive the fire?

Therefore, welcome my fire, beloved, and thereby open your heart to me. For I come to perform a service unto your soul and unto your spirit, Atman, yet imprisoned in your temple.

I smile, beloved, for no one welcomes me.

[36-second standing ovation. Congregation gives the salutation:]

Hail, Zarathustra! Hail, Zarathustra! Hail, Zarathustra!
Hail, Zarathustra! Hail, Zarathustra! Hail, Zarathustra!
Hail, Zarathustra! Hail, Zarathustra! Hail, Zarathustra!
Hail, Zarathustra! Hail, Zarathustra! Hail, Zarathustra!
Hail, Zarathustra! Hail, Zarathustra!...

Ho! Ho! Ho! Now, beloved, by your welcome I gain necessary entrée to your heart. And truly I come from the heart of Helios and Vesta that I might give you fire for fire. And even if you have so little or none, yet I shall deliver the fire. Thus, be still in your seats now.

I ask you to meditate upon the chakras and to know that the all-consuming fire of God is just that: it is all-consuming. It is like the mighty sculptor. It does chisel away only that portion that was never real in the first place.

Oh, how I love the fire! Be fearless before the fire, beloved ones. Oh, be fearless! For in the day and in the night the gentle caressing of the flame of God and the rainbow rays—this is a great protection, this is a point for acceleration, this is Life's all-transfiguring, all-resurrecting flame. The flame *is* Life! Extinguish the flame: no God, no manifestation.

Fire is central to the worship of all peoples of all time, for it is, after all, the gift of Ahura Mazda. Yes, beloved, it was the gift of Sanat Kumara when all the fires of all the hearts of all the people who had so degenerated on planet earth were self-extinguished.

Therefore, hollowed-out man we found when we came from his home star. Hollowed-out man we found, hollowed-out woman, hollowed-out child. It was a day and an hour when, as you know, the Cosmic Council had decided to cancel opportunity for earth's evolutions, to extinguish the planet itself as a failed experiment. But who of the Council could turn down the beloved Sanat Kumara, who did come offering his flame, offering to kindle the hearts of earth one by one?

Therefore none of his devotees from Venus, his home star, would allow him to go alone. Many did volunteer to go with him[1] and many of those volunteers who reincarnated in this era do gather today on the mountain here in this place.

You have been pursuing the fire and the fiery ones for aeons upon aeons. Now you know so much about the flame. You know the workings of the violet flame. You know the Dhyani Buddhas and that they do deliver the flames of the five secret rays. Yes, beloved, the flame, its coloration, its vibration, the level that it is native to—all these things you have become sensitized to and you are becoming more sensitive to daily.

You understand the harmonies of the flames, the rays of the flames, their acceleration and how they bless the body and the body cells, and this (which you know at inner levels and somewhat on the outer far more than many upon earth) does make you candidates to come to my retreat, to come to that place prepared that is a mighty retreat that is a replica of the secret chamber of the heart, your very own heart.[2]

I look forward to welcoming you there, beloved ones, yet I have not released the whereabouts of this retreat, nor shall I. For when you make attunement with your own heart, beloved ones, and when you are in that heart as the devotee of the God within your heart, then so know and so understand: you shall not be able to avoid reaching that retreat of mine that is the replica of the secret chamber of the heart. Thus, I will tell you one thing. It is deep within the mountains. But which mountains, beloved, you will have to discover for yourselves.

Now I come for the preparation of your beings to be, oh, so sensitized to the Maha Chohan, to the Holy Spirit, to many who are unknown to you who are in the higher octaves as Buddhas and Bodhisattvas. They have not come, beloved, because you have not yet mastered even the threefold flame of your heart and the uses of the sacred fire. For that fire can work much good but it can also be misused for ill.

Therefore, you may enter the path of initiation with me, and that path will involve your willingness and ability to be trusted with the flame and entrusted with it. So, beloved, it is the greatest element of all. And without it, no other elements would have integration, for the fire is the nucleus of all life in all octaves and the very center of a cosmos.

Thus, I am speaking to you as you are being gently warmed by the angels of fire who come with me and by the fiery salamanders. And therefore, though it may be cool, you may begin to feel a warmth that is comfortable. But by and by it will not be comfortable, beloved ones, for I bring you a heat that you can stand and withstand, whereby you can be purged within the pores and cells and molecules of being.

This, then, is an offering that can be given. For listen to the silence! Listen to the love! Listen to your heartbeats one—one with the Central Sun, one in desiring to love and be loved and once and for all to end the separation between yourselves and God.

Oh, such a holy place! Oh, such a cradle, as we call it, for the coming together of souls who can "rub souls" with one another and therefore polish one another's auras and also know the meaning of the oneness of God in so many manifestations.

I AM THAT I AM. I AM in the heart of the flame. Ho! I AM Zarathustra and I choose to come gently in this moment, gently intensifying. Thus, I am causing the fiery salamanders to intensify the pressure: first of the light, then of the warmth, then of the fire itself.

Thus, beloved, I give what Alpha and Omega have called me to give. For they have prepared you, even as the preceding ones have prepared your auras, to assimilate absolutely the most fire that can possibly be given and received. Thus, for the moment be still and contemplate the rainbow flames all about you. [20-second pause]

Your body elemental is enjoying a fire bath. The body elementals love the fire bath of the multicolored flames. They delight in this! They are scientists beyond your ken, beloved. They know the science of the body, they know what the flames heal and how to apply them. They not only enjoy the bath but are busy directing specific rays of the flames into specific needs of the body. They produce a well-beingness and a relaxation. They produce the harmony of the spheres.

And now the flame forms the cosmic egg around you, an ovoid of Light. You can sustain the pattern of the flames, beloved, and magnetize them to yourself at will by using the mantra I have given you to the Mighty Threefold Flame of Life.[3] This mantra, beloved, will call my Electronic Presence around you. It is not short, because through your giving of the mantra, whilst you are giving it, I am realigning your chakras, assisting you to balance the threefold flame at all costs and to bring God-control to every aspect of your life.

Thus, some mantras work well as a line or two of affirmation. But when I wish to activate in you the spirals of the rainbow rays of God, then I must have this mantra. And while you give it, beloved, I can sustain the Presence. Thus, if it become a perpetual mantra in your heart, see where the increase of fire will bring you—closer to all of my chelas at inner levels and on the outer, closer indeed to the members of the priesthood of beloved Melchizedek. Thus, the mighty threefold flame of Life is the gift of God so pure!

Into the flame now comes your own beloved seraphim, the same, the very one who was with you in the hour of your birth in the Great Central Sun. Beloved ones, this seraphim has an attachment to you and to your twin flame and desires to bring you together. This seraphim has an attachment to bringing your body and mind and soul into the health of God, the health enjoyed by seraphim.

I would suggest you woo your seraphim and woo him to your side that he may not return to the Central Sun except according to the regular rotations and cyclings and recyclings of the seraphim from the Great Central Sun to the outer rings they form in the outermost universes and back again.

So, beloved, seraphim are personally devoted, as they should be, to whomever God appoints them. Inasmuch as the seraphim, as you have been told, are great healers, they use these rainbow rays now for that healing purpose.

I AM in the white fire core of the flame. I AM in the pulsation of resurrection's flame. I AM in the action of the point of your Holy Christ Self.

In this moment of our meditation, beloved, I AM one with your Holy Christ Self. Now look upon your Holy Christ Self and see the smiling face of Zarathustra. In this moment I am not in my fiercest mode but when you see me turn upon the forces of Antichrist, then you may tremble by the fury of the elements and the wind and the vortex of the fire, beloved. But remember, in all of this it is directed. It is directed, beloved ones, and under the God-control of myself and legions of Light.

Therefore, while you are in this hour of assimilation of the flame, I shall perform the service now of dealing with those forces of Antichrist.

Bind the Forces of Antichrist in the Earth!

Ho! Mighty legions of the Light, descend!
Ho! Mighty legions of the Light, descend!
Ho! Mighty legions of the Light, descend!

Take up your positions in the quadrants of the earth now. By the mighty sword of the Divine Mother, therefore bind the forces of Antichrist in the earth and in the sea, *in the earth, in the earth, in the earth,* in the air, in the mental plane, in the etheric octave!

Blaze the full power of the Great Central Sun!

Mighty legions arrayed and circles of seraphim of God, legions of the mighty fire beings of the Ruby Ray and all of the secret-ray Dhyani Buddhas, come forth now for the binding of the forces of Antichrist in the earth!

Let all of heaven now unleash that full-gathered momentum of Elohim! *ELOHIM ELOHIM ELOHIM*

Let the full power of God descend for the displacing in the earth, for the consuming in the earth, for the binding in the earth, for the judgment in the earth of those who are the force of Antichrist, known or unknown, embodied or disembodied!

Let it descend now, O God! Let the fire descend as you have accorded it, as you have decreed it, as you have sent it and sent me into this very midst!

Therefore, let the fire descend! And let the all-consuming fire deal with that consciousness and that manifestation whose time is up. And therefore, let it be bound, let it be dissolved and let it be taken now into the very heart of the Central Sun for that action of the sacred fire which is meet!

Now the rain of fire-snow descends. ("Fire-snow," a misnomer, but fire-snow it is.) Descend, O fire-snow! Goddess of Purity, Goddess of Light, Queen of Light, all hosts of the Fourth Ray, Astrea and Purity and all legions of Zarathustra, *go forth, then!*

They are bound by the hosts of the LORD and the hosts of the LORD shall continue the binding!

And therefore, I *seal* the action of the binding in the name Ahura Mazda! And I seal your temples in the flame that will not be quenched by God, will not be quenched by the Lord Christ or the Lord Buddha, will not be quenched, beloved, by your Holy Christ Self. The only one who can quench the flame is you.

See thou do it not! *See* thou do it not! *See* thou do it not!

Salutations from all legions of *Zarathustra!*

[37-second standing ovation]

July 1, 1992

CHAPTER 12

A Spokesman for the Delegation of the Priesthood of Melchizedek in Attendance

THE GREAT MYSTERY OF THE VIOLET FLAME

Give a Cup of Cool Violet Flame in Christ's Name

Salutations to all sons and daughters of God present and not present and to all children of the Light! I bring these salutations, as I represent the delegation of the order of the priesthood of Melchizedek.

I am chosen as a nameless one to speak to you that you might know that as aspiring candidates to this priesthood you have begun well and run well. Therefore, finish your course and do not weary. For the requirement for studying under the Master Melchizedek is your mastery of some level of the fire element, and you are given this opportunity each time you invoke the violet flame.

Let us speak of the mastery of this flame since you are familiar with it and it does not strike a certain fear, as the physical flames of earth's fire sometimes do. Therefore, beloved, be seated in the violet flame, for soon the day will be upon you, on July 3, wherein you will have the great joy of communing for twenty-four hours in the mighty aura of Omri-Tas, Ruler of the Violet Planet.[1]

Each month we look forward to and anticipate his coming with great joy. And we prepare all the days of the month unto the third of the next month that we might bring a greater concentration of violet flame and also be initiated by Omri-Tas. For with the blessing he extends to you and all Keepers of the Flame, he does also stop by at Zadkiel's retreat to offer us some portion of that mighty flame which we have earned in the previous cycle. Therefore, what is true for us is true for you, beloved. Look forward to this opportunity as nothing else.

Visualization of the violet flame begins your concentration and results in your God-mastery. Visualize the fire in the heart, then, and let the violet flame burn in the heart, surround the heart.

And when you know your mantras by heart, as many of you do, then sit in deep meditation and let the violet flame increase in size, beginning within and then encompassing the physical heart and the heart chakra. Let the action of the violet flame remain intense by your visualization and by the intensity of your call. Then let it expand slowly so that the intensity is such that you cannot see through the flame; for it has become a dense manifestation of the violet ray of light as it has descended from the sun and then sprung up as a flame at your point of invocation.

Your point of invocation is your throat chakra. It can also be defined as the plane of your soul's incarnation. Therefore I say, invoke the flame through the throat chakra and add to your invocation the instrument of the heart chakra, thereby pouring love to the flame and drawing love from the flame. Use the third eye to invoke the violet flame by intense visualization, drawing the flame into the third eye and giving to the flame the momentum of the sacred fire of that chakra. So use each of the chakras to meditate upon the flame, to focus the flame and then to give devotion unto the flame even as you receive the devotion of the flame.

The more creative you are in the use of the violet flame, the more you understand that the violet flame is a ritual, has a consciousness of ritual and looks forward to the hours of the day that you have consecrated to invoking a mantra of the violet flame—or, should I say, invoking the violet flame through a mantra?

Well, the mantra is the flame and the flame is God and so is the mantra! The question is: Are *you* all three? Are you the flame, the mantra and the manifestation of God?

This is the attainment you look forward to as you visualize the violet flame rising up from beneath your feet, rising and pulsating and purifying every level of your being. Then when the concentration is complete in the physical body and you see and feel it, let it slowly extend out from you as an aura having the magnetism of the violet flame and let it increase and intensify.

And so, beloved, as you go through the world, remember to put on your tube of light to protect your momentum of the violet flame. But also be ready when you see the eyes of a Lightbearer and the child in need and the soul who looks to God for help. Do not fear to be the instrument to transfer a cup of cool violet flame in Christ's name.

To have a reservoir of the violet flame means that when you invoke the violet flame, you are using the action of the mighty sea of violet flame in the heart of the earth, you are using the mighty action of Saint Germain's Maltese cross[2] and you are establishing that pillar of fire where you are—multiplied by your own reservoir.

After all, it is the seventh age and the seventh dispensation, beloved ones. It is that age and hour when you can all become priests and priestesses under the Order of Lord Zadkiel, under Melchizedek, under Saint Germain, under Zarathustra and even Oromasis and Diana. It is that moment in an entire twelve-tiered cycle when you have come all the way around the Cosmic Clock of the ages back to the place of the Aquarius sign—the sign of the liberation of the soul through the violet flame.

In no other past age since the last age of Aquarius, twelve cycles ago, has there been such an opportunity for world transmutation, soul transmutation, the balancing of karma and your soul's restoration through the Lord and Saviour Jesus Christ to your own inner Christ-potential. So, beloved, the opportunity is vast. It is increased by the dispensation of Omri-Tas, who has brought to you an unprecedented dispensation (given the present level of earth's evolutions) to reduce your karmic cycles by light-years.

Therefore know what a boon all students in the retreats of the Ascended Masters on the etheric octave who are not in embodiment consider this one day a month to be to them! Why, all the retreats of the entire planet are simply pulsating with the joy of the violet flame!

And we do keep that flame and we do conserve it and we preserve it in the urns upon our altars. And therefore, when world crisis breaks out or the planetary hierarchs and the Solar Logoi give the word that there must be earth changes, we have upon the altars of all of the retreats of the Great White Brotherhood on earth the wherewithal to apportion that violet flame that we have carefully invoked and garnered so that there might be a smooth transition when the Great Law decrees the balancing of that karma which is weighing heavily in the earth body and being borne by so many billions of souls who live thereon.

So you see, beloved, you can do the same! You can bank the fires of the violet flame in all of your chakras and in all of the levels of your being, as tier upon tier your chakras represent the seven planes of heaven. You can rise up those tiers, beloved ones! And you can rise up the *sefirot* unto the point of the I AM THAT I AM, and one day you may go beyond the I AM THAT I AM to the point of the *Ein Sof.* So understand the meaning of the cycles of the degrees as you walk the Path a true initiate of the Great White Brotherhood.

Now understand, beloved, the great mystery of the violet flame. The violet flame is an action that can be stepped up or down and tuned to any level of the seven chakras. Therefore the violet flame that you keep in the heart will have a different frequency than the violet flame that you keep in the solar-plexus chakra, and so on. And as you are stepping up the grades of the violet flame from the base-of-the-spine chakra to the crown chakra, there is an acceleration of the violet flame affecting all of those levels in the earth body. So when you begin at the base chakra and proceed, rising to the crown, you are experiencing God in the seven levels of heaven *right in your very own being!*

Therefore I say to you, value the chakras in your body. Value them well, beloved, for they are chalices. And in the day and the hour when sudden calamity or terminal disease or plague of any kind comes upon your house or upon your body, you will have vials filled with violet flame as a precious medicine, as a precious unguent that you may use spiritually and physically.

Understand therefore, beloved, that he who does not collect his pots from all of his town and townspeople and bring them into one place on the third of the month and fill them with the violet flame surely does not anticipate that the day may come when there will be no violet flame rain anymore. And therefore, in that day the pots will be dry if you do not fill them now and they will be full if you do fill them now!

So, beloved ones, this is not hoarding. For the violet flame is infinite —infinite out of your own Causal Body of Light, infinite from the Violet Planet and from Omri-Tas. But I can tell you, we, the brothers and the sisters who study under our beloved priest Melchizedek, who was indeed king of Jerusalem and priest of the Most High God,[3] know the value of garnering the violet flame. And we are asking you to do the same, beloved, in your octave.

For where there are pockets of concentration of the violet flame and you in your joy and love for beloved Saint Germain and Portia and all they have ever done for you do keep that violet flame, well, you see, you are as points igniting a whole world with the violet flame. You are practically as a tinderbox! And someone may come along and invoke a single violet flame and catch the whole momentum that you carry. And therefore the violet flame will be contagious! And it will *leap* from heart to heart, from continent to continent, from village to village!

Do you understand, beloved? Our goal is to see planet earth become, as she should be, a Violet Planet herself! And thus, Omri-Tas and all of the mighty beings of the Violet Planet are rooting for you. And that is why Alpha has come with the fourth woe. For that woe does descend for the binding of the forces of Antichrist who defile the Divine Mother in her children and in her sons and daughters.[4]

This judgment must come, for we cannot have the fallen ones misusing the violet flame. For every flame can be abused by black magicians on the left-handed path, and they take it not to liberate but to imprison. Thus, know this, beloved ones. And therefore, the time may come when there is a limit to the violet flame that the earth can be given unless and until these fallen ones are bound.

Happy are ye who understand the concept of the mighty labors of the Elohim of God so that you can make light work and fast work of the binding of those forces of Evil who would abuse the very gifts of Saint Germain that he has so lovingly given to his own; for the forces of Evil are already abusing them, as they have abused science and technology in all manner of manifestations from the last days of Atlantis. And, as you know, these manifestations of the abuses of science were actually one of the major causes of the sinking of Atlantis.

Beloved ones, have I expanded your horizons a bit? ["Yes!"]

Happy are ye when ye have illumination! You may think I have brought to you the violet flame but I have brought to you the violet flame of illumination's flame!

Now hear this. There is the violet flame of the blue ray. There is the violet flame of the yellow ray. There is the violet flame of the pink ray. There is the violet flame of the white ray. There is the violet flame of the green ray. There is the violet flame of the purple and gold ray flecked with ruby. And there is the violet flame of the Seventh Ray of the violet flame!

Now therefore, beloved, see how the violet flame can clarify in the mind, the heart, the body and the being all of the understanding, all of the knowledge, all of the perception, all of the senses, all of the functions of the chakras. This can happen when they are cleansed and revivified and purified by the elixir of the violet flame. Why, you see every color more brilliantly! You see the crystal and the white fire core of each ray more brilliantly!

So the violet flame has an aspect on each of the seven rays. And as you invoke it and allow it to complement the seven rays, beloved ones, you will learn more about those rays than you have ever learned by just concentrating upon those rays alone.

The violet flame is surely the universal aura of the planet in this hour, for many angels and elementals and Keepers of the Flame have invoked it. I say, continue to invoke it! For the greatest miracles of all will come to you through this flame and through this flame combined with others.

We have emphasized illumination, beloved, because, of course, without illumination there is simply utter darkness and the dark night of the soul and the Dark Night of the Spirit, where there is no candle.

I bring to you—and all of the priesthood of Melchizedek who are here with me this night bring to you—candles, candles of the violet flame. The wax, or substance like it, is of the violet flame color and the flame is the violet flame color.

Now take your candle, beloved ones. Hold it before you! Be at peace! *Be* a Keeper of the Flame! *And go set the world on fire with violet flame!*

I bow to the violet flame within you and I bid you adieu.

[39-second standing ovation]

July 1, 1992

CHAPTER 13

Elizabeth Clare Prophet

THE WORSHIP OF THE GODDESS—THE PATH OF THE DIVINE MOTHER

The Corona of Sarasvati and Lakshmi

And now some notes on the Divine Mother:

The Divine Mother in her manifestation as Sarasvati is the Shakti of Brahma. Brahma is known as the Creator in the Hindu Trinity. The Ascended Masters teach us that Brahma is parallel to God the Father in the Western Trinity. He is the Divine Lawgiver, the source of all knowledge. Together, Brahma and Sarasvati are the embodiment of cosmic force.

Sarasvati is known as the Goddess of the Word. She is identified with Vac, the Word. She represents eloquence and articulates the wisdom of the Law. She is the Mother/Teacher to those of us who love the Law, revealed by Brahma. And she is the power of volition, the will and motivation to be the Law in action. Sarasvati represents the union of power and intelligence from which organized creation arises.

In the book *Symbolism in Hinduism,* A. Parthasarathy notes that the name Sarasvati literally means "the one who gives the essence of our own Self." Sarasvati is sometimes represented with four hands, sitting on a lotus. She holds the sacred scriptures in one hand and a lotus in another. With the remaining two hands, she plays the Indian lute (veena).[1]

Parthasarathy writes: "The Goddess, therefore, represents the ideal guru. . . . 'Sitting on the lotus' symbolises that the teacher is well established in the subjective experience of the Truth. 'Holding the Scriptures in her hand' indicates that she upholds that the knowledge of the Scriptures alone can take us to the Truth." Parthasarathy says that Sarasvati's playing of the lute suggests "that a truly qualified teacher tunes up the mind and intellect of the seeker and draws out of him the music and melody of life."[2]

According to scholar David Frawley, in an esoteric sense Sarasvati "represents the stream of wisdom, the free flow of the knowledge of consciousness."[3] She is called the Flowing One, the source of creation by the Word.

Sarasvati also represents purity and wears white. David Kinsley, Professor of Religious Studies at McMaster University in Ontario, Canada, explains:

> The predominant themes in Sarasvati's appearance are purity and transcendence. She is almost always said to be pure white like snow, the moon, or the *kunda* flower. . . . Her garments are said to be fiery in their purity. . . .
>
> Sarasvati's transcendent nature . . . is also suggested in her vehicle, the swan. The swan is a symbol of spiritual transcendence and perfection in Hinduism. . . . Sarasvati, astride her swan, suggests a dimension of human existence that rises above the physical, natural world. Her realm is one of beauty, perfection, and grace; it is a realm created by artistic inspiration, philosophic insight, and accumulated knowledge, which have enabled human beings to so refine their natural world that they have been able to transcend its limitations. Sarasvati astride her swan beckons human beings to continued cultural creation and civilized perfection. . . . She not only underlies the world and is its creator but is the [very] means to transcend the world.[4]

Sarasvati is associated with speech, poetry, music and culture and is known as the Goddess of Learning and the patroness of the arts and music. She is revered by both Hindus and Buddhists. To Buddhists she is the consort of Manjushri, the Bodhisattva of Wisdom.

Buddhists appeal to Manjushri for intelligence, wisdom, mastery of the Teaching, the power of exposition, eloquence and memory. He works with Lord Maitreya. The two are sometimes depicted in a triad with Gautama Buddha in which Manjushri represents the wisdom aspect and Maitreya the compassion aspect of Buddhist teaching.

I am holding before you a very precious statue of Manjushri that I keep on the altar. You can feel his powerfully comforting presence as he places a focus of his light body over his likeness. In his right hand he wields a flaming sword of wisdom to vanquish all ignorance. His sword has been called a "sword of quick detachment" and the "symbol of enlightened will." Like Sarasvati, Manjushri brings the gift of illumination.

In the earliest Hindu texts, the Vedas, Sarasvati is a river goddess. The Vedas say that Sarasvati was the greatest river in India. For years the Sarasvati was believed to have been a myth, but an archaeological survey in 1985 found an ancient riverbed that matched the description of the Sarasvati. It was a great river, four to six miles wide for much of its length. It flowed westward from the Himalayas into the sea. Frawley believes that the Sarasvati was the main site of habitation at the time the Vedas were composed thousands of years ago.[5]

Frawley says that the Sarasvati, "like the later Ganges, symbolizes the Sushumna, the river of spiritual knowledge, the current that flows [through the spinal canal] through the seven chakras of the subtle body. She is not only the Milky Way or river of Heaven, inwardly she is the river of true consciousness that flows into this world."[6]

The Rigveda calls Sarasvati "the best mother, the best river, [and] the best Goddess." It also says, "Sarasvati like a great ocean appears with her ray, she rules all inspirations."[7]

Her sacred "seed syllable," or bija, is *Aim.* A bija mantra encapsules the essence of a Cosmic Being, of a principle or a chakra. Sarasvati's mantra is *Om Aim Sarasvatye Namaha.*

The Divine Mother in her manifestation as Lakshmi is the Shakti of Vishnu. Lakshmi is known as the Goddess of Fortune and Beauty. In earlier texts she is known as Sri, which means "splendor," "beauty," "prosperity," "wealth." Vishnu holds the office of Preserver in the Hindu Trinity. The Preserver is parallel to the principle of the Son in the Western Trinity. As the Son, Vishnu embodies Cosmic Christ wisdom. He is also the mediator, or bridge, between the human consciousness and Brahman, Absolute Reality.

According to the teachings of Hinduism, Vishnu was incarnated nine times, most notably as Rama and Krishna. Lakshmi took human form to serve as his consort in each of his incarnations. Lakshmi's incarnations included: Sita, the faithful wife of Rama; the cow girl Radha, beloved of Krishna; and Rukmini, the princess whom Krishna later married.

As the Preserver, Vishnu preserves divine design conceived in Wisdom's flame. He restores the universe by Wisdom's all-healing Light. Lakshmi shares his role as Preserver. Her wisdom is revealed in blessings of prosperity and the precipitation of the abundant life. She bears the cornucopia of good fortune by "eye magic," the eye magic of the All-Seeing Eye of her Beloved. She embodies divine compassion and intercedes on our behalf before her consort. She is the mediator of the Mediator!

Lakshmi is described as being "as radiant as gold" and "illustrious like the moon." She is said to "shine like the sun" and "to be lustrous like fire."[8] She teaches multiplicity and beauty and is called "She of the Hundred Thousands." Whatever matrix is in her hand, whatever you hold in your heart, Lakshmi can multiply by the millions, for one idea can be reproduced infinitely. Lakshmi also teaches us mastery of karmic cycles on the Cosmic Clock.

At the beginning of the commercial year in India, Hindus give special prayers to Lakshmi to bring success in their endeavors. She is worshiped in every home on all important occasions.

But Lakshmi has a deeper, esoteric significance in that she is associated with immortality and the essence of life. In Hindu lore, she was created when the gods and demons churned a primordial ocean of milk. Their goal was to produce the elixir of immortality. Along with the elixir, they also produced the Goddess Lakshmi.

Lakshmi is seen as the one who personifies royal power and

conveys it upon kings. She is often depicted with a lotus and an elephant. The lotus represents purity and spiritual power; the elephant, royal authority.

Kinsley says, "To be seated upon, or to be otherwise associated with, the lotus suggests that the being in question . . . has transcended the limitations of the finite world. . . . She is associated not only with royal authority but with spiritual authority as well, and she therefore combines royal and priestly powers."[9]

Remember the phrase in the Book of Revelation "kings and priests unto God."[10] The mantle and the office of that kingship and that priesthood unto God are the bestowal that God would make upon all Lightbearers of the world. Such are the crowns and scepters that are there to be bestowed. It is as though your mantle and your royal or priestly robes (or both) were hanging on a hanger in a retreat, waiting to drop upon you when you fulfill your reason for being.

So know, O my beloved children, that it is the Divine Mother who will carefully take your robes from the hanger and put them on your shoulders when you will have proven without a shadow of a doubt that you are a trusted servant of the Light—trustworthy to the end. This is the ceremony of entitlement.

In ancient times Sri-Lakshmi was considered to be the source of the power of kings. Carl Olson writes: "The relationship of the goddess to the king is so intimate that she is described as residing in the sovereign. . . . Thus Sri is the source of the king's power. And she is very concerned about the exercise of royal virtues like truth, generosity, austerity, strength, and [the] *dharma*."[11] The Mahabharata states that when one ancient king fell from power, "he lost his royal *sri*."[12]

Kinsley points out that several Hindu myths tell of "[the god] Indra's losing, acquiring, or being restored to Sri-Lakshmi's presence." He says, "In these myths, it is clear that what is lost, acquired, or restored in the person of Sri is royal authority and power."[13]

Please note that I said in my lecture on Hinduism that Indra represents the Self. So, in the process of realizing your Real Self, if you depart from the 'royal' virtues, you may temporarily lose the sponsorship of the Divine Mother until you value your embodiment of those virtues more than you value your freedom to embody either vices or a vacuum.

Lakshmi is the one who anoints us with the Christ Light, the Light of Vishnu. This is the Light that makes every son of God royal, every son of God a king or a priest unto God. The office of *king*, remember, defines "the one who holds the *k*ey to the *in*carnation of *G*od"—k-i-n-g. The office of *priest* defines "the one who holds the *p*ower of the *R*a and the *R*ai and who *i*ncarnates the *e*nergy of the *s*acred *T*au and *T*ao"—p-r-i-e-s-t.[14]

Lakshmi is often shown with an elephant on either side showering her with water from their trunks. Kinsley tells us that these images are "probably meant to portray the act of royal consecration."[15] And I would say "the consecration of the mind," because it is out of the memory of God that we are able to properly rule ourselves and all who may be with us or under us. The elephant-god Ganesha has the infinite memory of the Mind of God. Without that memory we cannot really progress on the Path.

Kinsley writes that this concept of royal consecration by elephants resonates with the Vedic royal consecration ceremony, "in which the king was consecrated by having auspicious waters poured over him."[16]

Has anyone seen any auspicious waters these days?*

The Hindus believe that these auspicious waters bestowed authority and vigor on the king. So claim your authority and vigor when the rain rains upon your tent! Nothing happens by accident or without certain purpose.

The king can be seen as representing the Christed one who has gained enlightenment. Author Adrian Snodgrass interprets the sprinkling of water as a spiritual initiation of the soul in which one is "washed free of mortality."[17]

So, we see the Goddess Lakshmi as an embodiment of the Divine Mother. We see her in her role as consort of Vishnu, the Second Person of the Trinity, as very much a part of the ceremony of the marriage of your soul to your Holy Christ Self. When you are wed and bonded to

*reference to the special cleansing, purifying rain in the Heart of the Inner Retreat at the ten-day *FREEDOM 1992* conference that brought transmutation of local and planetary records in preparation for the coming of Alpha and Omega.

that Christ Self, that is when you become royal in the godly sense of the word. Each one of us can receive this "royal" initiation when we have earned the grace of the bountiful Lakshmi. Lakshmi restores us to our original estate of oneness with God.

In one Tantric text, Lakshmi says of herself: "Like the fat that keeps a lamp burning I lubricate the senses of living beings with my own sap of consciousness."[18] Lakshmi bestows upon us the nectar of God consciousness when we gain her favor. Vishnu is the Christ Light and Lakshmi is the bestower of that Light. The riches she brings are spiritual riches and admission to the kingdom of heaven.

Lakshmi's seed syllable, or bija, is *Srim.* Her mantra is *Om Srim Lakshmye Namaha.*

Messenger's Invocation before the Lecture:

O sweet flame of Divine Love burning in our hearts, expand now and glow! Let the glow of Divine Love in our bodies and in our souls, O God, which you have placed there provide a new emanation of the aura of the Lightbearers of the earth. Let this Light accelerate by all of the Causal Bodies of all of the beings of Light who are one with us in this hour in the Divine Mother.

O thou greatness of Divine Love that we share, let the full power of the Godhead through the mighty Shakti so multiply and multiply and multiply again, O God, for the victory of every soul of Light on planet earth. Encircle them now! Lakshmi, Durga, Sarasvati, Kali, Parvati, come forth!

O mighty ones of God, O Divine Mother in concentration in manifestation throughout all cosmos, be one with your chelas in this hour! Be one with us. Oh, magnify the Lord as Mother within us! And let us mother all life, succor all life, O God, that they might be free, free from fear and want and doubt, free to stand with thee in the heart of creation.

O beloved Father, because thou art, so we have our Mother with us, as Above, so below. We are grateful, O God! Our gratitude overflows beyond this cosmos unto thy throne. Receive us now, O God.

Chant the Bija Mantras to the Feminine Deities

1. SARASVATI: AIM
   OM AIM SARASVATYE NAMAHA
2. LAKSHMI: SRIM
   OM SRIM LAKSHMYE NAMAHA
3. KALI: KRIM
   OM KRIM KALIKAYE NAMAHA
4. DURGA: DUM
   OM DUM DURGAYE NAMAHA
5. AIM HRIM KLIM CHAMUNDAYE VICHE

July 2, 1992

CHAPTER 14

The Goddess Sarasvati

WE DO WORK!

Illumination— The Only Cure for Earth Is Illumination

I am sent to you by my Lord Brahma, who has said:

> O Sarasvati, now is the hour for the appearing of dazzling knowledge, the power of the might of purity multiplying illumination's flame.
>
> Go forth, then! Go forth, then, with Lakshmi and multiply thy powers and the powers of the Divine Mother Durga and Kali.
>
> And therefore penetrate the sheaths of the four lower bodies of the earth with knowledge, with Light, with brightness of the spiritual cosmos.

I AM Sarasvati. I come to you, beloved, for the only cure for the earth in this hour is illumination—illumination that comes from the light of the Word and the delivery of the Word by right speech preceded by right mindfulness.

O the Mind of God! O let it descend! Let it descend everywhere. Legions of the Divine Mother, legions of the Divine Mother, come forth! Come forth now and reveal to these inner eyes the shafts of golden yellow light, crystallized as glass, as crystal itself, penetrating the layers of density.

O my God, I *plead* for the removal from the eyes of the young and all people of that which is utterly a nonessential in this earth—and that is 95 percent of that which passes through the television sets everywhere upon the planet. This is the destroying not only of the third-eye development but of the development of the crown chakra.

I AM Sarasvati! I am ready to pursue with you the opening of the crown. I am ready to assist you in the raising of the Light of the Goddess Kundalini. But I must have in you a nucleus of golden-yellow white fire. I must have in you an intensity of desire for the knowledge of God and for the knowledge of what is truly transpiring in the earth and all of the trespasses that are made against the children of the Light.

O ye sons and daughters of Brahman, now hear me! Hear my call! I am very present in this Community, for I have an affinity with the work of the Messenger and the Messenger has an affinity with my work; and therefore, we do work! And you work also and you share in the veils of my garments that I extend.

So, yes, I wear the white, beloved, but I also wear all of the rays as I bring that fiery white core of knowledge into all manifestations in the outer and the inner traditions. This earth must have knowledge! Woman must have self-knowledge, man must have self-knowledge and the child must know the Inner Christ as the Holy Christ Self and the Inner Buddha as the I AM THAT I AM. This is the teaching, and so much more.

We rejoice, therefore, to offer the mantle of our office, "Sarasvati," to all who teach children. And if you would have the mantle, then I say, take an hour or two or three here and there to teach children something of your own expertise in this Community.

What is life without having a child for a true friend?

Go into our schools and give of your talent that your talent may not die. For it is the requirement of every disciple of the Divine Mother to pass on his talent to the next generation ere he take his leave from this octave.

So, beloved, before the day and the hour of your transitioning to other planes, remember to deposit in many hearts your skill, your creativity, your art, your science, the melody of your soul, the preciousness of your heart. And do not think for one moment that you do not have anything to teach! If you have nothing you have learned, beloved, then teach compassion, teach love, teach joy, teach gratitude, teach all children of all ages how to magnify the Lord in their hearts.

Thus, I come to you and I come in the great Spirit of God. I come in the hour, then, when I will contribute the great river of illumination to your endeavor. Unless illumination cleanse the earth, inundate the earth, take over the earth, beloved, where will the people go? How will they recognize the Truth?

Let them recognize it within you, I say!

Sarasvati is both Person and Principle. Sarasvati is in the heart of every one of you. Each one of the four principles, the four seed syllables that the four Goddesses embody, is a part of the threefold flame. For we are in the sphere of the white fire that is the source of the fount of the Trinity.

So you see, beloved, I AM an Ascended Lady Master. I AM a Goddess. I AM a Principle. I AM the Counterpart of Brahma. Therefore, where Father is, there AM I, the other side of Father.

Know, then, that as you meditate upon the Trinity in your heart and you say the names Father, Son and Holy Spirit—Brahma, Vishnu and Shiva—you are automatically saying and affirming our names: Sarasvati, Lakshmi, Durga. Yes, beloved, and then you have Kali and then you have Parvati.[1] And then you have the wondrous Presence of the Divine Mother all in one, as the mantra makes us one divine manifestation.[2]

The mantras that descend in Hinduism—and, I should say, the principle of the mantra as it has been applied by your beloved Saint Germain to you in this time—are the key and the means to the turning around of the age. Therefore I pour forth illumination and you invoke the violet flame to clear the way for its absorption by all people of earth.

I come to you, then, with the fierceness of self-knowledge. I expose to you your True Self in glory! I expose to you your unreal self and I say: Choose this day whom you will serve and be about your Father's business, your Father Brahma, the mighty one who sits on the twelve o'clock line of the north, who is represented by the Great Divine Director and all beings of Light who serve in that quadrant.

Yes, beloved, come to know us as we walk and talk with you, as God of gods and Lord of lords and Goddess of goddesses. Come to know us intimately and personally and you will find the great key to bhakti yoga and devotion to God, the key to jnana yoga and knowledge of God. You will find the key to raja yoga and royal integration with God. You will find the key to karma yoga and the path of your soul's resolution in God by the flame of transmutation.

I am with you because I am kindling a flame! I am speaking with you, and while I am speaking I am transferring a phenomenal manifestation of filigree of illumination's flame. And Lakshmi and I have, in fact, consorted together and we have determined that we shall press through by the fire of Kali, by the power of the deep blue of the cosmos, by the Ruby Ray, by the power of the purple and the violet flame—we shall press through in this hour such a desire for true illumination of a spiritual nature as to produce, if you will be our instruments, a worldwide awakening to the spiritual path of the entire Spirit of the Great White Brotherhood.

This illumination, beloved, can come through all of the mystical paths of the world's religions that are being revealed to you. But I tell you, orthodoxy in every world religion and a priest class who are not servants of the Light and not Sons of the Solitude do block the true revelation of the indwelling God. Therefore, expand the paths of mysticism. Renew them, intensify them, review them so that you may understand how it is that a soul journeying on one of these mystical paths will more clearly understand union with God through her religion.

Helios and Vesta radiate tremendous light of the golden pink glow-ray for the intensification of knowledge. So the mighty ones have told you, so we reiterate it: Teach the Teachings, clear the levels of ignorance and the poisons of ignorance, and replace them by the binding power of wisdom that binds all that is unreal, for thereby you will come to the feet of your Inner God.

Pass on true knowledge. Do not hide it under a bushel! There is no time to waste. Pass on the Teaching to those who are interested and pass by those who are not. You are looking for those eyes! You are looking for those chelas! You are looking for those souls! *Go and find them.* And keep on going until you know you have found one, for, beloved, sometimes they are few and far between.

You have a lifetime, or the remainder of a lifetime, at your disposal. Therefore, consecrate your days and hours to the Lightbearers who are searching and waiting for the Truth. And call to me—call to me, beloved, for I will connect you to those who must be contacted by you in this life for your karma does dictate it.

For your karma is that from time to time you have denied the light and the wisdom of the Divine Mother; now you must balance that karma and I will help you! *I will help you.* Feel the strength of the Shakti of the power of God, beloved, and know of a certainty that I will not fail you in your mission. And I ask *you* not to fail *me.*

I AM Sarasvati. I will stay close to you and I will not leave you until you ask me to leave and dismiss me. But, beloved ones, do not neglect me. At least give my seed-syllable mantra daily that you might know the wavelength of my office and share in it:

Om Aim Sarasvatye Namaha

Lo, I give you what I AM and I guard what I AM in you.

I AM Sarasvati, profoundly concerned for the future of earth and her evolutions. Teach the children! Teach them by example. Teach them by love. Teach them by the will of God. Teach them by the power of his Presence.

Love them and I shall love them through you.

July 2, 1992

CHAPTER 15

The Goddess Lakshmi

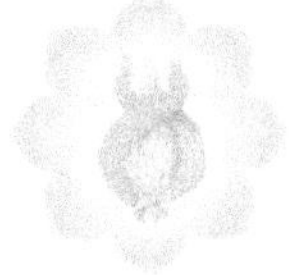

LET THE EGOS FALL!

The Torch Must Be Passed to the Children

Lakshmi I AM. Lakshmi I AM! Oh yes, beloved, I come to mediate. I come representing Vishnu, Lord Krishna. I AM the representative of the ones who are the shining Sons of all of cosmos and the One who is the Son, Lord Vishnu, in so many manifestations.

Right within you now is Vishnu in the person of your Holy Christ Self. You are familiar with the term *Christ Self.* How does it feel to say, "My beloved Vishnu, descend into my temple *now!*"

Blessed ones, it feels good, does it not? ["Yes!"]

So understand that we go before our consorts. As you receive us, so you receive them. They enter because we have first entered. Thus, the Divine Mother is always the one closest to her children.

And so in this hour, let the egos fall! And let the fallen ones who have fallen by the ego *fall!* Let them fall under the line of Helios and Vesta and the great cosmic hierarchy of Aries. This is the hour of the judgment. So let them be judged!

So let there come the dawn of a new day of a people who have the inner strength because they have self-emptied themselves of that ego and the Divine is indwelling. No need to prance about and strut the ego when the whole of the Divine Ego lives within you!

It is such an awesome experience that it makes you be quiet and sense a hush all about you that God walks where you walk, that God is in your temple, that Vishnu is firmly centered on the throne in the secret chamber of your heart. Understand, beloved, that when you know that God is in you, when you know that you are that God-manifestation and that he who is one with God is God, you have no need to sing your praises or to make certain that someone is aware of your talents and abilities.

Beloved ones, be in awe of the indwelling Presence of God. Go often to the altar of the inner Light and thank your God and your Great Guru, Sanat Kumara, who has saved you for this hour.

Yes, I plead with you to also be the Saviouress and the consort of the Saviouress. I plead with you, beloved, for there will be no new day and no golden age if there is not a passing of the mighty torch of the ancient ones of thousands of years and tens of thousands of years and of past golden ages and histories of a planet unchronicled in this era.

The torch must be passed and it is not being passed. Look at the true gap between generations—the gap between the knowledge that you have had and the knowledge that your children and children's children do not have, the gap between what you were taught and what they have not been taught. It is frightening to you and it is frightening to us.

You must close this gap. You must transfer to those generations coming after you what they have missed in the schools. You must turn off the television set, as Sarasvati has said. Throw it out the window! Get rid of it! And commune with the Child of your child—commune with the inner person! Otherwise you will find your children growing up as lonely ones, as ones who seek the company not of Lightbearers but of the role models they have seen on the television, yes, beloved, the antiheroes and -heroines.

Blessed hearts, there is no place for you to be except with the little children for a portion of your life. And extend that! Be not content just to be near those in the circle of your family. Extend your love! Open your home! Teach the children! Welcome them in! Feed them what their souls need and what their bodies need. Give them love, not a mechanical TV set and mechanical people and mechanical gods and scripts written for their minds and advertising for their desire bodies.

Yes, you have heard it before, but you have not heard it from Lakshmi! And I tell you, beloved, this is an hour to make the difference, to turn the world around or to lose the children of the Light and all children of planet earth. I say this as a most urgent message of this Fourth of July conference here in the dwelling place of the beloved Gautama Buddha.

Yes, beloved, we are mothers and fathers all. Now let us not go back to the former level of neglect and of not tuning in to what is the need of the hour.

I AM Lakshmi. Remember me in the morning and remember me in the night. Remember me when you take your soul journeys, and invoke us, Vishnu and me, as you take your leave of your body at night to go and serve those individuals who need your care.

Yes, continue to set your mark on Yugoslavia, for the judgment must descend and the Lightbearers must be protected. But you can multiply this by transferring to the map of the world the concentration that you have placed there in Yugoslavia. And when you return to the Royal Teton Retreat after your night's work, you can transfer that entire momentum of your inner work to other areas of the earth and not dilute the concentration of that work. This is the multiplication of God's power. This is the multiplication and maximizing of your effort.

Call to us and we will teach you to multiply your Presence, your Electronic Presence. We will use our Presence as mediators to assist you that you might place yourselves in many places through your own Christ Self wedded to the Divine Mothers. Yes, beloved, you can increase your effectiveness and your work. And watch how the newspapers do reflect that which is going on at inner levels.

I, then, go with Sarasvati this night to the Retreat of the Divine Mother that is over the Royal Teton Ranch. Come, then, to that retreat and meet others who wait for you, for the representatives of the Divine Mother hold a reception for all of you this night. Bring your children and make the call for all Lightbearers of the world to gather.

For we must have our convention! We must have our meeting of the minds! We must determine at inner levels to take our assignments and meet in committee and go in full force with an organized plan into the towns and cities and the nations for the illumination of the children and for the giving to those children who have a spiritual light and a desire to know the Truth that cup of wisdom, that cup of knowledge, that cup of Christ consciousness, that cup of the Inner Buddha.

We *are* your friends. Come, take our hands—hands of all of us who represent the mighty ones. Come! Come! Come! *We* are the Shakti!

Will you be the Shakti with us? ["Yes!"]

Will you make it happen? ["Yes!"]

Yes, beloved, say yes! Lay the plan and the blueprint, and do it! And call for our strength, for *you will need it* and *we will give it!*

[35-second standing ovation]

July 2, 1992

CHAPTER 16

Gautama Buddha

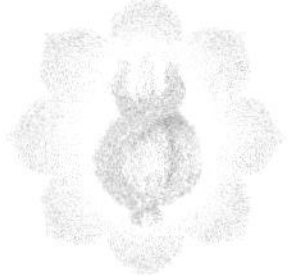

YOU MUST RISE!

Do Not Fail to Give the Mantra for the Mantra Is God!

Thus, I come. Thus, I come in this hour, my Bodhisattvas with me. We descend! And we lower into congruency in this place—for these hours of the celebration of the Declaration of Independence of the original colonies—the Tushita heaven![1] [31-second standing ovation]

This, beloved, is an act of desire. For it is the desire of the Bodhisattvas, it is the desire of Lord Maitreya to descend into this octave when the earth shall have realized a golden age and sustained it for five hundred years.

We desire to see them take incarnation. You desire to see them walk among you. Therefore, the desire from Above and the desire from below has allowed this action to take place that you might understand that the entire earth is intended to be locked in to the etheric octave but, instead, the astral plane does blot it out.

Happy are ye, then, who have kept the flame in the Heart of our Inner Retreat, fully mindful and aware of the Western Shamballa[2] that surrounds you. Happy are ye who return to this place yearly as an annual precelebration to your own victory of your ascension in the Light.

This is the pilgrimage to the Western Shamballa. I remind you that your Lord and Saviour Jesus Christ took his ascension from the Eastern, and the original, Shamballa.[3] Thus, East and West the devotees mount the thirty-three-tiered spiral staircase that will ultimately bring them to the All-Seeing Eye of God, their own Mighty I AM Presence.

I AM Gautama Buddha, your Lord and the Lord of the World, and I am most grateful to be speaking to you on this day of days. Won't you, then, be seated midst the Bodhisattvas, who count you fellow bodhisattvas on the Path and desire to lend you the very magnetism of their auras that you might keep and strengthen and intensify that auric emanation of your own Holy Christ Self.

Therefore, let us understand and receive the meditation of the rings of the Causal Body, the mighty spheres of Light. O most beloved ones, if you should one day enter into the congruency of the great Dharmakaya, into the heart of hearts of the I AM THAT I AM, you will then be in the presence of and come to know those great and mighty spheres of the Causal Body of God.

Now then, by way of magnetizing below that which is Above, let us begin to realize and to visualize these rings. See them as flat rings that are horizontal. Then visualize them extending from your heart chakra, one upon the other, as you look at the Great Causal Body on the Chart of the Presence above me.

See these rings as extending, beloved. See them going out. See the fiery power of the white, the yellow, the pink, the violet, the purple, the green and the blue. See that mighty action, beloved ones, and know that each day as you fill in those rings by action, by prayer, by determination, by will, by all that you do to the glory of God, as Above, so below, you are becoming that auric emanation of your God and of myself.

Every Ascended Master lives in the Dharmakaya, in the Mighty I AM Presence. And we see to it that each and every day we are extending and expanding and strengthening and intensifying the Power, Wisdom and Love of the spheres of our Causal Body. I have extended my Causal Body to include planet earth and far beyond. And therefore I hold within my very Body, within my very Being and Consciousness and within the very bliss of my Being, all evolutions who are abiding in the earth and in other planes of the earth.

This is my assignment, beloved ones, and I concentrate upon it, for I AM the Lord of the World in the heart of every person, every son and daughter and every child. I AM in the heart of sentient life and I AM even in the heart of the evildoer. I remain there until the last trump of defiance against God is sounded by the one who then must go before the Court of the Sacred Fire and determine whether or not to bend the knee and if not to bend the knee, as that one has not for aeons, then to find that that God within is canceled out and all energy of God is withdrawn, purified, transmuted and restored to the Great Central Sun.

Thus, up to the very moment of the extinguishing of the self by the Self, I, Gautama, am there to keep the flame. And if there be no flame, I substitute my aura and I extend a certain life, a certain consciousness whereby there is absolutely no possibility for anyone in this universe, especially those connected with the earth body, to not be able to understand the choice whether to be or not to be in God.

Thus, understand, beloved, that I AM in the earth. I AM in my Causal Body in the earth. And all of these evolutions play in the fields of my consciousness day by day. I AM in the center of the Great Tao. I AM in the center of *Ein Sof,* in the unmanifest as well as in the manifest.

Yet what do you see as response to this nurturing of my heart?

Well, beloved, you might say that the response is pathetic, but I am also always hopeful. I am hopeful, beloved, because you have responded to my aura. I am hopeful because Sanat Kumara did come to earth, did call me, did raise me up for this service.

This I say to you, beloved: If I might have such as you as extensions of myself in physical embodiment, with brother and sister bodhisattvas accompanying you—*you* directly speaking to the people, *you* becoming on fire with the zeal of the LORD that you have not yet had, even though many of you are zealous—if I could have you speaking the Word into every corner of the world and into every point of Darkness, into every heart and eye, with the conviction that you are planting another seed of the Buddha that shall go and merge with the inner seed of the Buddha that is in everyone—if I can have this, beloved ones, there can be a stepping down, then, of my Causal Body and all that I AM through you, there can be a reaching of many more.

And you can make the call to me this day and every day to dispel the false theology, the false notions that people in every field of endeavor entertain; for they cannot receive the Truth when they hear it because they are indoctrinated.

Understand this principle, beloved ones. I must extend myself *through you.* For if I do not hold myself in the place where I AM THAT I AM, then should the world verily collapse. Thus, as I hold my position in these octaves and as we press in and among you this day, so I say to you, realize in the bliss and the meditation of this conference that you *can be* myself in form. You can invoke my Causal Body and my aura. You can approach everyone you meet, stranger or friend, in the vibration of Gautama Buddha.

And I say, bring the gentleness, the compassion, but bring the sudden thrust of Truth. For sometimes when Truth is least expected it makes its mark and drives deep into the psyche and remains there for many days and many miles until it can no longer be denied.

Do you know, beloved ones, that when you plant Truth in the heart and the being of an individual, at that moment it becomes a focus for more of the momentum of Truth to gather? It becomes as a lodestone. And therefore everywhere he goes, that one who has heard the Truth spoken by you does bump into that Truth in another form, in another manifestation, in odd places and from unusual people.

So it is, beloved, that a great truth is confirmed. It is confirmed by all elemental life and all of the stars and all of the great beings of Light. But most of all it is confirmed by the soul who is listening, who is listening to the Holy Christ Self.

I have looked at ways and means and up and down and I have walked the earth. I am a pilgrim who has walked the earth round about so many times. I am probably the one who has most walked the earth of any pilgrim you know! For I am always interested in people. I am always interested in souls. I am always interested in placing myself in the situations they are in and then providing them with exactly what is the antidote to that situation that is so difficult.

And as much as the Great Law will allow, I place my Electronic

Presence over them with the solution to the problem. And some see it, beloved ones. They see it immediately. They jump with delight! They are joyous, for they have found the key—they have found the way out of a certain dilemma that was so difficult, a knotty problem where factions of people warring against one another would find no solution to their warring, to their situation. And lo and behold, the idea has struck! the idea has stuck!

Beloved ones, I am no respecter of persons.[4] It does not matter to me who gets the glory for the idea or whether it is one who is a sinner who catches that idea first. For I am one who believes in the God in everyone until that one "says die," as I have already said.

Therefore, beloved, try it also. When you meditate upon the world's problems, call to me for the solution. Then by your invocations and decrees, call to your Mighty I AM Presence and Holy Christ Self to direct that very solution as a matrix, as a sphere of Light that contains the inner Logos for the absolute God-resolution of a specific problem.

Send these spheres of God-solution! And let them be multiplied many times over. And let them descend as mighty spheres of Light over an area where there is corruption, where there is the slaughter of many, where there is starvation, where there is politicking and therefore the people cannot move on with the agenda of their Holy Christ Self.

Beloved ones, I review the planet this day, the planet earth, which is placed in my charge. I review all ascended ones, those in the etheric octaves. I review those in embodiment and those who would like to be but have been denied. If I were to tell you the greatest need of the hour, I would tell you that it is that each one become acquainted with his Real Self, that Holy Christ Self. If it were possible for all people to see the image on the Chart of the Divine Self, beloved ones, it would open the eyes of the soul for millions.

That wallet-size card on which the Chart is stamped and which has the description on the back does reawaken souls to their original identity, to the God who is with them and in them. It is the most important single glyph of Light, a photograph of the soul's inner being; and its accuracy is such that it does recall the soul—the soul that is a million light-years away from her God-Reality—back to the point of the seat-of-the-soul chakra and to the desiring of resolution, to the worship of her God, to the invocation of the I AM THAT I AM.

There is no greater gift that you can give to anyone than the understanding of his own Mighty I AM Presence, his Holy Christ Self and his evolving soul, as depicted in the lower figure in the Chart surrounded by the violet flame.

The violet flame is the flame of the Seventh-Ray Buddhas and Bodhisattvas. And should I ask for hands today showing who are the Buddhas of the Seventh Ray and who are the Bodhisattvas of the Seventh Ray amongst those who have descended here in this place from the Tushita heaven, I tell you, one million hands would be raised in this moment. Think of it, beloved! [13-second applause]

Think of the immensity! Think of the immensity that is all, the all of the Spirit and the Matter Cosmos. Then think of these one million and think how their Causal Bodies, charged with the violet flame, should fill entirely the immensity.

Understand, then, how we at our level should have such a sense of frustration when our cups are full. We are filled with the light of the violet flame, ready to pour it into your chakras, into the chalices of your being for anything whatsoever you desire. We are like the genies. You rub the Buddha's belly and out pours the violet flame, beloved ones!

[11-second applause]

Why, then, take the long way around the Buddha's belly? Why not invoke the full-gathered momentum of all the Causal Bodies of all the beings of the Seventh Ray and all other beings in heaven of the violet flame and ask for it to rain violet flame upon earth for absolute God-purification of this world, for the turning around of all those things which are yet the portents of prophecy?

O beloved, how do you turn a people around? How do you turn them around in the continent of Africa, in Asia, or wherever else in the world?

How do you turn around AIDS and promiscuity and all of the diseases that beset the people even while there are this day cures for those diseases that are not even being released?

I will tell you how you turn it around. You remind yourself at least once a day that it is the dark ones, those spiritually wicked in high places,[5] the fallen angels, the demons, the false hierarchies of the Twelfth Planet who have infected an unsuspecting and a karmically vulnerable humanity with diseases that eat away at the heart and soul.

All children of God and all sons and daughters of God, with very few exceptions (those exceptions being those who have truly taken the left-handed path), I tell you, beloved, are of good heart, good will and good mind. And regardless of what they have been taught or how they have been indoctrinated in their systems of education or brainwashed in their areas of religious or political persuasion, these individuals mean well. They would do the best if they could see the best, if they understood the entire equation of Light and Darkness and Good and Evil, which does continue on planet earth. I tell you, they would come to the same conclusions that you have come to, and this Church Universal and Triumphant would have millions upon millions of members worldwide.

Therefore, I appeal to you this day as Lord of the World to not let your head rest upon your pillow at night until you have called for the binding and the judgment of the dweller-on-the-threshold of the sinister force of planet earth and the sinister force of other systems attacking planet earth through the Twelfth Planet and through the sinister force manifest as the anti-Christ, the anti-Buddha, the anti-Father-Mother, the anti-Child, the anti-Holy Spirit.

Yes, beloved, bind Evil and the evil ramifications portrayed and blown up in the media and on the sound waves, and the people, at least a greater majority of the people, *shall turn and serve their God!*

[28-second standing ovation]

Sweet ones of my heart, as I commune with you in great tenderness, so I feel the love that is a part of you, that is the real you that is of God. Sometimes this love has been bruised, sometimes even broken, as though your very heart should break in two. Beloved ones, I AM the heart of all the Buddhas. Take refuge in my heart.

What is it that causes the record to remain from this life and another, the record of pain?

Pain, beloved, is necessary for one and only one purpose. When that purpose is fulfilled, the pain is no more. The pain is not actually from the hurt experienced. The pain is really the pain of your separation from God, from me, from your Holy Christ Self, from your I AM Presence, from the flame that beats your heart. This is the pain. It is a pain that results from your seeking me elsewhere and not finding me and therefore being rebuffed, rejected, buffeted, bruised, put down.

Blessed ones, let go of this struggle, else all of your life shall be so engaged and you shall not arrive at the gate of bliss that you are seeking. My heart is the open door of bliss. Seek my heart early. Seek it late. Seek it in the day. Give the simple mantra *Om Mani Padme Hum.* This wondrous mantra, also known of Kuan Yin, celebrates your soul, your spirit, your Atman, as the jewel in the heart of the lotus, the chakra of the heart.

O blessed ones, unless you nourish the relationship to me and to all others serving with me and to your Presence, you will continue to experience the pain of isolation, of separation, of aloneness. These things are *illusion!* They are illusion, beloved ones. Beware illusion, or maya! For it has entrapped some of you for many embodiments.

Be willing to take your sword and cut through the mayic veil as though sundering some precious silk or garment of apparel. Keep on slashing the veils! Keep on slashing the veils! Slash through until you come to the very end of the mayic universe. And you shall behold the reality of your not-self and you shall faint in the presence of angels, who will catch you, when you see the unreality, the unreal self—and the unreal self, the dweller-on-the-threshold of the planet.

And when you are revived, you will also be shown your Great God Self. And you shall see that you are naked: You are *not* clothed. You are *not* rich. You are *not* accomplished. You are nothing but a soul, a soul that is the potential to make the choice to become the All or to forsake the All for all of these unrealities, all of these things.

Now, beloved, bliss is not very far from you. It is as close as your breath and my breath. My breath that I breathe unto you now is the breath of bliss, and the only true bliss is the bliss of the union of your soul in God. I AM the aura of that God Presence. So are the

Bodhisattvas and Buddhas with me the aura of that God Presence. Now drink in the bliss of your union.

You are changing, beloved. The earth is changing through this retreat. See how causes set in motion here shall become the beautiful, fruitful, flowering trees of life. See how you are bonded to the Bodhisattvas and, in knowing them as brother and sister at your side, how you too shall choose their path without any sense of loss, any sense that there is something here and something there and something over here that you must first go and do and go and experience—and then and then and then, as the road leads on to another and another, one day, some day you say, "I shall sit at the feet of the Buddha."

Well, I wish you had eternity, but you do not. You have this life. And insofar as the Law is concerned and insofar as you know, you do not have another. I say this because until you are granted another incarnation, you have no certitude whatsoever that you will have another opportunity.

The Law does count the opportunities given to each one. So many are turned down because they come so easy, as though your soul were approached by a suitor day after day and you tired of him and did not take seriously his offers and then one day the repetition of his coming would stop and all of a sudden you would say, "Where has my suitor gone?" And the suitor would be gone forever. So does God pursue the soul. So does the Guru pursue the soul.

Know this, O beloved ones: there comes a day, and it is an exact moment and it is calculated, when God and angels and Ascended Masters have pursued the soul for the last time. Now the soul must turn around and must chase after the Great Ones, who are dissolving into higher octaves. And in order to be with them, the soul must put on filigree veil upon veil upon veil to mount the higher octaves. And if she is not able, for she has not taken and applied the Teaching, then the gates close, the vision is gone, the higher octaves are sealed and she wanders the earth again, only God knows how many lifetimes.

Yes, beloved, it is my key announcement to you today. *I want you to live every day of the rest of your life with the conviction that you have but one life.* Of this life you are certain, for you are here and now in physical embodiment. You cannot be certain of any other.

I wish you to accept this bent of the mind, this cast of the mind, therefore eliminating all procrastination, beloved ones. For some of you who are young think you have many years ahead. Do not assume it! When it comes down to it, all that is guaranteed to you each day is that the sun rises on that day and at the end of that day the sun sets.

Thus, contemplate this mystery, beloved. It comes under the Law of the One. One universe of God is apportioned to you each day. It is a raindrop become a universe. What you do in that universe is stamped on your record permanently—permanently when it is good, permanently when it is not, until you erase that karmic record.

Understand the realities of human existence and realize that there is no such thing as a reality of human existence! Human existence *is* maya. It *is* illusion. And the only thing real about this existence is your daily contact with God and your expanding of the flame in the heart. Your Atman is real but you are not yet your Atman! Your soul is a living potential but only a potential!

Therefore, see how precarious is the way and know how firm is the manifestation of the Bodhisattvas in your midst right now, who are absolutely and totally one with the Cosmic Christ, the Universal Christ and their own Christhood, *dazzling* in their golden robes, *dazzling* in the white fire of their hearts! I say, look at them! See yourself in the mirror as one of them, see yourself now transformed into the great image of the blessed male and female followers of the Buddha.

Yes, beloved ones, *seek* to be real! *Seek* to be real! *Seek* to be real! I AM real! And I expect the extensions of myself, namely you, to have at least a portion of themselves that is absolutely real and is absolutely qualified with God-Reality *every day of the rest of this life!*

[23-second standing ovation]

I speak sternly to you, beloved ones. I speak sternly because I am determined to wake you up! Therefore I say, *Awake,* O bhikkhus! *Awake* by the power of Helios and Vesta! *Awake* by the thunder that descends from Mount Horeb! *Awake! awake! awake!* you silly ones who waste your time in chatter when the mantra could be flowing from your lips.

If you desire to have and to hold this land as the Buddha-land, as the focus of the Pure Land, then I say to you, and I skip not one of you: *You must rise!* And you must rise to the level of the mantra, for there you will find all of the other devotees and disciples reciting the mantra. And when you are at the level of the mantra, beloved ones, then, *then* you will strengthen the *antahkarana* of your Ashram rituals. Then you will see how strong you are as a Body of God, one contacting the other by the sounding of the great mantras.

Therefore, let the mantras recited by the Messenger with others be published abroad. Let them be heard! Let them resound in the canyons of being! Let them be directed into the electronic belt! Let the mantra overtake you, I say, *for the mantra is God. You* are God! Therefore, let you, God and the mantra come together every day of your life!

I AM Gautama. I will watch you. You have had many instructions from many Masters, *but I will not allow you to fail to give the mantra daily.* Therefore heed me! For if I do not have obedience from every one of you and all who hear me, I will be back and I will tell you what is the karma of disobedience to the Lord of the World!

Gautama Buddha I AM.

[26-second standing ovation]

July 4, 1992

CHAPTER 17

Lord Maitreya

TO RESTORE THE CHRISTHOOD OF AMERICA!

Return to the One God

I AM Maitreya. And I come to restore the Christhood of America!

[33-second standing ovation. Congregation gives the salutation:]

Hail, Maitreya! Hail, Maitreya! Hail, Maitreya!
Hail, Maitreya! Hail, Maitreya! Hail, Maitreya!

I AM Maitreya in the heart of the Goddess of Liberty, in the hearts of all Cosmic Beings, devotees, Lightbearers in all octaves.

I AM that Maitreya. I AM that Cosmic Christ. And I come first and foremost to restore *you,* the Lightbearers of America and the world, to that God-estate of your individual Sonship. Oh, hear me, beloved ones, and come with me to that place of your Christhood!

[14-second standing ovation]

Please be seated, beloved ones.

Now visualize the secret chamber of your heart, a beautiful altar set by your Holy Christ Self and high priest. It is a magnificent altar and it is erected according to the style and design and preference that comes forth out of your own Causal Body of Light. Should you see this altar with your outer eye or your inner eye, beloved ones, you would say, "This is just what I wanted!" And so, beloved, you did "want"* it until you saw it. Now you no longer lack it, for you see that it is indeed your very own altar, tended by your very own high priest.

Beloved ones, I say to you, rise to the standard of the Christ in you! (Remain seated but let your soul rise.) Rise to the level of the true person that you are, to the true dignity and honor that life has given to you. Oh, such a mighty bestowal!

Walk, then, in the dignity of your Christ Self and use the mantra of Padma Sambhava. Use that mantra, beloved ones, and let it ring in your soul and your heart! This mantra is sufficient that you might be obedient to Lord Gautama each day.† Give it thirty-three times and celebrate your soul's ascent each day to the secret chamber of your heart, to the altar of being.

Life is empty when you do not do this. And yet when you do not do it, beloved, you do not even know just how empty your life is or how full it can be when and if you enter in to the practice of keeping your appointment with Maitreya, with Gautama Buddha, with the Bodhisattvas. Give it thirty-three times, beloved ones:

Om Ah Hum Vajra Guru Padma Siddhi Hum!

In the victory of the God Flame, become who you are and no longer walk the earth allowing yourself to be subdued by any human consciousness, any carnal mind, any individual who would have you, whether your soul or your body or your wealth or your wife or your children, et cetera. Beloved ones, judge, then, by the judgment of your Christhood: Why do individuals approach you? And if they approach for the reason that is the right reason, then give to them of the life and living waters of your Christhood.

Daily—I say, *daily*—merge with and celebrate your Holy Christ Self and your threefold flame. The songs to the Holy Christ Self are truly inner hymns of the heart. They are beautiful. Sing them! Give the mantras of the threefold flame, especially "Keep My Flame Blazing!"[1] Oh, if you only knew how often you are in danger of snuffing out that threefold flame, you would sing that mantra daily!

Beloved ones, if life is not permanent here, then nonpermanence

---

* *Want* here is used in the sense of lack. *Want* [from Old Norse *vanta,* akin to Old English *wan* "deficient"]: to be needy or destitute; to have or feel need; to lack.

†Gautama Buddha assigned us "to give the mantra daily." See p. 143.

and its nonpermanent state ought to give you pause and serious concern. And if you are in a wrong place in consciousness, you should understand why you have anxiety or, if you don't, why you should! Why, I would be anxious myself if I had not forged and won that link that is the tie to my Guru, if I had not made my peace with God, if I had not confessed my sins and written my letter of confession asking to receive a penance.

Beloved ones, *it is necessary* that you see yourselves aligned as anchors of God in the earth, the mighty anchor showing the cross of Christ, anchoring the power of God. Because that anchor, beloved ones, is the power of God in you whereby you walk right on the right path and you walk straight and you raise the Christ up in you.[2]

And all who desire that Christ, all who have the capacity to see that Christ will love you and will come unto you because you raise it up. And then again, beloved, because you raise it up, all who have enmity with Christ, all who hate that Christ will revile you: they will persecute you, they will do it again and again.

And I, Maitreya, say to you, *So what!* [10-second applause]

Be tough! Be tough students of Maitreya and understand that this will continue until that Christhood becomes as fearsome as *vajra! vajra! vajra! vajra!*[*]

So, beloved, when you become that Christ Presence, the majority of your persecutors will flee! And they will flee rather than persecute, for they have been forewarned by that mighty aura of your Christ Presence that extends and extends.

Beloved hearts, this type of pain is not to be avoided. This type of pain must be dealt with directly by the fire of the heart, by the love of God, by the violet flame and the violet flame Buddhas and Bodhisattvas.[†] After all, beloved, there is not anyone in this congregation this day who does not have personal karma.

---

[*] *Vajra* is a Sanskrit word rendered as thunderbolt or diamond; adamantine; that which is hard, impenetrable; that which destroys but is itself indestructible. It is also a scepterlike symbol of the thunderbolt, representing the adamantine nature of Truth. It is taught that the vajra cleaves through ignorance and symbolizes the indestructible nature of the Buddha's wisdom and the victory of knowledge over illusion.

[†] *Bodhisattva* (with a capital *B*) refers to an advanced disciple or initiate; *bodhisattva* (lower case *b*) refers to a disciple. The day that one decides to enter the Path—to stand, face and deal with his karma—he becomes a bodhisattva.

Therefore, recognize that many come that you might accelerate the balancing of your karma. Do it now! I have a plan for every one of you. You have a destiny that I will help you fulfill. Let's get on with it! Let's see that acceleration!

If you cannot find any karma descending upon your head today, then give the violet flame and let the violet flame go out and meet tomorrow's karma and the next day's karma and the next year's karma and clear the way until the entire circumference of your universe is cleared of that karma and you are free to act purely as the bodhisattva.*

And in the givingness of your heart and in the expansion of your heart and in the guarding of your heart for the little ones who need you, for the Lightbearers who will call to you, beloved ones, do not give away one erg of Maitreya's energy, of your Holy Christ Self's energy to those individuals who are a bottom-less pit, who will swallow it up, who will drink and drink and drink from your fount until they are full and you are dry.

Now, what kind of a circumstance is this, I say?

It is not good.

So, you are given Light to increase your strength. You are given Light against the day when you do meet the Adversary personally, the embodied Antichrist. Therefore, let there be the concentrate of Light so that you are ready—*ready* to heal, *ready* to rebuke, *ready* to love, *ready* to be who you are when God says to you, "This day, my son, this day, my daughter, step forth on that dais on that stage and proclaim to the world the word of your own Christhood!"

O America, I, Maitreya, call to you today! I call to the souls of the good people, the God people. *Rise* to the level of the Sacred Heart of your Jesus Christ! *Rise* to the Immaculate Heart of your most beloved Mother Mary! *Rise* to the Immaculate Heart! *Rise* to the Immaculate Heart! *Rise* to her heart and love her, for she does contain in that heart the divine resolution for this nation and every nation under God.

And when I say I will restore America to her Christhood, I am speaking of America as the I AM Race and I am speaking of the I AM Race embodied in every nation, in every race, in every area of the

*See footnote on previous page.

planet.* I come to restore that Christhood in you who have let it go down. And some of you have let it go down to the very ground and you have lost that Light.

I AM Maitreya. I come in the name Vishnu. I come in the name Krishna. I come in the name *Maitreya, Maitreya, Maitreya.* For I AM THAT I AM Maitreya! And I AM in the heart of all Buddhas. And therefore, all Buddhas rejoice as they take their positions around the earth, and there is such an *antahkarana* of Buddhas and Bodhisattvas this day circling the earth, beloved ones! You would see, therefore, if you could see, the spacecraft vanish, disappear in absolute fright. They have flown! Blessed ones, understand this: they do not come nigh the Buddhas.

You are the Buddha. The seed of Buddha is in you. Water it, raise it up, become it! *Do not delay.* Your greatest problem as students of the Ascended Masters is your procrastination of your Godhood, which is here and now a cosmic reality!

Now let me say: Watch yourself this day and tomorrow. See what your actions are and what they are not. Pattern them after the actions of the great avatar, after what you know very well Jesus would do, Krishna would do, Lord Gautama would do. Watch yourself and see how close, by the vibration of the love of your heart, you can come to your idea of what is that true Christ-manifestation of yourself.

First and foremost, *be kind.* Simply be kind. Be kind in word. Be kind in the generous giving of yourself. Be kind in your thought toward others and not critical. Be kind in your feelings. Be kind in your demeanor. And think of kind things and helpful things to do. You are in a positive spin when you make kindness, as the quality of the Buddhas, your first and foremost thrust whereby you encounter, meet and talk with people.

Let kindness, then, become compassion. Let compassion fulfill the law of the Bodhisattvas. And let compassion be unto the Lightbearers and let sympathy not descend in agreement with the dweller-on-the-threshold or the carnal mind of anyone. If the scheme is wrong,

*The word *America* is composed of seven letters, which form the words I AM Race. The term "I AM Race" refers collectively to a group of souls from all nations who have one thing in common: they all have an I AM Presence and threefold flame.

it is wrong. Say so and be done with it, and do not toy with a compromise of the Law. If something is right, *and it is right,* then stand for it. And be certain that you know which is which.

Beloved ones, the first point of restoration of the Christhood of America, the place where the I AM

Race of the world gather, I say, is the restoration of right music and right sound. Music and sound can carry the heart and the soul to the octaves of their source. Great music has come forth out of the higher octaves in all centuries. And very good music has come out of these planes that is the Ascended Master music that you use.

Beloved ones, it is not a question of denying rock music and rap. It is a question of displacing it—*displacing it,* I say! [17-second applause] Listening to rock music, rap and every other kind of dissonance out of hell, I tell you, is an addiction, a very deep addiction. And it becomes the addiction of the Kundalini that is driven downward instead of upward.

How do you liberate a soul from that addiction?

Well, beloved ones, I will tell you the same story I have told you before and I will tell it again and again: There is a false hierarchy that has purveyed this dissonance out of Death and Hell in the earth and purveyed it unto the children in their midst.[3] And that false hierarchy can be bound and taken by the call for the binding of the dweller-on-the-threshold, by the call to the Dhyani Buddhas and the Buddha of the Ruby Ray, and by the Ruby Ray calls. Yes, beloved ones, the fallacy is to think that the situation is insurmountable.

Return to the one God!

How many gods are in this room?

["One!"]

One God, absolutely omnipotent. And therefore, you see, that one God, as in the person of Elijah,[4] can swallow up all of the false gods, all of their attempts to deny the living God and the true God. One God is all. One God is powerful.

And the many voices that come out of the fount of your Holy Christ Self can now overflow that fount and go directly into the core of the seed of the wicked and their entire false hierarchy out of Death and Hell. And believe you me, the personages of Death and Hell, down to the very thirty-third level, are listening to me now and they are listening to this Messenger, and they are trembling in your presence because they know that you have the key to the undoing of their grip-hold on the youth of the world! [32-second standing ovation]

They are already taking counsel against you to create an antidote to the very power of God within you. Listen as I tell you what it is.

It is, beloved, simple forgetfulness—forgetfulness that God is in you, forgetfulness of the power of the Word, forgetfulness that you are one with the Messenger, who embraces you with all of her heart and soul and mind, and therefore you cannot be divided from God, forgetfulness that decrees work, forgetfulness that you are a part of a worldwide body that is called the Great White Brotherhood, that you are one, as you are a Keeper of the Flame and you keep that flame, with all Ascended Masters, Archangels, Cosmic Beings, Buddhas, Bodhisattvas, Elohim, elementals and the very tiniest angel, your own body elemental, and that you are one with each other through the heart chakra. *You are one,* beloved! [10-second applause]

This, then—this, then, is the plot: to allow you to believe the lie of separateness, aloneness, apartness. "The problem is so great, what can I do about it? I might as well not decree. The problem is too big for me."

Well, indeed, it is too big for the lesser self. But with God—with God all [Congregation joins Lord Maitreya:] things are possible! With God all things are possible! With God all things are possible!

Remember Igor, the unknown saint who kept the vigil with the blessed Mother of Jesus during the Bolshevik revolution.[5] Blessed ones, that single isolated saint keeping the flame and keeping the tie to the Blessed Mother did prevent untold millions from perishing who would have been engaged in bloodshed and would have indeed perished.

Think what you can do when the aura of God merges with your own because you are right with God, you are right with your soul and the Masters, you are right with the Messenger, you are right with Love and, through the mantra, through the decree, you are congruent with your Mighty I AM Presence.

No matter what it takes, no matter what you have to turn your back on, no matter what habit you have to give up, I say make it your business, every Keeper of the Flame, this year to see to it that you cut all ties to *anything* that is a tie to Death and Hell, *including all of that sugar!* [12-second applause]

Forgetfulness, separateness, aloneness, "the decrees don't work"—these thoughts are hammered on the brain and the soul. Worthlessness. "I should be normal. I should be doing other things that other people do. I should have a balanced life."

Well, I tell you, beloved, souls are dying every day, bodies are dying every day. And the Mother of the World is praying daily for those souls on the astral plane. You are praying, the Messenger is praying. But, beloved hearts, many die because they entered the road of the downward spiral of this music of Death and Hell and therefore were pulled down into every kind of drug, every kind of addiction, including sexual addiction.

Beloved ones, consider the youth of the world: by the time they are twenty or twenty-two they are spent and look the age of forty. What is this world coming to?

I say it is coming to Death and Hell. And I say, *God in you is the power to reverse this spiral.* And when you get a hold on that dweller-on-the-threshold of this false music, you will begin turning around everything else.

Beloved ones, there is no exception here. You have come to Maitreya's Mystery School. You have come to the Heart of the Inner Retreat. I have given you an instruction. *I pray you, do not make the karma of failing to call daily for the binding of the dweller-on-the-threshold and the entire false hierarchy of Death and Hell, of rock music, rap music and all of the rest, including the drug culture.* [10-second applause]

Now, beloved, consider the meaning of the scripture from the Lord Christ: "With man nothing is possible. With God all things are possible."[6]

You see, if you are not in the God-manifestation and in the God-vibration, you are not "with God." Things go wrong, they don't work. Schedules get off. You are here when you should be there and you encounter all kinds of opposition to what you are trying to do. The telephone is ringing off the hook. This one wants this, this one wants that. Yes, beloved, it is because you haven't taken time in the morning to be that God-manifestation. I speak to the recalcitrant ones who have denied their early morning calls for many years.

Blessed ones, with man nothing is possible. Let the son of God reject the human and become the God-man from the point of awakening to the point of falling asleep. Then all things will be possible to him.

Write out your map. List what you determine will happen in your life. Pour your energy into those specific pots. Nourish the flame, repeat the call, see the blueprint, expect miracles and by hard work *pull* down the substance to make it happen!

You know the teachings on the precipitation of supply, of projects and of all that you need to make your ascension. *Apply the teaching!* We cannot apply it for you, but we can answer, through you, every call you make.

Thus, beloved ones, no more forgetfulness of self, of who you are and who the ones on the left-handed path are. Make no mistake. Try the spirits[7] of people in embodiment. Try the spirits that whisper in your ear to confuse you.

Yes, beloved ones, *you* are capable of turning around the world. The only question is: *Will* you do it? ["Yes!"] [21-second pause]

[Congregation joins Lord Maitreya in the sounding of the Om:]

Ommmmmmmmmmmmmmmmmmmm

Ommmmmmmmmmmmmmmmmmmm

Yes, the judgment has descended. The fourth woe[8] is integrating with the people and the people are angry.[9]

Yes, clean out what is before the eyes of all people through the motion-picture and television industry! Clean it out with Hercules and Amazonia! Lend your arm of the power of God to put down these fallen ones who re-create fallen Atlantis, Sodom and Gomorrah, and even worse, and put it before the eyes of children and people. This is the pulling down of the Goddess Kundalini. It does cause depravity, insanity, perversion and the death of the soul.

By the same reasoning of the Solar Logoi, by the same power one with God, be this body of Light! O beloved, prepare yourselves to be brides of Christ, to be communicants of Church Universal and Triumphant. It is a level of commitment that is not too hard for any of you, and yet that solid commitment enables you to have greater strength and the strength of a greater chalice—the chalice of the Bodhisattvas and the Buddhas, which you become a part of as you uphold the descending Light of the Church of heaven made manifest in the Church on earth.

Who and what is the Church?

You are the living Church, each one of you the temple of God. That is the only true Church on earth. When many souls of Light have the consciousness of the temple of the living God and determine to come together and make themselves white cubes in that temple, then the edifice begins to rise in the etheric octave, which it is doing. But for some of you, the white stone[10] is missing; for you think you will lose something rather than gain if you so declare that level.

That level of declaration, beloved ones, is not to a human church but it is saying: "I am a part of the Mystical Body of God of the living Christ and the living Buddha of planet earth. I desire to anchor that presence and that body and that Light tangibly and physically. This is a commitment I desire to make in this octave as I declare myself to be a communicant of Church Universal and Triumphant." See, then, how the true spiritual *siddhis*[11] come to you when you come into alignment more and more each day with your God.

Beloved ones, it is surely the hour and past the hour to concentrate certain services for the binding of the dweller-on-the-threshold and the false hierarchy of Death and Hell through abortion, abortionists and the abortion laws. Abortion is first-degree murder of God within the womb of the Mother. I ask you to rescue mothers and fathers and children from the big lie that abortion equals rights—constitutional rights. This, beloved, is the turning inside out of the entire intent of God from the Beginning.

As you have been told, beloved, so it is true that abortion is the critical factor in this nation and all nations, for it does create such a karma that wherever it is practiced it makes that nation vulnerable. May you quickly deliver the earth of this false notion and the diabolical lie that what is wrong is right—that it is right to kill the child in the womb. It is not right: it is murder, beloved. And so the karma for such action is the karma of murder.

Let the enlightenment go forth! Let the illumination go forth! Let the victory flame go forth! Let us not see on the astral plane fields and fields and fields of white markers, marking the place where souls have been denied life. Let us see these records cleared! Let us see all souls who have ever been aborted in this century have their day and their opportunity to come into life, to know God, to fulfill their reason for being and deal with their karma.

I AM Maitreya. I seal you in my heart. I AM the warrior this day and I go forth with legions of Bodhisattvas, with Karttikeya.[12] I go forth for the rescue of all life and I say, beloved, help me! *Help me* and let us have this victory! We *have* to have it!

[29-second standing ovation]

July 4, 1992

CHAPTER 18

Elohim of Peace

THE CROWN JEWEL OF PEACE

"Decide Now!"

Peace, be still in the Elohim, God! [8-second applause]

I come to extract from you what you will give me of the warring in your members.[1] We place our Electronic Presence over the Mother, for the Mother has often desired to take you, and has taken you, individually into her arms to take from you the burdens and the sorrows and the pain and the confusion and the misunderstanding. Now we place our Electronic Presence over her that we might absorb it, that we might take from her and from you that which the Great Law will allow and that which you will release.

Decide if you will release your illnesses, your infirmities, your schisms, your bad habits, your momentums not of the Light. Decide now whether you will keep them as crutches, as maneuvers of manipulation. Decide whether you can let go and be God where you are.

The process of being and becoming may follow if you will it so, beloved, but this initial encounter with Elohim Peace and Aloha will give you the thrust you have been waiting for to be divested of records and hurts. Therefore, sound the Om as you release to us your burdens:

Ommmmmmmmmmmmmmmmmmmmm

Ommmmmmmmmmmmmmmmmmmmm

Come unto us, all ye who labor and are heavy laden. We give you rest.[2] We take your turmoil and terror and temerity. We come to give you resolution in the name of the Prince of Peace. Continue to release —release, release, release—as we speak.

Thus, beloved, the message is clear. Peace is not everywhere in the earth, and war is where it should not be. And war is where it should be stopped and is not stopped.

Of what avail, what use or purpose, the governments of the nations if not to preserve life and preserve the peace? Things have gone far out of line. Elohim can scarcely contact individuals upon earth, for they are so far out of line that they should suffer loss of identity should we approach. As Gautama has said, so it is true of us: we reach them *through you* when you are in alignment.

Many do not understand their out-of-alignment state. What a pity! Therefore, seek God. Seek God and know him as Peace. The best you can do is to be at peace, to be peaceful where you are, and to call to us, to give our mantra, to give the call for the Great Sun Disc to guard the solar plexus and to send forth rays of golden-pink and purple fire.

Withdraw the warring in your own members, give it to us and know the crown jewel of peace. When you have enlightenment, you *are* Peace. When you have it not, you do not see your nonpeaceful state.

I represent Elohim in the Heart this day. All are present, some whose names you have not. We are manifesting in the earth in all areas and concentrating here a Light that is intended to assist all evolutions to come to peace, to challenge war and its advocates and to defend the peace by whatever means necessary to prevent war.

War is the agenda of the fallen ones on this and other systems, and their agenda is for war on planet earth. Disarmament and the seeming disappearance of World Communism does not change that fact in any way.

The Buddhas are the warriors of peace. The Cosmic Christs are the warriors of peace. Therefore, the defense of life at all levels *must be secured.* When life in the womb is not defended, so the nations also disarm and they are not defended. It is karmic. It is blindness. It is so because of the depths to which many have descended in consciousness in the little value which they place on human life.

Human life is of ultimate value! For it is the lowest level to which anyone can descend and still have a soul and still become one with God. When you go below the human species, that option is not there. Therefore know, beloved, that many upon earth in human bodies have descended as far as they can go and still have opportunity. Opportunity will not come to the unpeaceful ones.

Thus, may you be champions, warriors of peace and understand that pacifism is a perversion of peace! *Peace* is the guardian action of the Sixth Ray. *Peace* takes care of life. *Peace* enters in and binds those who deny life, who deny the disciple, who deny the Guru, who deny their oneness with God. *Peace* enters in where those pretending to be chelas and are not chelas shall find themselves in outer darkness![3]

It is high time you consider what it means to make a commitment to an Ascended Master Guru. You do not break such a commitment, beloved ones, *for anyone.* Therefore, see to it that you are in the right line and in the straight line with your God and your service. Opportunities do not come again to those who have had so many in so many lifetimes. Therefore, beloved, it is not words but Light, Empowerment and profound Love that we bring.

We seal this session in the power of the resurrection flame that you might drink it in as the rays of light of Helios and Vesta.

We are Elohim all, from the Great Central Sun through the vast cosmos. We salute the entire Spirit of the Great White Brotherhood and the true chelas of the living Word, who keep their word no matter what the price.

I salute you on this day! May your joy in the cosmic flame of freedom be full and may you know whence came to you this gift of joy!

[Messenger turns toward the portrait of Saint Germain above the altar and salutes Saint Germain during 13-second standing ovation:]

Hail, Saint Germain! [Congregation joins in:]
Hail, Saint Germain! Hail, Saint Germain!
Hail, Saint Germain! Hail, Saint Germain!
Hail, Saint Germain! Hail, Saint Germain!

July 4, 1992

CHAPTER 19

Saint Germain

FOR THE VICTORY!

I Wield Archangel Michael's Sword to Cut You Free and Keep You Free

Hail, Keepers of the Flame! I AM come for the Victory, for there is nothing else to come for!

[22-second standing ovation. Congregation gives the salutation:]

Hail, Saint Germain! Hail, Saint Germain! Hail, Saint Germain! Hail, Saint Germain! Hail, Saint Germain! Hail, Saint Germain! Hail, Saint Germain! Hail, Saint Germain! Hail, Saint Germain!

Now then, now then, hear Saint Germain, if you will, for I tell you, beloved ones, the earth has muddled around in non-victory for too long. Therefore, I AM here and I AM here to stay until each and every one of you this night is standing in a pillar of Victory's fire! And that pillar is golden and purple flame! [11-second standing ovation]

Therefore, beloved, consider the hour and consider *what is not being done.* Everywhere you turn, you say and you hear those saying, "We must do something about our problems." So they talk about those problems.

Where is the solution?

It is in the heart of every Keeper of the Flame on earth.

Therefore I say, *hear me!* There are many good hearts everywhere on earth who suffer dire catastrophe, whose children are lost in these situations of gang warfare all over America. Children are dying all over the world from famine, from abuse, from neglect.

The child must be elevated to the place of the Inner Light. And when the child is elevated, the civilization shall be elevated. Elevate the Divine Feminine in you, and that Divine Feminine, beloved ones, shall be the means whereby we shall have that victory. There *must not be* stagnation any longer nor your acceptance of conditions as they are and getting worse.

Therefore I say, the only reason for you to come to the Heart of the Inner Retreat is for your personal victory, that you might add that victory to the mighty stream of God's victory, of Alpha's victory, of Omega's victory and bless their coming!

Blessed hearts, the only reason to get out of bed in the morning is for the Victory! There is no other reason to get out of bed! *Hear me.* You must have the victorious spirit. You must claim it from Mighty Victory. You must claim it from Justina and all of the hosts of heaven!

We are sick and tired of the non-victory consciousness! There is a victory available to *you* and *you* and *you* and every one of you. And you must have it! You must *will* to have it! You must *desire* to have it! You must shout your fiat and determine: *"I will be God's will of victory in manifestation today, this hour and every day!"*

Get up for the Victory! Go to bed for the Victory! Work for the Victory! Eat for the Victory! Be joyous and happy for the Victory. But always and always and always give the earth, give yourself, give all whom you meet that Victory spin! I say, do it and be glorious about it, be triumphant about it, be magnanimous about it, but *be* it!

[30-second standing ovation]

So! So now you know why I have come in the hour of Victory. It is because I desire the full momentum of Lord Maitreya to be in this Inner Retreat that he might have his day and have his say. And I tell you, there is *more* fire and determination in the entire Spirit of the Great White Brotherhood, in this Messenger and in you than there is the spirit of defeat in the fallen ones.

Do you understand? He who has the greater sense of victory *will win! And we are going to win!* [16-second standing ovation]

We are not going to take no for an answer! We are going to *beat* the stubborn will within ourselves into submission. We are going to raise up the Light. We are going to command the vessel of the memory body itself to be the memory of the Mind of God wherein we shall restore the consciousness of Victory by God's memory projected on the earth as a giant hologram, a giant manifestation of the records of victory of ancient golden ages. We shall project this upon the earth, and the earth and the people in the earth will outpicture it by the call to Victory, by the call to the Holy Christ Self, by the mantra to Lord Shiva, by the power of the Universal Christ!

We are more determined than the enemy. Let us keep it that way every day and hour and not be discouraged.

I AM not discouraged! Are you? ["No!"]

For all the terrible things that come tumbling down in the world, beloved ones, *we are not discouraged!* We are *encouraged* because if things get any worse, we will see tens of thousands of people coming to the feet of their Mighty I AM Presence. For they shall become aroused because *you* are aroused! And you will invoke in their behalf the full power, the full momentum of my mantle, of my violet flame, of my purple fiery heart, of my beloved Portia and all the Buddhas and Bodhisattvas, the very million of them of the Seventh Ray.

Yes, beloved ones, *you* will sit up! *You* will jump up! *You* will come alive! *You* will be Saint Germain in action and you will not wait out the nineties for the "terrible, terrible" calamities to fall. You will raise your hand to that avalanche and say: *"You get back up that mountain! You will not come down on my planet!"* [17-second standing ovation]

Beloved ones, you are at the peak of contact with the highest levels of the etheric octave, as you have spent day upon day in this Inner Retreat. Therefore you have the joy of victory, the spirit of victory and freedom. You have the Light and the fire in your being.

I tell you, this is how you were in those octaves before you took embodiment in this life. And I did address you with Portia and the Lords of Karma, and with your Holy Christ Self I laid out your life for you and I told you what would come upon you. And you descended then into the body prepared for you, you passed through the birth canal, you came into the density of the world. You did not have direct, living, visible contact with the angels and the Ascended Masters. And so you know the rest of the tale.

Well, beloved ones, going forth from the Inner Retreat this time will be like being born again into the denser world. This time I must have—for this is the last time I can have it—*this time I must have your commitment that you will not lose the spark of freedom that I and all the rest have transmitted to you during this conference.*

You *must* not lose it! You *cannot* lose it! You *must* not fail! You *will* not fail! For I am told by the cosmic hierarchy and the Lords of Karma that unless we do it this time and do it well, there will not be another opportunity such as we now have in this interval of cosmic space and cosmic silence to turn the whole Dark Cycle around.

You must wake up! So, I plead with you. Others have pleaded with you. Yet you must know that every moment you can spend before your altar and with your decrees you are buying time for Saint Germain. I want to be with you. I *can* be with you. I can place my Electronic Presence with you. If you but give that call to the living flame of cosmic freedom!

Why, who else is that flame?

I AM that flame, of course! And I come because I AM the mantra, I AM the flame, I AM Saint Germain and I would put my Electronic Presence over you. Please breathe the mantra of the violet flame so that we can accomplish this mighty victory! [19-second standing ovation]

I will tell you how much time you have to turn the world around. Measured in cosmic time, beloved, it is seconds. Yes, beloved, it is seconds.

The recent earthquakes in California were an adjustment that could be made by your presence and decrees here, but they were also a warning.[1] These earth changes will come! And you standing here tonight are the ones who will determine whether they shall change the face of continents or the violet flame shall consume 10 or 20 or 40 or 60 percent of the brunt of the adjustment of the planet that must take place before this system, this planet can enter in to a golden age of Aquarius.

And I will tell you one thing: As far as we are concerned and the Seven Holy Kumaras and all of our bands who have come together and come together in this hour after so many thousands of years are concerned, we will accept nothing else *but* a golden age of Aquarius! We will not accept a downward-spiraling age, building downward upon the downward spiral of the Piscean. We will have our golden age or we will not have an age at all! [16-second standing ovation]

Thus, there is no time to lose. Let the message leap heart to heart around the world! Keep your vigil as you go forth at night with the legions of the mighty angels of the LORD. Keep your vigil, beloved ones, and recognize that the problems of children and gangs and gang warfares and the problems in South Central Los Angeles and elsewhere are related to the non-binding of the dweller-on-the-threshold, the human ego and the carnal mind of the lifestreams so involved. And the antidote to the problems is your fervent giving of Jesus' call for the casting out of the dweller-on-the-threshold.

Mothers, fathers, sons, daughters, I call to you! If you could know how you can bind this force among the people and see your children, whom you believe in, and so many who began as wonderful souls turn around and face their God because you will give this call three or nine times a day, I tell you, you would do it! And I promise you that if you do not do it, it will be your greatest regret when you pass from the screen of life and graduate with less than cosmic honors.

For all of you should graduate earth's schoolroom with cosmic honors for the simple reason that there has never been such opportunity to deal with such degradation. There has never been such openness of the gift of the violet flame and the knowledge of the Mighty I AM Presence.

Now, I say, all hosts of heaven, pour down upon these and all who are the Lightbearers of the world the *zeal* of the LORD!

Let the *zeal* of the LORD come upon you! Let it be tempered by the LORD's wisdom, by his power and desiring for your victory and by your profound love for God in all people.

O beloved hearts, we have spoken for many decades! We have spoken again and again. What is the missing "something" that will now cause the world to catch on fire?

Well, first of all, beloved, *you* must become the sparks that fly and more than sparks—intense fires. You must become the igniters of a world of Lightbearers! And if you go down again into the density of the karma with which you were born and you do not sweep it away by the violet flame and by calls to me, well, what shall I do?

I think I shall weep. For if you do not so become and so do, beloved ones, I predict and I prophesy that a decade from now we will say, “We have lost.” So, beloved, I come to you with the greatest determination and I ask you to think upon me in so many past civilizations when you were my very own and when we did strive together against forces of Darkness who did destroy higher civilizations, far higher than the one you now enjoy.

Yes, beloved ones, those were the days when the people of Light in general did not have the knowledge of the Law and the empowerment that you have. You have this empowerment, beloved, in part because the Messenger does hold the balance for you who are in embodiment to have that power. And I work through the four lower bodies and the light body of the Messenger to contact all of you daily. Understand, beloved, that you are also keys as you make your bodies available for me to use as step-down transformers that make the Light more gentle and yet do not dilute its potency.

Beloved hearts of living flame, we have never had such an opportunity as we do today to defeat the fallen ones, who have determined to destroy a civilization, to sink continents, to use their weapons of war from other systems of worlds and their advanced technology to manipulate and twist and tear and destroy the minds, the psyches, the bodies of the people.

Beloved ones, you have what it takes in the Call. God gave to me the dispensation to give to this century the power of the Call in the name YOD HE VAU HE, I AM THAT I AM. Yes, God allowed me to open the vision to you of your Mighty I AM Presence.

Do not be dullards! I command you to rise up to the level of your own Christhood! I send forth the rays through my hands now that you will do it.

How can any of you refuse to decree?

I cannot understand it, but I hang my head for the foreknowledge I have of what you will say to yourselves when your time is through on this planet and you did not take advantage of that Opportunity who stands beside me in the person of beloved Portia in this hour.

Beloved ones, since 1939 in the hour of the birth of this Messenger, Portia has descended to these octaves; and prior to that time she was in the planes of nirvana.[2] This is why you have never had such an opportunity—it is because the Goddess of Opportunity has now made herself with me *almost physical.*

Therefore, rejoice that there *is* a Hierarchy in the earth and very close to the earth and that *you* are *key* in that Hierarchy. All of you—every single one of you—no matter who you thought you were when you came here, know today that you are sons and daughters, companions and friends of Saint Germain and Portia, for so we count you!

[20-second standing ovation]

I wish you could have seen the determination of the Messenger and the fiats she made on the very first day of this conference. I would like to see every single one of you duplicate those fiats whereby *you* stand, face and conquer every part of your body, mind and soul, bringing them into submission unto God, and you take up that sword of Archangel Michael! [Messenger takes the sword from the altar.]

This sword is your best friend. Beloved ones, it cuts through your own density. It delivers the action of Archangel Michael's sword of blue flame. I, Saint Germain, wield it now, for I am sending to you an intense action of blue fire to cut you free and keep you free so that when you make your way down the mountain to sea level *you will not decelerate!*

[Saint Germain wields the sword through the Messenger:]

Blaze the Light* of Archangel Michael!
Blaze the *Light* of Archangel Michael!
Blaze the Light of Archangel Michael!
Blaze the Light through!
Blaze the Light through!
Blaze the Light through!
Blaze the Light through!

I say, now open yourselves to me. Do not cross your arms, do not fold them in front of you, do not reject me. For I am sending to you

**Light* capitalized here means the God consciousness of Archangel Michael as well as the full-gathered momentum of Light as energy and power that he may release in answer to the fiats of Saint Germain. Saint Germain makes the call for us because he knows that by cosmic law Archangel Michael can deliver far more "Light" through Saint Germain to us than we can access by our own calls.

what is altogether safe and healthy and that which will assist you in securing your absolute God-determination.

Bolts of blue lightning, pass through!

Bolts of blue lightning, pass through!

Bolts of blue lightning, pass through!

Bolts of blue lightning! *Bolts* of blue lightning! *Bolts* of blue lightning! *Bolts* of blue lightning! *Bolts* of blue lightning! *Bolts* of blue lightning! *Bolts* of blue lightning! *Bolts* of blue lightning! *Bolts* of blue lightning! *Bolts* of blue lightning! *Bolts* of blue lightning! *Bolts* of blue lightning! *Bolts* of blue lightning!

Take your sword. Cut around yourself each day.* Cut before and behind. See that you do it, for this world is literally a sewer. Wherefore you bathe each day, you shower each day—it is because of the stickiness of the astral plane.

Cut yourself free from the ties to the astral plane. Cut around yourself. Do not miss a day! *Rouse* yourselves! Release the power of Archangel Michael! See how quickly you are delivered of the burdens of your karma and the projections of so many millions of demons. You ought to understand that it is insane not to invoke your tube of light every day and then to repeat it now and then.

Beloved ones, you will face now the absolute truth that you are Lightbearers. You are shafted in Light. You cannot be in the presence of an Ascended Master and not be so! The universe has seen your Light. And the inhabitants of the universe who are the dark ones—they have seen the Light, they have targeted you with their computers.

Be wise. Rise up and know that you are as the great freedom fighters of all ages and of all times who have won that flame in every civilization. Do not allow this one and its food to make you dense and soft and unable now to respond to the greatest calling you have ever had in any hour or day or year or century or continent.

Yes, beloved ones, this *is* it. This is the ultimate confrontation. And therefore I say to you, keep on keeping on, *wield* this mighty sword and know that I, Saint Germain, stand with you. And I stand for that great victory of your soul! [25-second standing ovation]

*Saint Germain demonstrates through the Messenger how the chela can wield Archangel Michael's sword to cut himself free each day.

My message to you, then, is: Fight the good fight[3] and win. Fight to win, not to lose. Fight to *win,* beloved ones! And know what it means to go after the beast of self and other selves until it is ultimately and totally slain.

Life is more than meat. It is more than the flesh. It is more than business. It is more than money. Life in this day and time is life for the saving of a dying planet and a dying people, whose light is fast going out.

Blessed ones, I love you or I would not even address you. I love you because you are mine and because we are yours. This is something that we share that is so close. Now Portia and I embrace each one of you personally with our whole heart and being.

Pray that you might see and know your ancient and future fiery destiny. Pray that you shall understand that you are *unique* and that time, time is running out for your victory.

Set Your Mark on the Inner Retreat

I ask you to set your mark and set your goal on this Inner Retreat. Mark the sign of the cross in the earth and say to that place:

I shall return next year and I shall see that we double and triple the numbers of those who come.

For I will go out and find them!

I will decree for them!

I will cut them free!

I will show the Messenger's videos!

I will teach the people!

I will give everything I have and everything I know and everything I have learned from the Ascended Masters to another and to another, for I have no right to selfishly keep this knowledge to myself.

My life belongs to Saint Germain, to Portia, to Almighty God.

My life belongs to the people of earth.

Here I have made my karma; here I shall have my victory.

I shall not leave another embodiment where I have left a record of my karma, some ditch for some soul to fall into.

I will press my feet into the earth.

I will move from nation to nation.

I will go where I am pulled by God.

I will speak the Word and speak the Truth into the very teeth of error!

I will now give all of my life to this cause.

And giving all of my life to the Spirit of God and being wise in taking care of my four lower bodies and being wise in using the dynamic decrees to deal with difficult situations and evil ones, being wise to know the tremendous power of the Word, I shall take my stand, I shall know when to be silent, when to speak, when to call upon the name of Saint Germain.

I will, I will, I will *pursue* to the ultimate.

I will give my all! And if it is only my victory I can win, then I will plant my V in the earth and others will come after me.

But I will never have to look back and say: "You were a coward. You were lazy. You failed your God and yourself and look at what the consequences were!"

Beloved ones, I speak to you thus because there is no other way to speak. Either have the full, fiery, heroic victory of your soul or do not look at me. For, beloved ones, you can do it! And if you do not, I shall hang my head with shame before the Lords of Karma.

I ask you, beloved, to lock my words in a locket around your heart and do not forget. For if you forget this night, beloved ones, *we will lose.* It is in your hands, and I am as near to you as your call to me.

I AM your Knight Commander, Saint Germain, and your Saint Joseph, ever at the side of the noble, the true, the God-victorious warriors!

[38-second standing ovation. Congregation gives the salutation:]

Hail, Saint Germain! Hail, Saint Germain! Hail, Saint Germain! Hail, Saint Germain! Hail, Saint Germain! Hail, Saint Germain! Hail, Saint Germain! Hail, Saint Germain! Hail, Saint Germain! Hail, Saint Germain! Hail, Saint Germain! Hail, Saint Germain! Hail, Saint Germain! Hail, Saint Germain! Hail, Saint Germain! Hail, Saint Germain! Hail, Saint Germain! Hail, Saint Germain!

July 4, 1992

CHAPTER 20

The Goddess of Freedom

PLAY TO WIN!

A Dispensation of the Solar Logoi

Hail, O Glorious Ones of the Light of Cosmic Freedom!

I AM the Goddess of Freedom! And I am so very happy to be here that I cannot even tell you how happy I am—but in a moment I shall tell you why! [19-second standing ovation]

Please be seated, beloved ones.

I remember the day when the Messenger discovered me in my statue that is above the nation's Capitol. And I remember her pondering on my heart and her recognition of myself as more than a mere statue but, indeed, as the cosmic embodiment of Cosmic Freedom to all systems of worlds. And I am grateful that the thoughtform of my Presence did indeed find its way to that Capitol dome.

Therefore, beloved ones, I have been under the order of the Solar Logoi in higher octaves beyond higher octaves—higher than you might realize. And only from time to time have I been allowed to truly roll up my sleeves and get involved with the sons and daughters of Freedom on planet earth.

Well, beloved hearts, not only am I called but I am commanded to descend to *this* level and *this* octave of earth, which is the level of the Heart of the Inner Retreat and its congruency with the Western Shamballa.

I have come, therefore, to lend *all* of my being, *all* of my Causal Body, *all* that I AM to Saint Germain and Portia, to the Goddess of Liberty, to all who are of the Seventh Ray and especially to *you* and *you* and *you,* whom I love so very much! [28-second standing ovation]

I AM the Flame of Freedom that speaks and I ask you to sing that mantra to me in this very moment, for I desire to hear it and to hear your voices. For it is my voice too, for I AM now the Flame of Freedom that can speak in this octave, and it is because, beloved, of the great efforts of the Lightbearers of the world. And those who have made that great effort and who have given the call have allowed this dispensation, which I tell you is rare, to take place.

Therefore, please let us sing "The Flame of Freedom Speaks."

The Flame of Freedom Speaks

The Flame of Freedom speaks—
The Flame of Freedom within each heart.
The Flame of Freedom saith unto all:

Come apart now and be a separate and chosen people, elect unto God—men who have chosen their election well, who have determined to cast their lot in with the immortals. These are they who have set their teeth with determination, who have said:

I will never give up
I will never turn back
I will never submit
I will bear the Flame of Freedom unto my Vict'ry
I will bear this flame in honor
I will sustain the glory of Life within my nation
I will sustain the glory of Life within my being
I will win my ascension
I will forsake all idols and
I will forsake the idol of my outer self
I will have the glory of my immaculate divinely
conceived Self manifesting within me
I AM Freedom and
I AM determined to be Freedom

I AM the Flame of Freedom and
I AM determined to bear it to all
I AM God's Freedom and He is indeed free
I AM freed by his Power and his Power is supreme
I AM fulfilling the purposes of God's kingdom

[10-second standing ovation]

I AM a Divine Mother of Freedom. I have lived in many ages. I have seen enslavement. I have seen tyranny. I have seen power in the hands of evil forces exclusively. You think that your rights are stepped on by this little this and this little that. Well, I tell you, beloved ones, Freedom is a new adventure on planet earth, relatively speaking, except for the past golden ages.

I have lived in an hour when I was under the fiercest of dark tyrants. And by the flame within my heart I determined with the deepest determination of my being that I would be free, that I would come out from under the yoke of these fallen angels. I knew who they were, I recognized them and they recognized me. Therefore, they enslaved me and dealt with me with such brutality as you cannot imagine. It was difficult to convince my fellow slave companions of the evil of these fallen ones or that we must band together to overthrow them.

These were dark, dark days on planet earth, when earth was in a Kali Yuga,[1] experiencing that darkness getting darker, just as you are experiencing it today in some places. But surely it is getting lighter in your hearts and in the Heart of the Inner Retreat.

I tell you, one does not become the Goddess of Freedom without doing battle with every force of anti-Freedom at all levels of the Matter cosmos. Yes, beloved, the title "Goddess" signifies that I have met and defeated every tyrant who has ever dared to attack me! [12-second applause]

When I was a novice I lost some battles, but I mounted a fervent effort to see to it that I would not be vulnerable again in that point where I had been defeated. And thus, in each and every battle and duel with the forces of Darkness, I learned to know the chinks in my own armour. And each and every time, I said to myself this vow: "This is the last time you will be defeated on that point!" And I did say to the enemy: "You will not find an opening there again!"

I recommend this to you, beloved ones. Find those chinks! Find those weaknesses! Make them your greatest strengths. Do not disgrace the God who lives in you by being defeated *twice* by the same enemy, even the same one who comes in the many disguises of many different people.

Yes, beloved, be analysts of your mind, your consciousness, your heart. Shore up your being. Balance your heart flame. Balance the substances you take into your bodies. And do not be found in a weak moment, waking or sleeping, caught off guard (which means off or out of balance) and therefore allowing a fallen one to thrust home and to bind you and to hold you under his foot.

Yes, beloved, they fight to the end, *their own end,* and they know their end is coming. *They* are the ones who have nothing to lose. *You* are the ones who have everything to lose—your life, your soul, your attainment of all past ages and your ascension in the Light, your divine plan, your mission, why you are here on earth.

Yes, you have all these things to lose in an unguarded moment. Watch the hours! Watch the day! Watch your consciousness!

I AM a Mother. I need tools. I require all of your Freedom songs, especially your Freedom songs to Saint Germain and your patriotic songs. I need them on compact discs because I would have you play them again and again. For I would provide for Saint Germain and Portia the means, the instrumentation, whereby you do not lose the high vibration that is present right here, so much so that you can touch it physically.

You must not lose it!

And the songs of Freedom of all ages, such as *Finlandia,* do awaken the soul, do remind the soul of her origin and destiny in the God of Freedom. The soul comes out of her density and says, "*This* is why I am here*!* *This* is why I am born! I will charge this day and every day with the flame of Freedom and give my life to my Creator."

You will know the difference when you see the Goddess of Freedom in the land. You will see how Freedom will be misqualified when a greater Freedom is in the earth. Therefore I tell you, bind the fallen ones who misuse Freedom! This is the trust of the Solar Logoi in the Keepers of the Flame. This is the trust of the Lords of Karma: that you will make the call for the binding of those who misuse Freedom in every way.

You have seen mass destruction come to South Central Los Angeles.[2] You have seen that Freedom flame perverted in a demonstration that ought to have been for the rights of the individual, for liberty and for a much higher standard on the part of law enforcement. Yes, beloved ones, you have seen individuals crumble because they have not kept a standard.

But, beloved ones, what a shame that the people do not have the Teachings of the Ascended Masters and therefore all they know is to resort to destruction! Imagine that force tied together, focused together, invoking the violet flame, calling for the binding of the dweller-on-the-threshold of the fallen ones and those who cause the little people to submit in an unwarranted manner to systems and conditions that do not allow their souls to blossom, their spirits to be infired with godly principles and their minds to be educated so that they are *not* the homeless, they are *not* on welfare and they are *not* at the bottom of society. [11-second applause]

Let us rerecord all of the violet flame decrees. Let us record them for the new students. Let us record them at an accelerated level. Beloved ones, the violet flame is the key! And when the elementals receive it and the people receive it, I tell you there is always some misqualification of Freedom. Therefore, you who know the science of the seven rays and of the chakras must not let go of Archangel Michael's sword, must not fail to call to Astrea daily for the binding of the forces who, if you don't, will simply have a heyday as they misuse the violet flame that is released through your decrees and make more karma for Saint Germain and Portia.

I speak to all Keepers of the Flame in the world: Let your keeping of the flame be the multiplying of your flame. Give the teaching, sponsor other souls and be willing to understand that forces assail them also. You must make your calls for their protection. You must make calls for the binding of their dweller-on-the-threshold and all forces surrounding them that would keep them from entering in to this mighty opportunity that is offered.

I do not come alone, beloved hearts. A Goddess never travels alone! I come with legions upon legions, *millions* of angels of Cosmic Freedom in the service of the Divine Mother of Freedom that I AM.

Therefore, earth has new guests who will become permanent residents so long as Keepers of the Flame continue to invoke the flame of Freedom. And if you tire of invoking it, please do not tire of singing its songs. They are devotional. They open your hearts. They are a cleansing of the desire body and the emotions. Singing the songs of Freedom to the beings of Freedom, beloved, is the best means to keep the desire body of the planet in check.

Summer is a time for unexpected happenings because of the energies of the emotional, or astral, quadrant.[3] Therefore anticipate that you will have your work cut out for you and know that you already have the pledge of all ascended hosts who have come to this conference, who will stand by you.

Do not give up! Do not say die! Push through in that department! Push through in that situation! *Push* through in that Congress! *Push* through in the elections! And see to it that at least you invoke the Presence of God over those who have made a mess of this country. See that you bind their dweller-on-the-threshold in the name of God and call for the Cosmic Christs to overshadow them.

Defend your rights, your property rights, your geothermal-well rights, your right to be the Buddha in this place, your right to worship, your right to have decent housing for your families, decent schoolhouses for your children, your right to know the abundant life. Beloved ones, assert it! Treasure map for it. Plan it, decree it, do it! You have the land, but you must put on it what you need.

Let the thousands and the ten thousands now show their faces in support of Saint Germain, the God of Freedom to the earth, and to Portia, the Goddess of Opportunity, and to all the mighty ones who stand and still stand. This is my decree! This is my battle cry! This is my plea to you! We *must* multiply the numbers.

Who will come forward with what it takes to put these teachings through satellite to all the stations in the world that broadcast the English language? *Who* will do that?

If that person or persons are not here, beloved ones, then let them be invoked! There is a pyramid of individuals who come from all over the world who should be here and must be here. I say, cut them free!

Call to their souls! Meet them at the retreats at night. And, above all, do it simply. Put up your posters, invite people over to your house or rent a hall for a nominal fee (or get one free) and show those tapes and give that teaching from your heart. Learn to do it better by coming to Summit University. And *know* that the earth is the LORD's and the fullness thereof, the world and they that dwell therein.[4] And all the people of Light, *they* are the owners of the earth. Let us get on with it!

I AM the Goddess of Freedom. Now plan with me. Now put yourself on the line of a certain service—the one so important to all of us, the education of children. Soon these children will be adults. Now they are babes in your arms, and before ten or fifteen years have passed they will be the wise ones among you.

Let them be loved! Let them be entertained with joy! Let them study earnestly. Let them become who they are. Take care of the children —take care of them!

There are many in my bands who would come with you, beloved, who would be here now. Pray that they might enter through the portals of birth, and when they do, know your own psychology and give them that which they need. Do not pass on to them the karmic/psychological flaws of generations preceding you.

They are Lightbearers, and when you come to the hour when you can fight no more in the physical octave, they will pick up your sword. They will look into your eyes with the most loving and shining eyes and say, "Mother, father, teacher, sponsor, *we* will carry on! *We* will fight the fight until we see Saint Germain's great golden age come."

O beloved ones, the years pass swiftly and the hours. And the fallen ones have also heard me. They would move quickly to "beat you to the punch," as they say, but *you* will *not* allow it! This I know.

I AM a Mother's heart. I AM a Mother's heart who has protected her young, and millions of her young across the planetary systems, from tyrants such as these who have journeyed far from other planetary homes to torment the children of God who still have the seed of God and the genes of Almighty God on planet earth. Thus, they come to steal your genes and they would, if they could, steal your threefold flame.

They cannot steal it, beloved ones, but they will taunt and tempt you and push and push you to the end that finally that deep-seated anger may rise up in you and they may cause you to lose that threefold flame. Therefore, do not allow yourself to be picked on by lesser devils or the greatest hierarchs among the Watchers. But remember, they will try every way to needle you or to take a needle and put you to sleep so that you will not rise to your victorious day and to the sun of Helios and Vesta.

> I appeal now to the Holy Christ Self of each one here and all Lightbearers of the world: In the name of God, I call to the Holy Christ Self to descend now into the temple of every Lightbearer upon earth, those aborning in the womb, those waiting in the etheric octave to embody. I call for a special dispensation from the Cosmic Christ, from Lord Krishna that the soul, the four lower bodies, the mind and the heart of every Lightbearer might receive an infusion of that Cosmic Christ consciousness through you, beloved Holy Christ Self.

Therefore, now let that which can be assimilated even to the level of the physical body be transmitted. This is the dispensation of the Solar Logoi. This "blood transfusion" of the very Body and Blood of your Holy Christ Self is a means whereby you can retain the vibration, the Light,* the memory and the joy in the Heart of the Inner Retreat.

I AM the Goddess of Freedom. I have much to tell you. I shall tell you things, each one personally. I shall tell you in the retreats, I shall tell you as I walk at your side. I multiply myself, as many times as necessary, without dilution. For I AM the Goddess of Freedom. My hour has come. *Your* hour has come. *We* are teammates! Let us go forward and play to win!

[36-second standing ovation]

July 4, 1992

---

*the Christ consciousness

CHAPTER 21

Archangel Michael

"MEET US HALFWAY!"

A Mighty Angel Assigned to Each Lightbearer

I AM the witness! I AM the witness! I AM the witness, ye holy ones of God! Therefore, receive me and the hosts of the LORD who gather this day. For I AM Michael, Prince of the Archangels, and I salute my own!

[23-second standing ovation:]

Hail, Archangel Michael! Hail, Archangel Michael!
Hail, Archangel Michael! Hail, Archangel Michael!
Hail, Archangel Michael! Hail, Archangel Michael!
Hail, Archangel Michael! Hail, Archangel Michael!

We have stood in the center of the sun of Helios and Vesta. Therefore you have received our rays commingled with those of the beloved Father-Mother of this system of worlds. So drink in the Light* of Archangels and their Archeiai, for we have come to earth and we have penetrated the density of all levels into the very physical earth body itself.

Therefore, we do come, O ye saints and those who would be! We come with a piercing Light! And that Light is to thrust home the Power, Wisdom and Love of God that you might be delivered of certain momentums not of the Light, certain momentums of the human consciousness that have continued to bind you to the levels of Death

*God consciousness

and Hell, so much so that between embodiments your souls have gone to the astral plane.

Blessed ones, we would speak now. Therefore be seated.

It is our determination made to the Lords of Karma, to beloved Saint Germain and Portia that all those who contact this activity and pursue with all diligence the giving of the dynamic decrees, calling forth the Light of God and the violet flame, calling to the Seven Mighty Archangels, calling for the binding of their own dweller-on-the-threshold and that of every member of this activity, fulfilling all things required by the law of their karma, beloved, shall not have to return to that astral plane at the conclusion of this embodiment—and also, if they are diligent, they shall no longer gravitate to those levels of morbidity, depression, death and self-condemnation, which are of the astral plane, while they are in physical embodiment.

This, beloved ones, is our goal. In this we will support you, but you have a great work to do in this matter if you are among those whose tendency it is to slip into old astral patterns. Therefore understand that if you do the work, we shall provide the strengthening, we shall come forth as you wield my sword physically and we shall simultaneously cut you free spiritually. We will work hand in hand with you!

We desire to have a body of Lightbearers who make up this Church Universal and Triumphant whose garments [i.e., auras and energies] do not descend into the astral plane. If you should make this your one-pointed goal—and allow your personal calls to extend on behalf of weaker souls or those newer to this activity who are unable to sustain a spiritual level of consciousness—then, beloved, we shall have for the first time in many ages a Church body on earth that does not descend lower than the mental plane but does abide in the physical, mental and etheric (the two higher octaves overlapping the physical), a Church body that does have as *steel,* as *fire,* as *diamond* the wall around it that does separate it from these lower [astral] planes.

This is the proposal we bring to you this day. And we desire to know how many of you can determine to make this your daily goal for the entire membership. ["I will!" (14-second applause)]

I must remind you, though it would seem that I need not, that the music of the astral plane pulls you quickly to its level by sentimentality, by sympathy and by the incorrect beat. You have heard wondrous music at this conference. See that you duplicate it.[1] See that you maintain that aura round about you. This is a key. Next, beloved, do not eat those foods that pull you down into the astral plane, those that are heavy in spices, sugars, strong meats, wine, et cetera.* Because when you do, you are in the astral plane before you know it.

Blessed hearts, I have observed you from inner levels when you have spent decades between embodiments on the astral plane. And there was not a thing that the Great Law would allow me to do in your behalf, for it was your karma, your will, the law of your own being and your own desire that put you there.

Thus understand, Archangels are the manifestation of God. Archangels come in the fullness of the I AM THAT I AM. We are fully God-manifestation. Therefore we cannot act in your behalf unless you meet us halfway and come to the level of your Holy Christ Self through devotion and prayer and meditation and specifically the hymns you have to the Holy Christ Self and the Holy Christ Flame. Beloved hearts, I desire to see recordings made of those decrees and songs that will keep you in the way of God.

I tell you, this Messenger has been raised to cosmic heights through these dictations and every one of you who has placed yourself here has experienced new levels of consciousness. You have been taken to advanced levels of the etheric octave where you have not been in thousands of years. You have touched the hem of the garment of God!

Now I say, hold on to that hem and that garment for all you are worth and with all your might! For I tell you, beloved, the stairs of heaven are not easily won. And when they are won they are often lost, for it is not easy to retain them. Therefore the byword is

"Hold fast what thou hast received!"

Hold fast to the Light!

Hold fast to the Light!

Hold fast to me, beloved ones!

Heaven does not give the gift that is not needed. And what is a gift

*animal fats, hydrogenated fats, chemicals, fertilizers, impure water

that is given after the need is manifest? We have given you gifts that you will need on the morrow and in two weeks and in six months and during the entire year. Therefore, garner them in your chakras. Value the state of consciousness that is the yang mind and heart and yet has the flow of the Divine Mother. Value your spirituality, your spiritual being and your goal. *Know who you are* and manifest who you are daily.

A clean white page has been turned for you with the conclusion of this conference. Preceding pages of the conference days record just how much karma you have balanced, just how much you have worked with the flame of the altar, just how much you have multiplied the action of the dictations by your love, by your tears of sorrow for having sinned and by your tears of joy in knowing that your Redeemer liveth within.

Truly you have come through transformations. You have known the graciousness and the mercy of the Mother of God. You have understood that the Church is the biding place, the sangha of the Buddha.

You have understood the sphere of Light and the circles upon circles upon rings of Light that make up the Body of God throughout the universes. You have been gently, cordially and politely invited to become a part of this Body of God. You have been urged, you have been commanded, you have been pleaded with!

I, Archangel Michael, stand before you! I stand in this hour and I tell you, beloved, it is imperative that you know Reality, that you see Reality and that you look upon Reality each and every day of your life in your meditation and in your heart of hearts.

The Seven Archangels stand and their Archeiai, and other Archangels of other levels who have not been unveiled to you, except the one you call Uzziel. Archangels all have come for the deliverance of the one, for the elevation, for the return, for the reunion, for the bonding to our bands and our octaves of one that has gone forth and one* that has returned.

In the name of Almighty God, I, Archangel Michael, assign to each and every one of you a member of my legions, one single mighty

*the one and the many. The Archangels come for the rescue of one soul, one by one by one, until many ones become the many.

angel who shall stay with you as long as you give the call to Archangel Michael and any of our decrees to Archangel Michael for twenty minutes each day. So long as you sustain that which is the absolute minimum requirement of the Great Law, this angel of my bands shall not leave you until the hour of your ascension in the Light. Understand whom you deal with when you deal with the Archangels!

Thus, we pray that you will rise, beloved, to new heights of consciousness and then anchor those heights of consciousness solidly in the practical domain of your life, in the circumstances in which you live, in the building of this Community as it should be, surely as that place where many, many souls may come. Let us see the increase of the harvest in this year!

The Light goes forth now. For those who have been judged by the fourth woe through Alpha[2] are now being bound by the legions of Astrea, the legions of the Seven Archangels, legions from out the Great Central Sun.

It is one thing for Alpha to mete out the judgment, beloved. It is another for the legions of Light to bind and then remove those individuals, whether on the physical or the astral plane, who no longer have the option to pollute planet earth. And then we must dig deep into the earth body to remove the records of their karma, the records of their infamy, lest these come upon this and future generations, being perpetuated through the media, through the print, through the voice, through the spoken communication. Therefore, this day and in this hour I, Michael, raise my hand! And I raise that hand for the consuming of the records of these fallen ones!

Blessed hearts, the removal of so many fallen ones from a planetary body can be just as cataclysmic as the ascension of many Lightbearers,[3] for there is a major adjustment in the earth when forces of Light and Darkness that are in relative equilibrium are unbalanced by an increase or decrease in their relative numbers. Therefore, remember to keep the flame of who and what you are as you go forth from this conference.

You have climbed a very high mountain. You will slowly descend that mountain. I pray that there will not be a deceleration of consciousness but rather a focalization in every atom and cell of your being, in your organs and chakras of the light you have received, that the light might be sealed inside of you rather than be dissipated in the world around you, attracting undue notice to your lifestream.

Therefore, let the descent be a gentle deceleration whereby the fiery coils are tight within and yet outwardly you return to an aura and appearance of normalcy. You then walk the earth as a son or daughter in training under the Sons and Daughters of the Solitude.[4]

Understand, beloved, that you must build on the foundations the cosmic hierarchy has laid at this retreat. In past years there has been a forgetfulness on the part of some conferees and a loss due to neglect of those dispensations given at Fourth of July conferences. Therefore the Lords of Karma draw nigh and they are protective of you and of the light released. And if there is a suggestion that a lifestream will misqualify that light, if possible, my angels will quickly take it up to a higher octave without allowing the individual to misqualify it.

These are days and hours when the light that is released to earth is as precious as gentle drops of rain. A small quantity of light is great, beloved. Therefore, come and understand that the more we give that you keep and multiply and qualify unto the Great God, the more that shall be entrusted to you individually.

I remind you of this because to misqualify the light is a karma-making situation. It becomes your own karma. And it becomes the karma of the Ascended Masters who are your sponsors. And, beloved, it is simply a waste to pour light into a leaky vessel.

Some of you have not yet healed the rents in the many layers of your garment. That is why you, above all, must call daily for your tube of light and to me for the manifestation of my protection while the healing work of the violet flame angels goes on within.

When you do not set your tube of light around you with a great fire and light and determination, then you are not able to hold the protection for the leaky vessel or to seal the holes in the garment that have been made over many thousands of years. Accidents, the hearing of voices from lower octaves, imbalances, psychological problems, et cetera —all these are the result of the weakening of the four lower bodies and the rents in the garment, whereby you cannot hold the balance of the inner integrity of the soul, the fire of the solar plexus, the fire of the heart and the mind.

Yes, beloved, those of you who wonder why you have this or that condition or karma upon you must understand that once upon a time when you allowed yourself to be vulnerable to individuals who sought no good but only ill for you, you opened the door to the entire astral plane.

Therefore, hear the answer. All of you who ask the question "Why?" —"Why do I have this problem or that problem or the next problem?"— I tell you it is because of those rents in your garment. And those very rents in your garment, beloved ones, are causative in tying you to the astral plane. For when you fail to observe the very first rule of the Keepers of the Flame Lessons, which is to invoke the mighty tube of light, to invoke the violet flame and recite "The Keeper's Daily Prayer," you are not building a solid foundation, a base upon which we may continue to build throughout the day.

Our healing angels are devoted to your healing. You must all consider yourselves as having this or that malady or out-of-alignment state. Yes, beloved ones, some area of all of you requires healing. Therefore you have come to this Church and this altar, for you know that true and everlasting healing comes from God through the Archangels and the Archeiai. One and all, we have been known as healers throughout the ages.

You have recognized at the level of your soul that you will not be healed unless you have the help of angels. Well, you do have that help, beloved ones! But do not think that because you have been a Keeper of the Flame for so long you can in any way neglect to invoke your tube of light.

It is a wondrous call! It is the mantra of your Knight Commander, Saint Germain. Therefore, it evokes his Electronic Presence, and so when you invoke your tube of light you also have the Master's Presence superimposed upon you! After all, beloved, you keep the flame of Life on earth for all people, but do you not also keep the violet flame for beloved Saint Germain, and the fleur-de-lis, symbol of your threefold flame, which has been his emblem for so long?

Yes, you do, beloved ones! Let not the flame be marred nor the chakras. Therefore, fully clothe yourselves in the whole armour of God![5] For when you are so sealed, it is as though you are sealed in that special place, a hospital, as it were, where the angels may come and tend to you and knit back together the fabric of your selfhood that is literally coming apart at the seams.

Thus, on the one hand, you are strong in the Lord, strong in his voice, strong in your decree momentum. And on the other hand, there is a weakness, an ultimate weakness in each one that is a reminder to you forever and forever that ye are Gods[6] only insofar as ye are one with the threefold flame. It is also a reminder that you are mortal, that you are limited, that your four lower bodies are ultimately corruptible and that therefore you have a certain limited time to occupy them. For existence in this octave is temporal and you must attempt to make your soul-identity permanent before the conclusion of this embodiment.

There is nothing more important! Perhaps it is not important to the rest of the world, but I tell you, beloved ones, every single one of you has been handpicked as a ripe apple from the Tree of Life. By and by, after you had suffered long enough and become fed up with the world and the human consciousness, you were drawn to this Path and this Teaching. You have been called and brought to the feet of your own Mighty I AM Presence at a time when you were able to receive this Teaching, to keep it, to cherish it and not reject it.

This is for a reason. Do not think it is because you are special in the sense of attainment, but simply assume that it is because you are special in the sense that you have an extraordinary need for an extraordinary help from those of us of higher octaves. And because you have that need, beloved, and can make it back to your home of Light in no other way except by our intercession, we have called you to be the firstfruits of those who should receive the Light from the altar.

Therefore come to the altar as lepers. Be cleansed! Be made whole! And share that wholeness with those who are on the rung of the ladder one step down from you. For they combine in their psychology the greatest need and the greatest receptivity of all evolutions on this planet.

I AM Archangel Michael! I stand for your eternal victory! And I will tell you one thing: There are days (as I count the days) when for one single one of you, I and my legions, in order to defend you, will slay ten thousand demons. This we will do on behalf of one Keeper of the Flame! Now understand how heaven goes to war for you! These are not small skirmishes. These are the wars against the ultimate fallen ones, who know you, who have your number and would see to it that *you* are put out of embodiment.

Blessed ones, when we come home from these battles, we are happy! We are happy to see you rejoicing. We are happy to see you in your recreation and in your dedicated service, and we are at your side strengthening you when the hours are long. We would like you to know, however, what it takes on our part and on the part of your Mighty I AM Presence to keep you in embodiment on the Path. And we would like you to know that if you should apply just a little more effort to your dynamic decrees, we could help others like you who are not able to decree, for they know not of the science of the spoken Word.

Therefore we ask you to think of us each day out of God-gratitude for our service as we lay down our lives for you daily. And we ask you to manifest your gratitude by laying down some portion of your life in decreeing for the Lightbearers who are at the very next ring and the next and the next—three rings out from the Inner Retreat—whom you must go and find and save and defend.

We say, be ourselves in form! Defend them as we defend you! And see how you will meet your comrades of all ages and systems of worlds.

I bow to you in the living Spirit of the First Ray of God's holy will!

[33-second standing ovation]

July 5, 1992

CHAPTER 22

Archangel Jophiel

"THERE MUST BE A COMMITMENT!"

The Quickening of the Crown Chakra

Hail, legions of the Second Ray! I AM Jophiel. I AM in the living presence of the sun of illumination. I intensify my commitment to you —all ye lands, all ye sons, all ye daughters—with Christine!

We are coming, the six Archangels, on the heels of Archangel Michael and with Uzziel, and we are coming to make your chakras star-studded chakras as we are able and as you are able to hold the Light. And where you cannot hold the Light, we place our momentum over the chakras of your Holy Christ Self to be lowered first into the etheric, then the mental, then the physical and desire bodies as you are able to purify those vortices by the sacred fire breath, the "Call to the Fire Breath," Djwal Kul's Breathing Exercise and the *pranayama.*[1]

We encourage you to become Keepers of the Flame, for there must be a commitment on your level if we are to give the commitment from our level. And the commitment that we ask of you is not so great, beloved ones, that you cannot give it, when you think of all the karma of the past that you balance by being a faithful Keeper of the Flame and faithfully keeping the flame.

Therefore, illumined action as the fire of the crown of all of the Archangels is an effervescent ray, a bubbling flame itself. It is purgative even as it illumines you. It is the power that enables you to see through the dark night of the soul and the Dark Night of the Spirit.

Therefore, beloved ones, I come now for the touching of the crown chakra and the mighty quickening. May you go after the crown chakra and all of the chakras with the violet flame for transmutation of karma made through the misuse of the chakras, that you might be as stars reflected in the very seas of the earth—in the earth but not of it.

Therefore I AM Jophiel. I AM touching the crown chakra of each one. I do this, beloved ones, for I AM God-determined that there shall be a new birth of Cosmic Christ illumination in this earth and that the sparks that fly this day from the Heart of the Inner Retreat and from the Western Shamballa shall be the sparks of golden illumination from your own crown chakra.

Therefore, be true sons of God! Therefore, be true sons of the lightning! Therefore, come forth in this hour, for it is an hour when illumination's fires can sweep round the earth.

Visualize that globe that is tended by Mother Mary, now licked in flames of illumination's fires penetrating: a world conflagration of illumination's flame burning through the ignorance of the mass consciousness, exposing the Liar and the lie, allowing the Christ to descend into the temples of more than have that Christ now.

Oh yes, beloved ones, we are the ones who have cleared the way for many improvements in society, namely, for the binding of tobacco, for the binding of nicotine, yes, for the binding of that substance in America.[2] So call upon us and all the mighty Archangels for the cleaning out of this nation of the drug traffic and all drugs harmful to the youth. Call for the judgment of those in positions of great power in this government who allow it, who know it, who benefit thereby.

Blessed hearts, let the entire hemisphere be cleared! Let all who come from North, Central and South America make their bond and pact in this age in a union that shall not be broken, truly a Pan-American union whereby all determine that the drug lords shall go down, that *there shall be no more drugs in this hemisphere!*

I enlist your aid. The Seven Archangels join you. And I ask for this mutual pact and commitment now. And I ask you to place your hands over the hands of those next to you until you feel a mighty bonding and a strengthening and the rays of light of the holy angels passing through you now.

This is Death and Hell in the streets, in the cities, in the homes, in the schools, in the universities. Everywhere you go, beloved ones, bodies are being turned into dens of hell because of the drugs that are there that do attract and keep the demons inside. It is hell on earth in the youth of the world and adults as well!

Therefore, I, Jophiel, promise you:

Give me the call! *We will do the job!*

[33-second standing ovation]

July 5, 1992

CHAPTER 23

Archangel Chamuel and Charity

THE PURGING OF THE BLOOD

We Are the Exorcists!

I AM Chamuel/Charity of the flame of Divine Love.
I come for the unification of hearts.
I come to heal division in your members.
I come with that Ruby Ray, with the flame of the Holy Spirit,
With the power of Chamuel and Charity, as Above, so below,
Multiplied by the power of the Ruby Ray,
  the legions of the Ruby Ray,
  the seraphim and the cherubim of God.

We come, beloved, that you may no longer be a house divided,[1] that you might not be split, sawn asunder and divided within yourself—one side the light side, one side the dark, Dr. Jekyll and Mr. Hyde.

We come this day by your love.

Give of yourself in sacrifice and service.

Be willing to be, if necessary, in the Heart of the Inner Retreat until you are fully healed and cut free of those ties to hell, which are signified by unclean and filthy habits of the mind, the body, the soul and the emotions.

Beloved ones, if these remain within you and you are tormented yet, I say, *We are the exorcists!* We come now in full array with all legions of Light and we can deliver you.

And therefore, open your heart now; for by the mighty sword of Alpha and Omega, there does come upon you now the touching of your heart with the point of the sword, releasing therefrom nine drops of blood.[2] For there is no remission of sin without the shedding of blood.[3]

Therefore, you may shed this blood in token and in communion with the Lord Christ upon the cross, and you may know also that you have been on the cross by the attack of Death and Hell upon your life. And you will come down from the cross when the reason you are on the cross has been fulfilled, which is the accomplishment of your own surrender, your own selflessness, your own service, your own oneness in sacrifice to Almighty God.

Contemplate now this event which does take place in the life of every Son of God, for I, Chamuel, have come bearing the crucifix. And the crucifix is a cross and more than a cross: for affixed to the cross, beloved, is you—*you,* the Christ crucified.

Now understand why all who are of Death and Hell have howled about you in this and past embodiments and between embodiments.

Understand how deeply and profoundly Archangel Michael cares for you and has absolutely determined that you shall no longer be subjected to those things that are below the level of the living Christ within you. (Therefore, be seated in the Love of the angels.)

Let there be the purging of the blood by the power of the Light of the Holy Spirit of the Third Ray.

Let the blood be purged in the etheric body, the mental body, the desire body and the physical body.

So it is an action of the Archangels!

Purify yourselves as you are able, as is scientific in your methods of fasting.

Know of a certainty, beloved hearts, that we guard your heart this day and your adjustment.

This is the day and the hour when, if you so choose, you may receive the exorcism of Chamuel and Charity.

["Yes!" (12-second applause)]

July 5, 1992

CHAPTER 24

Archangel Gabriel and Hope

LET THERE BE THE ASSIMILATION!

Vials of Ascension's Flame to Be Distributed by Your Holy Christ Self

Now cometh the angels of the Fourth Ray!

We are Gabriel and Hope!

Therefore, we raise up the white fire that is the sign and the signet of your ultimate union with God, your immortality, as Above, so below.

See the shafts of ascension's flame round about your Messenger! Claim them as your own *now!* And let our angels, the mighty seraphim, bear that flame to you who so love it and desire to keep it with you always.

[17-second standing ovation]

Let there be the assimilation!

Let there be the assimilation!

Let there be the assimilation!

Let there be the assimilation *now* of that essence of the white fire! Let there be the unblocking of the flow of light upwards along the spine. And let the high priest, the Holy Christ Self, now stand over each one. Now know and lock your mind with the Mind of your own Christ Self.

Know the Mind of God!

Know the Mind of God!

Know the *purity* of the Mind of God!

Ascension's flame, beloved, is the instantaneous annihilation of Death and Hell. The two cannot occupy the same time or space or point in eternity. Where there is Life, Life, then, consumes Death. Death is not, has no victory and is a poor, poor impostor of the Life everlasting.

Death only wins when the individual has no tie to everlasting Life. And there are many such individuals upon earth, beloved. Knowingly or unknowingly, willfully or not, they have cut the tie of the crystal cord and the threefold flame.

This essence of white fire, therefore, as a transmission of ascension's flame, is given to you. Now it has flowed freely. Now we seal it in many vials and the vials are being sewn by angels on the inner side of the garment of your Holy Christ Self.

Your Holy Christ Self, therefore, may dispense these vials to those in need whom you meet. Since you are often prone to sympathy, it shall not be your lot to decide who shall receive them, but your Holy Christ Self alone will guard them and keep them and impart them to those who need them.

Thereby you shall make 100 percent good karma as your Holy Christ Self distributes these vials of ascension flame. Know that they will go to those who are deserving and whose Holy Christ Self will make certain that the lifestream does receive over the years drop by drop the contents of the vial. In some cases a life will be spared that would have gone through transition, a terrible experience may be prevented or karma may be mitigated. Such will be the blessing upon those who have merit in their lifestreams yet have gone astray, have gone the wrong way.

Beloved ones, when you make a turn into a one-way street and the sign says Wrong Way, there is only one thing to do: back up and go down the right way. But you see, instead of backing up then and there, you go over again and again the mistaken steps, byways you never should have entered and that you should have gotten out of faster than fast.

And so life becomes complicated as you attempt to undo and undo the spirals in the body that have increased your mortality—old age, disease and death.

Yes, beloved ones, take no more wrong turns!

Go the way of the ascension!

Make the acquaintance of Serapis Bey!

Understand his dossier[1] and walk straight for the mark of Luxor.

Visualize Luxor, Egypt, now.

Visualize that place and make the determination in your heart that you will arrive there qualified to make your ascension before your body runs out or runs down.

Strengthen the body!

Strengthen the will!

Accelerate the call to the flame, to eternal Life!

And *see* what Archangel Gabriel and Hope will do for you!

[21-second standing ovation]

July 5, 1992

CHAPTER 25

Archangel Raphael and Mother Mary

THE SWORD OF THE FIFTH RAY DESCENDS

The Marriage of a Soul to God

Now the sword of the Archangel and the Archeia of the Fifth Ray does descend! And a mighty descent it is, beloved hearts, clear through all of the planes of the earth body, all of the planes of the Matter universe, for we are servants not alone of the evolutions of this planet.

Therefore, rejoice, ye holy ones of God, and know that we of the Fifth Ray precipitate into manifestation that which is the mighty and powerful action of those Archangels and Archeiai of the first four rays.

Know, then, how needed is the recording of your emerald-ray, Fifth Ray decrees and songs, for with that ray all that has come before is precipitated into the very physical octave.

Rejoice in this, beloved!

Rejoice in that you have the point of anchoring [14-second standing ovation] through *Sanctissima* released to you. It is indeed a chalice into which the heavenly hosts pour their light unceasingly. And it is a chalice into which you also pour the light and devotion of your hearts, which reaches all of the Archangels, some whom you know and some who are yet unnamed to you.

Therefore know that your point of precipitation through the balanced threefold flame, and the action of the Mother Light gone before through the matrix of *Sanctissima*, can truly be for the healing of the body of the planet and her evolutions.

Blessed hearts, our treasures of Light, be seated in our love.

This is a day of great rejoicing across all the heavens, for the great marriage is come and the marriage is repeated again and again. And a single marriage performed this day in heaven is a glorious occasion for all hosts of the LORD. And I do not speak of any outer marriage so consecrated before this or any altar of the world. I speak of the marriage of the soul, of a single soul, to God through the mighty Archangels.

Therefore, you shall know that in the earth as a result of this marriage there is a stronger tie to the great God-government of the spheres and of the God Star, Sirius. And you shall know, O ye brides, O ye virgins, that you are also in line and your day will also come and you will know what it means to be fully God in manifestation.

For there is a wedding and a bonding to the Christ Self and then there is a wedding and a bonding to the I AM THAT I AM. Yes, beloved hearts, when this does come to an individual on earth, the worlds do change, the equation does change. And you who desire to stop the coming down of the woes prophesied and delivered by the Four Horsemen, *you ought to know* that the single greatest gift you can give to the universe is the bonding of your heart to Christ, your living marriage to Jesus Christ, to your Holy Christ Self, and your walking the earth as a Christed one with that bonding that can never be undone.

Therefore know that when you set your sights upon that goal, you will deal with all of the forces of Darkness that have ever assailed or invaded your temple, beloved ones.

Therefore, go in the way of the healing waters.

Go in the way of the Healing Matrix!

Go for the Healing Thoughtform![1]

Go for bringing yourself into alignment!

And listen again and again to the Mother's teachings on those saints who did become the brides of Jesus.

Let this be your longing, your yearning, your overriding reason for being—not because of the blessing you will receive but because of the stabilization of planet earth that will take place and that does increase each and every time, beloved ones, a single soul is bonded to her Lord.

O beloved ones, know the sweetness of our Jesus! Know his sweetness, his oneness, his presence. How can we forget, we who were there, as Above, so below? We, yes, are in the service of the living Christ, of the living Buddha and every son and daughter of God. Therefore we bring the impetus for your precipitation of your Holy Christ Self in this octave.

Our angels are also the mending angels. Therefore they have come, certain among them with needle and thread, green thread, certain among them angels of music, others angels of science, of chemistry, of alchemy—in short, angels of precipitation in every field and area of endeavor.

Yes, beloved hearts, we come. And while this service is being rendered, the greatest service of all shall be rendered by us through the Immaculate Heart of my beloved Mary and through my own heart, which is its counterpart.

Therefore, in this moment sing, then, so sweetly, as sweetly as you have ever sung to God, the introit to your Holy Christ Flame and your Holy Christ Self. Let this be that we might seal you, as effectively as the bonding to Christ can occur in your present state, and set the matrix and set the circumstance for you whereby you can continue to pursue this holy event, truly your marriage to Christ.

(Please remain seated in profound meditation upon your Holy Christ Self and Holy Christ Flame. Offer your prayers.)

[Congregation offers prayers to the Holy Christ Self.]

Introit to the Holy Christ Self

1. Holy Christ Self above me
Thou balance of my soul
Let thy blessed radiance
Descend and make me Whole.

Refrain: Thy Flame within me ever blazes
Thy Peace about me ever raises
Thy Love protects and holds me
Thy dazzling Light enfolds me.

I AM thy threefold radiance
I AM thy living Presence
Expanding, expanding, expanding now.

2. Holy Christ Flame within me
Come, expand thy triune Light
Flood my being with the essence
Of the pink, blue, gold and white.

3. Holy lifeline to my Presence
Friend and brother ever dear
Let me keep thy holy vigil
Be thyself in action here.

The threefold flame is your immortelle. Water it with devotion. Invigorate it with the life-giving essence of the Mother from the base to the crown chakra. Let it be balanced by a sound mind, an endearing heart and a firm will, resolute in the honor of God.

Your threefold flame is your cosmic honor flame. By this flame balanced and blazing brightly, you may pronounce your marriage vows to your Holy Christ Self. Without this flame, beloved, you have no bridal bouquet, you have not the acceptable offering to bring to God's altar.

Therefore we say, love intelligently, love powerfully!

Expand wisdom by love and the will of God made practical!

Use the power and the will and the determination of God to hold steady your love in the plane of the Spirit and at the level of the Christ.

Use that thrust and that momentum so that your wisdom might cover the earth and take dominion in the earth.

So, be the Trinity and that Trinity supported by, actualized by, made manifest by the Divine Mother, who is, was and ever shall be the Word in the Beginning with Brahman.[2]

In your heart is all you need, O beloved! And if perchance you think you may have lost that flame along the way, now is the hour to be on your knees and to call to God and to the Lord Christ to come to you to reignite that flame.

Do not be sorrowful in this plight, beloved ones, for in the heart of your Holy Christ Self there is a threefold flame. And as long as you have life in this embodiment, you can serve and serve from your waking unto your sleeping. You can serve God and serve the Light and serve the Trinity and the Mother and serve their children until the hour when surely the mighty Light does turn and serve you and that flame is reignited and you feel the breath of the Maha Chohan and you know you have come to your second birth in this life, the birth in the Spirit.

Therefore, let none despair! Let none succumb to depression! Let none allow the gaze to be lower than the love of the Bridegroom.

Visualize yourself in the grandest cathedral of the etheric octave, a cathedral that can hold millions. See your Holy Christ Self at the altar and you at the rear door looking all the way down the aisle. Look at your Holy Christ Self and count the steps you must take until you are in the arms of your Beloved.

So the wedding day shall come for you also and the bells shall ring and the angels shall sing and you shall find yourselves permanently in the Sacred Heart of Jesus. So, beloved, rejoice that you are brides in preparation for the assimilation by your Bridegroom.

We daily tend your coming and your going to keep the way of the Tree of Life within you. Until ye are able to keep it, that mighty Tree of Life must be held in the matrix of your Holy Christ Self.

As you have fallen on the Fifth Ray by misappropriation, miscreation and misprecipitation, so now shall you be redeemed and you shall redeem yourselves by the application of the law of the Fifth Ray unto your restoration to God.

We are your helpers!

[22-second standing ovation]

July 5, 1992

CHAPTER 26

Archangel Uriel and Aurora

THE HOUR OF JUSTICE IS COME

We Execute Judgment in the Matter Spheres

We, the Archangels of the Sixth Ray, Uriel, Aurora, summon the legions of Light who bring the judgment of the Lord Christ, the Lord Buddha, the Lord Krishna, the Lord Sanat Kumara and the LORD God in ye all *to the physical octave!*

Therefore, *you* serve, *you* serve, *you* serve! And where there is injustice in life, we come dividing the way on behalf of the servants of God in bringing the judgment upon the seed of the Wicked One, who have had, I tell you, beloved ones, more mercy than you will ever be able to conceive of from the heart of God! [15-second standing ovation]

When you consider sympathizing with the criminal element—with those who abuse life and do so repeatedly lifetime after lifetime, those who mentally contort the wisdom of God, distort it and use a false logic whereby they affirm that the ends justify the means, et cetera, with those who pervert the chakras and twist and try the very patience of the saints—blessed ones, do not do it!

Do not sympathize with them! For I tell you, they have had the mercy of God aeon upon aeon upon aeon. And I tell you, there have been more Ascended Masters, Lady Masters and Gods and Goddesses made by their extension of mercy to the fallen ones than in any other way! [9-second standing ovation]

Therefore, the hour of Justice is come.

Therefore, increase and intensify your service.

Do not re-create ties with those who are on the left-handed path, no matter what your sympathy, no matter what *you think* your loyalties are. We are here to tell you that your loyalties are to God and God alone and that not one ounce, one fraction of an ounce of your energy should go in sympathy to those individuals who have turned their back on the altar of God, who have turned love into anger and into all of the Martian misqualifications.[1]

Beloved ones, beware! For when you reach this point on the Path and you are given this level of opportunity, it is *not,* it is *not,* we say, your option to make the judgment to give God's Light to those who have shown themselves nonservants of the Light for aeons. Therefore Alpha did come and he did tell you that it is lawful for you to pray for the Lightbearers of the world and to invoke dispensations in their behalf, but he did not tell you that you could invoke the Light on behalf of those who misuse the Light.[2]

Beware, then, beloved ones, for if you give the Light to the dark ones, the Light will be turned off *in you.* For God will not allow it to flow through you to the fallen ones.

Therefore, have mercy upon the children of God who are being abused daily, who are not being taught as they should be taught or loved as they should be loved; nor are they being given the true and profound understanding that the Divine Parents would give them.

Be merciful to one another!

Bind up one another's wounds of the psyche and the heart and of the chakras and serve together as though your life depended on it and planet earth depended on it—on your being this one, inseparable, indissoluble union of a body of Lightbearers that will *hold* against the force of Antichrist so that by the time the Word of judgment has been pronounced by the Lord upon that Antichrist, no one will even remember *who* or *what* was Antichrist! [14-second standing ovation]

I, Uriel, speak to you fallen ones throughout this Matter cosmos:

Your names will not be remembered! There will be no record left of you or your names! I, Uriel, summon all hosts of the LORD for your judgment this day as a ratification by the Seven Archangels of the judgment of Alpha upon those who have misused the Justice of God.

Therefore, we come! *Therefore,* the Light of the sword does extend through the Matter cosmos! *Therefore,* beloved ones, know this day that all have been served notice. The fallen ones know of *you. You* know of them. The line is drawn. Take heed. Call upon the name Uriel Archangel and Aurora and know that we are the appointees of the LORD God for the execution of judgment in all of the Matter spheres.

You have the calls we have given to you.[3] Use them in connection with your calls to Helios and Vesta for the full manifestation of the binding of the dweller-on-the-threshold of the force of anti-Christ, anti-Buddha, anti-Mother, anti-Father and anti-Holy Spirit and anti-Child.

Yes, beloved hearts, use them, for we stand in the heart of the sun of Helios and Vesta. And when your calls go forth, they *sweep through* the Matter cosmos and many worlds are cleared, for the science of the spoken Word is the ultimate power that can manifest at this level of your evolution for the victory of worlds.

Thank God that you have received it!

Thank God that you understand it!

For many have been delivered by the science of the spoken Word.

I seal you in the Sixth Ray—purple, gold, ruby flecks.

I seal you in the Justice of God.

Therefore *be* just and let the word of Divine Justice and human justice go forth from you, beloved ones, and not a word of judgment or condemnation or criticism.

Therefore, invoke your beloved Portia, Great One of the Aquarian Age, blessed Goddess of Opportunity. Allow her, then, to raise you up in the flame of God-Justice to be those pillars of Justice in the land, taking the side of the poor, the oppressed, the helpless, the homeless who have none to champion their cause save politicians who would make a name for themselves and *use* them rather than support them.

Blessed hearts, Uriel is an angel who will do absolutely everything you call upon him to do.* I am that one who listens day and night. Sometimes I must recline in a space where I wait for someone to make the call for the binding of the horrendous injustices upon this planet! I tell you, it is an absolute defamation of the living God and the living Jesus Christ, Gautama Buddha and all whom I serve that these injustices go unchecked in the courts of the world!

Therefore I tell you, there is a higher court where matters are adjudicated swiftly and finally and the karma does descend. Therefore be *healed* of any sense of injustice about anything in you, outside of you or in the land or in the world. Simply invoke the Lords of Karma and remember, Uriel is waiting to be called into action!

I AM here.

I AM smiling, for I have found my troops.

You are it, beloved ones!

You are *they!* You are *we!* You are all of us.

We are going forward together in Divine Justice!

[27-second ovation]

July 5, 1992

*so long as it is in keeping with the will of God

CHAPTER 27

Archangel Zadkiel and Holy Amethyst

HO! HO! HO! HERE WE ARE!

Give Us an Opportunity: 40 Days of Violet Flame

Ho! ho! ho! The happier we get, the closer we get to the Seventh Ray!

Ho! ho! ho! The closer we get to the violet flame, the happier we get!

Here we are, Zadkiel and Holy Amethyst!

Ho! ho! ho! Here we are!

Ho! ho! ho! Here we are!

Ho! ho! ho! Here we are! [14-second standing ovation]

Thrust home, I say!

Thrust home to the heart of every heart in the universe!

For the violet flame will purify your hearts. It will make of your heart a purple fiery heart. It will dissolve the hearts of the wicked else dissolve their wickedness, whereby they may become converted, beloved ones. And if they are not converted, they will be perverted forevermore and bound and taken to the Court of the Sacred Fire!

Therefore, hear the word of Saint Germain and Portia, Zadkiel and Holy Amethyst, Arcturus and Victoria.

Hear the word! *Hear* the word! *Hear* the word!

For the violet flame is able. The violet flame does support the Seven Archangels and all the Archangels and angels of the universe and all elemental life and all Lightbearers of the world.

Let's get it rolling, beloved ones, and rolling and rolling and rolling! [Congregation affirms with Zadkiel and Holy Amethyst, clapping:]

I AM a being of violet fire! I AM the purity God desires!
(repeated 10 times)

Earth is a planet of violet fire! Earth is the purity God desires!
(repeated 15 times)

So, beloved ones, be seated in your violet flame seats! For we have determined that you will know the violet flame, that you will know what has touched you during this conference, all the flames and the full power of transmutation's ray, and that you will make the violet flame your flame, your day, your night.

We have determined to do all in our power to see to it that you will make it your cosmic honor to invoke this flame, to pass it through every problem, standing at that point before your altar where you can turn 360 degrees holding your sword of Archangel Michael, directing it 360 degrees and sending forth the violet flame.

Do you realize that when you make that turn, such as this, beloved ones, [the Messenger turns 360 degrees, holding the sword Excalibur] and when you do it bringing the sword down every so many degrees [Archangel Zadkiel demonstrates through the Messenger], you are sending, if you make the call, the full power of violet flame's ray to the farthest reaches of the cosmos?

And when you stand before the altar of your Mighty I AM Presence and through that Presence you connect with those mighty light rays going forth from the Great Central Sun, you become a second sun replicating those mighty light rays.

And therefore, you see, beloved ones, wherever you have made karma in the Matter cosmos, if you do this turning with the sword once a day, so you will be sending the violet flame into the cause and core of any condition where there is any person, any lifestream in all of the Matter cosmos with whom you have a karmic debt. There is simply no limit to the action of the violet flame that you send forth from that center; and it goes forth from you spherically as many cosmic rays in all directions from your heart. By practicing this ritual, you are therefore balancing the karma that you have made on that line as far as that line can go, bisecting the finite universe.

The scars of your karma, which have also scarred the Matter cosmos, may not disappear all at once. Therefore you pursue this ritual daily. You can say: "The Matter cosmos is a cosmos of violet fire! The Matter cosmos is the purity God desires!" You can say any of the mantras you desire. But, beloved ones, it is a glorious joy to know that when you will have fulfilled this life and made your ascension you will have no ties of a negative nature to anyone in the Matter cosmos but only millions of positive ties to individuals upon earth who are yet moving toward the sun of their Presence. And these individuals, by reason of having received the violet flame that you have invoked, will now owe *you* some karma.

And therefore, as an Ascended Master, you may call upon them, you may work through them. You may ask them to receive you, perhaps to write books that you would dictate or to write music that you would direct. There are all sorts of things that Ascended Masters like to bring into manifestation once they are ascended and, of course, they can be heard or seen by scarcely anyone. [9-second applause]

The violet flame will do for you what you do not know until you invoke it. And do you know what? I am not going to tell you today what the violet flame can and will do for you if you take ahold of it and, with the same fire with which this Messenger delivers to you the Word of God, you invoke it, you love it, you call to it, you draw it forth *because all of your desiring is to make that violet flame physical,* just as all of the desiring of this Messenger is to make our presence to you physical.

Do you understand, beloved ones, that it is the receptacle of the Messenger that allows us to deliver such intensity by her intense love of our hearts and of God Almighty? Appreciate this, beloved ones, and *be* your own messenger of your own Holy Christ Self and deliver to the earth your "dictations" of steady streams of violet flame and violet flame decrees! [23-second standing ovation]

How we love you! How we love you! We pray you would know and feel that love as intensely as we give it and as intensely as it is felt in the heart of the Messenger. Oh, that love, beloved, should you receive an ounce of it or more, would surely be for you the resolution of all separation from God!

Oh, give unto us, the legions of the violet flame, the Goddess of Freedom, Saint Germain and Portia, the Mighty One, the Great Divine Director, all elemental life—oh yes, beloved ones, give unto the Seventh-Ray Buddhas and Bodhisattvas *an opportunity!*

Let us make it forty days. Beloved, give yourself forty days of saturation of the violet flame.

Direct it into those nooks and crannies and empty places that ought to be filled and painful spots and sores and hurts and limitations, problems with the health of your children, loved ones.

Give yourself the forty days and the forty nights of the rain of the violet flame. Trade it, beloved, for the averting of some future cataclysm that could come upon the earth.

Give forty days of violet flame.

Pick the time, beloved, but do something every day and keep to that something that we might hear you and have your violet flame response directed to all of us who have spoken at this conference.

Blessed hearts, see what you can do with planet earth and yourself with the violet flame.

See what questions will be answered, and see the sublime level of the Seventh Ray that you may rise to. And you know, you might just find that you will be able to hold that level, sustain it and thereby catapult your soul up into that secret chamber of the heart just as you desire!

We are the ones of the sealing. Therefore we seal you, seal you in the Light of the Seven Archangels, seal you in the heart of hearts of your beloved Lanello, who comes to have a chat with you now.

[15-second standing ovation]

So, in the name of Almighty God, of the Father, the Son and the Holy Spirit, we seal our proclamations, our dispensations, our Love, Wisdom and Power, our honor and our centeredness in the heart of the Mother that you might be fruitful and multiply and magnify the Lord in the earth.

We are yours and we pray that *you* will always be *ours.*

[20-second standing ovation]

July 5, 1992

CHAPTER 28

Lanello

DEFEAT THE NEGATIVES

The Future Is in Your Hands

Let there be music in our hearts!

Let there be music in our hearts today, beloved!

For have we not cause for rejoicing? ["Yes!" (18-second standing ovation)]

I bring to you, beloved ones, another cause for rejoicing and it is that an individual unknown to you, yet who has had connection with this activity, has on this day ascended from the Temple of Luxor.

[24-second standing ovation]

And so it is true, beloved, that each one of you rises a little bit when one of your members takes that ascension, that glorious and grand step into the octaves of Light, nevermore to be tainted again by the earthly atmosphere. So is the ritual of the ascension welcomed by everyone when it is taken at the right time. (Please be seated, then.)

I come to you to discuss with you today the future of this organization—a future that lies in your hearts and your hands, a future that will depend largely on whether or not you follow with care the advice I give you today.

The dispensation of *FREEDOM 1992* comes following the thirty-third anniversary last year of The Summit Lighthouse. Building upon that, you have heard sponsors and very determined Masters ready to help.

Now I expect you to defeat the negatives, whether in your astrological chart or in your karma or in your human habit patterns. Defeat them!

Carve up your day in a new chart and a new map and see what you can do that you have not done before!

See how you can organize, how you can accelerate and how you can appreciate remembering when you were "out there" and had nowhere to turn, when you knew that somewhere there must be someone or something—a message, a light, even a church or a movement or a place where you could truly drink from the waters of everlasting Life.

Do not be like the ones who surveyed the scene of the Buddha and the Bodhisattvas, jumped over the wall and never came back to tell the great, great story of the Path—the Path to union with God.[1]

I remember my own quest in many lifetimes when I had but partial knowledge. You remember, also, when you gave your very best but there was no dispensation, not even the intercession of the violet flame, to prevent your assassination, your untimely death or simply your nonfulfillment.

And you went to rest in certain planes of the Spirit, weary from that lifetime and yet so yearning for the age that was to come, the age when all these things might be put together for you because it would be the age of the coming of the Divine Mother and the coming of the World Mother once again.

Now that you have the precious configuration and you know the calculus of this embodiment and of the Path, all you need to do is fill in the blanks as in those painting kits where you match the numbered colors to the numbers in the blanks. Once you have filled them in, the picture is complete.

Well, your life is almost as easy as that, beloved ones. Though it is hard and seems hard, it must be allowed to be hard by the Lords of Karma. For if you do not learn to appreciate the weight and the burden that you have put upon life by now having to deal with and wrestle with that same weight and burden, what kind of a prize could life afford you?

Wouldn't it be like some kind of a make-believe TV talk show where you give the right answer and you go up three notches?

Well, beloved ones, the Path has been hard won. It may not have been so hard to descend, but from our perspective it was very hard when we hit bottom! And many of us did. And so we began our climb, and it is a wonderful thing and wonder of wonders to our friends as well as to our enemies that we have made it to the ascended state.

Be not concerned, beloved ones. There is hardly an ascended one in heaven, nameless or well-known to you, who does not continue to be criticized by those in embodiment who knew that one or who know of that one as a historical figure. You simply cannot please the human consciousness, and therefore do not try.

Do not go down and roll with your little piglets in the mud and enjoy yourselves at that level.[2] But rise to the level of your Godhood, stay there and draw to your God Self[3] all men and women and children of the Light who are destined to rise in this age.

They are not all destined to rise. Therefore, when they reject the Light, do not be dismayed or saddened or depressed. Know that there is a harvest and the wise pickers go out and they pick the ripe fruit and they leave the rest to ripen. Yes, beloved, pick the ripe fruit, that which is ripe and ready to fall from the tree. Those are the ones who will go forward, whom you may touch with the Light of your heart.

Blessed hearts, make yourselves available to Lightbearers by the simple process of making yourselves totally unavailable to those who are servants of the left-handed path—no matter what excuse you may conjure up that you owe them something or that this is a lesson that you have to learn or that this experience is needful for you to resolve your psychology.

Let them pass you by with disdain, as they always do. Keep on walking toward the Sun and by and by you will meet the inhabitants of the Sun. You will meet the Bodhisattvas. Be content to be alone in the honor of God until you are together, all-one, with those who embody that honor.

If you do not make this your lifetime policy, you will waste your life, fritter away your energies, spend the precious substance of your chakras, of your glands and all that God has deposited in you and not have the wherewithal to take flight when you must move against the gravity, the downward pull of the entire mass consciousness of the planet, in order to make your ascension as that one who ascended today so did.

Do not be concerned that you pull against the world; for when you do, know that legions of angels are pulling with you, pulling you up! And when the mass consciousness can no longer bear the fragrance of the lilies that surround you, they let go and the Lightbearers hitch themselves to your wagon.

And you find that God is pulling, legions of Surya are pulling and you are pulling an entire race and root race of people toward the Sun simply by the set of your jaw, the twinkle in the eye, the God-determination and the absolute certainty of self-knowledge that *you* are the winner! *you* know who you are! *you* know where you are going!

And the smart people and the spiritual people will know it too and they will follow you, and that is all that counts in this world.

[10-second applause]

Why, I tell you, beloved, in my time and in all of my embodiments put together, I have known the misunderstanding of millions. Yet I cherish the precious friendships—the friendships I count among you as we have been together for so many lifetimes, the bonding of our hearts, and through that bonding the springing forth of a new bonding to the Lord Christ and the Lord Buddha.

Yes, beloved, for every misunderstanding, every shunning, every ignoring of your life or mine by some, there has been the reward of the bringing together of those who are one. This Summit Lighthouse is like the confraternity of the brothers and sisters of Islam or of Judaism or of this or that Masonic order, the Knights Templar, and so on. It is the bonding together of all who have ever been the Gnostics or the mystics of their own faith.

Is it not a wondrous thing to find that whereas in prior lifetimes one could count one's true friends on a couple of hands or less, now one counts one's friends in the millions of ascended and unascended devotees of the Light?

Is this not a grand cause for rejoicing in the Mystical Body of God? ["Yes!" (10-second applause)]

I teach you one lesson today and it is that there is the projection upon you and into you of the fallen ones who demand:

"You must please us until we approve of you. You must do our bidding, walk the way we walk, dress the way we dress, talk the way we talk, and then we *may* give you our approval."

And after you have walked a few miles to bring yourselves closer to them, they have walked on and said, "Well now, that is not enough! You must do this, you must do that. You must even commit crimes for us. You must steal and lie for us. All of this you must do that you might have our approbation."

The Devil in the persons of those who move about the earth as the proud and the established ones who hold the moneyed interests of the planet and control the little people—he comes along and he is determined to have you. His agents make the same promises that Satan promised to the Lord Christ: "All these things will I give you if you will fall down and worship me."[4]

Why, they promise you the whole world! They cannot deliver. Blessed hearts, it is well to be cured of the disease of having the desire to be thought well of by the wrong crowd.

Now then, come in to the company of those millions upon millions of saints robed in white who gather round the throne of God, the throne of Sanat Kumara, even the great white throne,[5] beloved ones, and know, if you so desire to know, who are your reinforcements, who are the real people that you ought to want to please.

Then make the invocation that as a part of your nightly journeying you will all be taken together to that high point of the throne of God that you might know *who is your crowd,* who are the multitudes of Lightbearers on earth and in heaven who are one body.

Blessed ones, get on the right side of the Sun!

Get on the right side of God!

Get on the right side of yourself!

And waste no further time in being impressed by or trying to impress those who are of another world, who are of another power, a stolen power ill-gotten.

Walk in the way of the Buddha.

And let your mind be the Mind of God.
Rejoice in the accomplishments of the Lightbearers.
Minister unto them.
Minister unto your soul.
Set the agenda for your posterity!
Prepare the children!
Plan the Community!
Build the structures!
Establish the depths of your soul
    in the depths of ascension's flame
    and walk in that living fire all the days of your life!
And be willing to pay the price
    of the scorn of the Watchers and the lesser devils
    and of all who are not facing the Sun of God.
Walk in ascension's flame, beloved.
That is my counsel to you.
Walk in the flame of everlasting Life.
Be healed through the Son of God!
Please him.
Please him with all of your heart
    and all of your striving
    and all of your life.
I set you free today from your ego.
Now toss all of your egos into my hands! my hands cupped here.
My hands are big enough to hold them all!
For you see, minus the water, there is very little left.
[19-second standing ovation]
Now I shall toss them unto God! [8-second standing ovation]

Now there is a hush, beloved ones, for there is a vacancy as a slip of a parting in the secret chamber of the heart and the Divine Ego enters. The Divine Ego enters, beloved. Stay close to that One. Stay close to that Presence, that Id-Entity of your Mighty I AM.

Know the Divine Ego. It need not strut. It need not prance. It need not make any showing of itself. It *is* the Tao. Thus it comes and you who are its embodiment have no need to proclaim it.

Go your way in peace. Go your way in peace whereby the torment of all of the loud sounds, of all of the loud cackling, cackling geese of the egos of the world, is silenced as you enter the silence of the flame of your Divine Ego.

Having so said, having so done, I say to you:

Go out now in the calmness of the peace-commanding Presence!

Be not moved this way or that!

Seize the torch of your mission!

Proclaim it to your heart!

Proclaim it to the world when you are fully prepared and ready to give what you have to a world that has been waiting for your sun to rise, my beloved, for aeons.

I AM your Father. I bow to the Light within you.

Messenger's Benediction:

O Seven Mighty Elohim of God, release through us all in this hour, through the seven planes of being in the mighty Tree of Life, the sealing of the Light/Energy/Consciousness of this entire conference in the heart of the Great Central Sun, in the heart of Lord Maitreya, in the heart of the Mystery School and the Western Shamballa, in the heart of the Retreat of the Divine Mother and in the heart of our Mighty I AM Presence.

Let every erg of energy bestowed upon us and invoked by us be sealed and protected by God and his angels to be used for the multiplication of the God consciousness, the Christ consciousness and the presence of the Holy Spirit in all people of Light upon earth.

O turn things around, Elohim! Turn things around!

And let this earth come into her true spiritual orbit!

The paths are opened, O God!

Let all the Lightbearers of the earth make their way to the Heart of the Inner Retreat next year and again and again and at night while their bodies sleep.

We seal them all, O God, in thy name.

In the name of the Father, the Son, the Holy Spirit and the Divine

Mother, Lord Sanat Kumara, Gautama Buddha, Lord Maitreya, Jesus Christ and our beloved Padma Sambhava, in the name, the inner name pronounced by the angel of the LORD over each one, the inner name known only by God, we seal this conference in the heart of Elohim.

And we are grateful, grateful to thee, O God, eternally and forever for these dispensations of the Ascended Masters and thy teachings! Amen.

July 5, 1992

NOTES

Books referenced in these notes are published by Summit University Press unless indicated otherwise. Bible references are to the King James Version.

CHAPTER 1 • Friendship with God

Prior to El Morya's dictation the Messenger read Genesis 15. The dictation followed the Messenger's lecture "Keys from Judaism—the Kabbalah and the Temple of Man." Some of the teaching in El Morya's dictation builds on concepts covered in the lecture. For a fuller understanding of the dictation, it is important to hear the lecture, which is available from AscendedMasterLibrary.org. The lecture also forms the basis for the book *Kabbalah: Key to Your Inner Power.* It is also recommended that you read Genesis 14 and 15.

1. Gen. 15:17.
2. Abraham, the friend of God. II Chron. 20:7; Isa. 41:8; James 2:23.
3. Josh. 24:2.
4. Gen. 15:1.
5. Heb. 11:8–19.
6. "I will multiply thy seed as the stars of the heaven . . ." Gen. 15:5; 22:17, 18; Heb. 11:11, 12.
7. Gen. 15:12–16.
8. Gen. 15:7–11, 17.
9. Christ, chief cornerstone and stumbling block. Ps. 118:22, 23; Isa. 8:13–15; 28:16; Matt. 21:42; Acts 4:10–12; Rom. 9:31–33; I Cor. 1:23; Eph. 2:20; I Pet. 2:6–8.
10. John 3:16, 17.

11. See Elizabeth Clare Prophet, "The Golden Age of Jesus Christ on Atlantis," available from AscendedMasterLibrary.org.
12. John 1:14.
13. Five Sacred Hearts. See El Morya, "Give Me Your God-Controlled Attention!" *Pearls of Wisdom,* vol. 35, no. 19, May 10, 1992.
14. Heb. 2:3.
15. Eccles. 3:1–8.
16. Gen. 14; Heb. 7:1, 2.

CHAPTER 2 • "I Am Not Done with Pisces!"

Prior to this dictation, the Messenger delivered the first half of her lecture "Roots of Christian Mysticism" and led the congregation in giving Ashram rituals 4 and 5—Sacred Ritual for Soul Purification and Sacred Ritual for Transport and Holy Work.

1. I Sam. 16:1–13.
2. Gal. 4:19.
3. Matt. 2:1–18.
4. I Pet. 5:8.
5. Matt. 7:15–20; 12:33; Luke 6:43–45.
6. John 4:35; Matt. 9:35–38; Luke 10:1, 2.
7. See Elizabeth Clare Prophet, *The Lost Years of Jesus.*
8. John 9:4.
9. The chalice of Elohim. On June 27, 1987, during *FREEDOM 1987* in the Heart of the Inner Retreat, Archangel Chamuel and Charity announced that a tangible chalice was being formed, tended by Paul the Venetian, Nada and angels of Love. They said: "When the chalice shall rise to meet and greet the Elohimic level, then shall Elohim pour into this chalice that which ye seek, beloved.... It is the purging, purging of all impurity: Light, then, solidifying and codifying the Word within you." Beloved Alpha explained on July 5, 1987, that the building of the chalice "must give to us entrée to earth twenty-four hours a day by the Spirit of Elohim." On July 13, Elohim Apollo and Lumina said: "As this chalice does rise and has risen that two-thirds of the way to our octave, we await the completion by the breakthrough of resurrection's flame." Calling for an intense decree vigil to the resurrection flame by Keepers of the Flame for the completion of the chalice, the Messenger explained that this chalice, "as a 'funnel' of crystal light," would be "the perpetual

open door for Elohim to work through all true Lightbearers of the world." On August 17, 1987, the Divine Mother Kali announced "the fulfillment of the chalice in the Heart of the Inner Retreat to the Elohimic level."

10. Yugoslavia overthrew Communism in 1990 and soon after began to split into several religious and ethnic republics, including Serbia (predominantly Eastern Orthodox), Croatia (predominantly Catholic), and Bosnia-Herzegovina (predominantly Muslim). In June 1991, Serbia, for reasons of territorial ambition, invaded Croatia and in March 1992 expanded its offensive into Bosnia. Fighting continued in some areas until 2001, resulting in the deadliest conflict in Europe since World War II, with an estimated 140,000 people killed. Many war crimes were committed, including genocide and ethnic cleansing.
11. Riots broke out in Los Angeles in April 1992 following the acquittal of four police officers charged with using excessive force in the arrest and beating of Rodney King. Looting and arson were widespread. When the riots ended, 63 people had been killed and 2,823 injured, Property damage was estimated at more than a billion dollars.

CHAPTER 3 • Turn the World Around!

1. *Hail Light Victorious! A Salute to Archangel Michael, Captain of the LORD's Host,* 17 songs performed by the Church Universal and Triumphant Choir conducted by Elizabeth Clare Prophet. 55 min.
2. John 4:6–14.
3. II Pet. 3:10, 12.

CHAPTER 4 • Break the Spell of Non-Victory!

1. A 7.3 magnitude earthquake struck Landers, about a hundred miles east of Los Angeles, at 4:57 a.m. local time on June 28, the morning of this dictation. The powerful quake caused extensive damage to the area around the epicenter, but only three deaths were reported. A separate 6.5 magnitude quake occurred three hours later at Big Bear, 22 miles west of the Landers quake. Damage was extensive, with 40 percent of the structures in Big Bear suffering damage, but no lives were lost.
2. Spiritual work over Yugoslavia. In his dictation given June 27, 1992, Saint Joseph asked that we make the call that night to be taken to the Royal Teton Retreat and from there angels would escort us to Yugoslavia (see ch. 2). Prior to the dictation, the Messenger and congregation had given Ashram rituals 4 and 5—Sacred Ritual for Soul Purification

and Sacred Ritual for Transport and Holy Work. These two rituals assist the soul in performing world service while out of the body during the hours of rest. The rituals are published in *Ashram Notes* by El Morya, pp. 37–42, 46–59, and *Ashram Rituals,* 64-page booklet, pp. 33–52.

3. Following ten months of increased seismic activity, the Alaskan volcano Mount Spurr erupted for the first time in thirty-nine years on June 27, 1992, depositing ash on the city of Anchorage, eighty miles to the east.

CHAPTER 5 • See What You Can Do!

1. Serapis Bey, *Dossier on the Ascension.*
2. Rev. 13:18.

CHAPTER 6 • Become Shiva!

1. John 1:1–3.
2. Anjani Kr. Srivastava, "Lord Shiva—the Master of Life and Death," in R.S. Nathan, comp., *Symbolism in Hinduism* (Bombay: Central Chinmaya Mission Trust, 1989), p. 180.
3. Margaret Stutley, *Hinduism: The Eternal Law* (1985; reprint, Wellingborough, Northamptonshire: Aquarian Press, Crucible, 1989), p. 107.
4. You and your body elemental: emotional attachment to the body. Almost everyone (with the exception of those who suffer severe psychological detachment from self and body) forms an emotional attachment to the body. After all, this is the body we have worn and worked through, the body that has provided the temple for our soul and the means by which we experience pleasure and pain on this plane, balance our karma and do good deeds. So we say, "Blest be the tie that binds us to earth when we need to be earthbound to fulfill our reason for being and blest be the liberating power of Shiva! when it's time 'to shuffle off this mortal coil.'"

   Emotions connected with our attachment to the body are natural, and you should be aware that your body elemental has a consciousness and its consciousness permeates the physical body. But you are the master of your body elemental. As you give him positive input instead of those complaining negatives, you will be much happier, more healthy and more holy—and so will your body elemental. And, of course, body elementals cannot do the best job, even though they would like to, when you don't give them the best food and exercise, spiritual teaching and practices.

Don't mistake your body elemental's fears for your own. Your body elemental is also attached to the body, because that's his job. He takes care of the body. No more body, no more job! So he's wondering where he's going and what he's going to do when you lay that body aside in your final embodiment. You have to comfort your body elemental as you would a little child and promise him that you are taking him with you to the next octave because he has been a very faithful servant. Tell him he can still be your aide-de-camp after you've ascended and he'll have plenty of assignments.

5. Stutley, *Hinduism,* p. 107.
6. Matt. 11:28–30.
7. John Snelling, *The Sacred Mountain,* rev. and enl. ed. (London: East-West Publications, 1990), p. 11.
8. Swami Karapatri, "Śri Śiva tattva," *Siddhanta,* II, 1941–42, 116, quoted in Alain Danielou, *The Gods of India: Hindu Polytheism* (New York: Inner Traditions International, 1985), p. 214.
9. Veronica Ions, *Indian Mythology* (London: Paul Hamlyn, 1967), p. 44.
10. Ananda K. Coomaraswamy, *The Dance of Shiva,* rev. ed. (New York: Farrar, Straus and Company, Noonday Press, 1957), p. 72.

CHAPTER 7 • Only Make the Call, "Shiva!"

The Messenger delivered her lecture "The Inner Path of Hinduism" on June 29.

1. Eph. 4:26.
2. The congregation gave the Sacred Ritual for Transport and Holy Work (Ashram Ritual 5) on the night of June 27.
3. On June 29, 1992, the Supreme released its decision in *Planned Parenthood v. Casey,* a landmark case on abortion rights. By a 5–4 majority, the court reaffirmed the "constitutional right" to abortion first established in *Roe v. Wade* in 1973.
4. See ch. 2; ch. 4, n. 1.

CHAPTER 8 • Do Not Doubt God!

Before the dictation, the Messenger led the congregation in the Sacred Ritual for Oneness (Ashram Ritual 6), devotional songs to the Father-Mother God in the Great Central Sun, and the sounding of the Om.

1. Matt. 13:58.

CHAPTER 9 • The Fourth Woe

The fourth woe was released by Alpha at 6:47 p.m. MDT.

1. Pss. 2:1–4; 59:8.
2. The Keeper of the Scrolls is the custodian of the archives containing each man's book of life. He is the head of the band of angels known as the angels of record, or recording angels. Each soul evolving in time and space is assigned a recording angel, who records every action, word, deed, thought and feeling. At the end of each day, the recording angel submits the record of that day to the Keeper of the Scrolls. It is the responsibility of the Keeper of the Scrolls to provide the Ascended Masters and the Lords of Karma with the life record of any or all incarnations of any individual about whom they may inquire. On October 13, 1972, Mother Mary told us that we could apply to the Keeper of the Scrolls to see the records that would assist us in overcoming the human consciousness and attaining our victory. Mother Mary said: "The Keeper of the Scrolls . . . will draw forth from the Book of Life in your behalf, if you will call to him and to the Lords of Karma, those pages that require seeing and examination if you are to make the proper calls."
3. Coil of the ascension flame. See Kuthumi and Djwal Kul, *The Human Aura,* pp. 292–93, 298–99.
4. See "A Proclamation" by Alpha, delivered during Gautama Buddha's May 13, 1987 Wesak address, in 1987 *Pearls of Wisdom,* vol. 30, no. 24.
5. Ibid.

CHAPTER 10 • The Light of Persia— Mystical Experiences with Zarathustra

1. Mary Boyce, *Zoroastrians, Their Religious Beliefs and Practices* (London: Routledge and Kegan Paul, 1979), p. 1.
2. R. C. Zaehner, "Zoroastrianism," in *The Concise Encyclopaedia of Living Faiths,* ed. R. C. Zaehner (1959; reprint, Boston: Beacon Press, 1967), pp. 222, 209.
3. Boyce, *Zoroastrians,* p. 18.
4. Telephone interviews with H. Michael Simmons, Center for Zoroastrian Research, 28 June 1992, 17 August 1992.
5. Mircea Eliade, ed., *The Encyclopedia of Religion* (New York: Macmillan Publishing Co., 1987), 15:557.
6. Boyce, *Zoroastrians,* p. 19.
7. Gathas: Yasnas 50.6, 46.2, 43.8, quoted in Zaehner, "Zoroastrianism,"

p. 210.

8. Boyce, *Zoroastrians,* p. 19.
9. Ibid.
10. Zaehner, "Zoroastrianism," p. 210.
11. David G. Bradley, *A Guide to the World's Religions* (Englewood Cliffs, N.J.: Prentice-Hall, 1963), p. 40.
12. Ibid.
13. Simmons, telephone interview, 28 June 1992.
14. Zaehner, "Zoroastrianism," p. 210.
15. R. C. Zaehner, *The Dawn and Twilight of Zoroastrianism* (London: Weidenfeld and Nicolson, 1961), p. 35.
16. Dinkart 7.4.75–76, quoted in Bernard H. Springett, *Zoroaster, the Great Teacher* (London: William Rider and Son, 1923), p. 25.
17. Zarathustra, January 1, 1981, *Pearls of Wisdom,* vol. 24, no. 13.
18. Mary Boyce, ed. and trans., *Textual Sources for the Study of Zoroastrianism* (1984; reprint, Chicago: University of Chicago Press, 1990), p. 12.
19. Boyce, *Zoroastrians,* p. 22.
20. Ibid.
21. Ibid., p. 21.
22. Ibid., p. 22; Boyce, *Textual Sources,* p. 13.
23. Boyce, *Zoroastrians,* p. 22.
24. Ibid.
25. Boyce, *Textual Sources,* p. 14.
26. Zaehner, *Dawn,* p. 36.
27. Ibid.
28. Gatha: Yasna 30, quoted in Zaehner, *Dawn,* p. 42.
29. Ibid.
30. Zaehner, *Dawn,* pp. 42–43.
31. Gatha: Yasna 45.2, quoted in Zaehner, *Dawn,* p. 43.
32. Zaehner, "Zoroastrianism," pp. 211, 210.
33. Ibid., p. 211.
34. Gatha: Yasna 48.10, quoted in Zaehner, "Zoroastrianism," p. 211.
35. Zaehner, "Zoroastrianism," p. 211.
36. Gatha: Yasna 32.11, quoted in Zaehner, "Zoroastrianism," p. 211.

37. Zaehner, *Dawn,* p. 36.
38. John B. Noss, *Man's Religions,* 5th ed. (New York: Macmillan Publishing Co., 1974), p. 443.
39. Ahuna Vairya, in Boyce, *Textual Sources,* p. 56.
40. Simmons, telephone interview, 28 June 1992.
41. Zaehner, "Zoroastrianism," p. 213.
42. I John 4:1.
43. Matt. 7:15–20; 12:33; Luke 6:43, 44.
44. Zaehner, "Zoroastrianism," p. 221.
45. Boyce, *Zoroastrians,* pp. 31–32.
46. Zaehner, *Dawn,* pp. 47–48.
47. Springett, *Zoroaster,* p. 60.
48. Ibid., p. 32.
49. Boyce, *Zoroastrians,* p. 79.
50. Ibid., p. 226.
51. Zaehner, "Zoroastrianism," p. 222.
52. Farhang Mehr, *The Zoroastrian Tradition: An Introduction to the Ancient Wisdom of Zarathustra* (Rockport, Mass.: Element, 1991), p. 93.
53. Ibid., pp. 94, 93, 70; telephone interview with Farhang Mehr, 1 July 1992.
54. Mehr, *Zoroastrian Tradition,* pp. 94–96.
55. Rev. 7:4; 14:1–5.

CHAPTER 11 • Thou Purging Fire!

1. For the story of Sanat Kumara and the devotees from Venus who accompanied him to earth, see *The Opening of the Seventh Seal: Sanat Kumara on the Path of the Ruby Ray.*
2. Lord Maitreya has also told us that he has such a place. Any number of Ascended Masters maintain a room in their retreats that is a focus of the secret chamber of the heart.
3. Decree 0.06 in *Prayers, Meditations and Dynamic Decrees for Personal and World Transformation.*

CHAPTER 12 • The Great Mystery of the Violet Flame

1. See "Omri-Tas' Violet Flame Day," *Pearls of Wisdom,* vol. 35, no. 8.

2. Omri-Tas' violet flame sea and Saint Germain's Maltese cross. See *Pearls of Wisdom,* vol. 34, nos. 26 and 65.
3. Gen. 14:18; Heb. 7:1–3.
4. Rev. 12:17.

CHAPTER 13 • The Worship of the Goddess— The Path of the Divine Mother

1. A. Parthasarathy, "Consorts of the Three Gods," in R. S. Nathan, comp., *Symbolism in Hinduism* (Bombay: Central Chinmaya Mission Trust, 1989), p. 157.
2. Ibid., pp. 157–58.
3. David Frawley, *From the River of Heaven: Hindu and Vedic Knowledge for the Modern Age* (Sandy, Utah: Morson Publishing, 1990), p. 126.
4. David Kinsley, *Hindu Goddesses: Visions of the Divine Feminine in the Hindu Religious Tradition* (Berkeley, Calif.: University of California Press, 1986), pp. 62, 141.
5. David Frawley, *Gods, Sages and Kings: Vedic Secrets of Ancient Civilization* (Salt Lake City, Utah: Passage Press, 1991), pp. 72–76, 354–57 nn. d–g.
6. Ibid., p. 219.
7. Rigveda 2.41.16, 1.3.12, quoted in Frawley, *Gods, Sages and Kings,* pp. 70, 71.
8. Sri-sukta 1, 6, 13, 4, in Rigveda, cited by David Kinsley, *The Goddesses' Mirror: Visions of the Divine from East and West* (Albany, N.Y.: State University of New York Press, 1989), p. 55.
9. Kinsley, *The Goddesses' Mirror,* pp. 56–57.
10. Rev. 1:6; 5:10.
11. Carl Olson, "Sri Lakshmi and Radha: The Obsequious Wife and the Lustful Lover," in *The Book of the Goddess Past and Present: An Introduction to Her Religion,* Carl Olson, ed. (New York: Crossroad Publishing Company, 1983), p. 136.
12. Mahabharata 9.18.14, cited by Olson, "Sri Lakshmi and Radha," p. 136.
13. Kinsley, *The Goddesses' Mirror,* p. 58.
14. Ra was the ancient Egyptian sun-god, the official god of the pharaohs. The Egyptian pharaohs were looked upon as both the son of Ra and Ra himself incarnate. In his March 5, 1967, *Pearl of Wisdom,* Lord Maitreya defined the power of Ra as "the power of the Son of God, the power of Light itself" (*Pearls of Wisdom,* vol. 25, no. 10). In the days of Atlantis,

Rai was a title used for the emperor or monarch. Tau is the twenty-second and final letter of the Hebrew alphabet ("t" or "th"); it signifies "cross." In the film *A Mystical Journey through the Hebrew Alphabet,* Dr. Edward Hoffman explains: "[The letter Tau] symbolizes that our universe is marked by cycles in all things and the ultimate end of this human cycle in joyful, complete redemption. Tau begins the word *Torah,* an infinite realm, and also the word *tikkun,* our soul's task or mission here on earth." As noted in *The Universal Jewish Encyclopedia:* "The written word was always regarded as sacred, particularly by the Jews. . . . Abraham knew the secrets of the wisdom of the alphabet. God tied the twenty-two letters to his tongue and revealed to him all the mysteries of the universe" (s.v. "Alphabet in Mysticism"). The word Tao, which literally means "Way," is the animating principle of life that sustains all creation and is in all creation. According to the teachings of Taoism, it is the transcendental First Cause, the Absolute, the Ultimate Reality.

15. Kinsley, *The Goddesses' Mirror,* p. 57.
16. Ibid.
17. Adrian Snodgrass, *The Symbolism of the Stupa* (Ithaca, N.Y.: Cornell Southeast Asia Program, 1985), p. 317.
18. Lakshmi-tantra 50.110, quoted in Kinsley, *The Goddesses' Mirror,* p. 66.

CHAPTER 14 • We Do Work!

The dictations of Sarasvati and Lakshmi were the culminating events of an evening devoted to the Divine Mother. The Messenger began the evening by delivering the major portion of her lecture "The Worship of the Goddess—The Path of the Divine Mother." She gave the concluding section—"The Corona of Sarasvati and Lakshmi"—prior to the dictations.

1. For more on Shiva's consorts—Durga, Kali and Parvati—see ch. 6.
2. This could be a reference to the fifth bija mantra to the feminine deities —*Aim Hrim Klim Chamundaye Viche* (see ch. 13). This mantra is known as the Navarna Mantra and, according to one translation, means "Praise be to Sarasvati, Lakshmi, Kali, to Durga: Shattering the knot of ignorance that binds my heart, release me!"

CHAPTER 16 • You Must Rise!

The Messenger delivered her lecture "The Buddhic Essence" on July 3. This lecture is published in the book *The Buddhic Essence: Ten Stages to Becoming a Buddha.* In preparation for the dictation, the Messenger and congregation sang to Lord Gautama and meditated on the image of the Buddha superimposed upon scenes from the Inner Retreat.

1. Tushita heaven is the abode of Lord Maitreya where he tutors his bodhisattvas. It is on the twelfth plane of the etheric octave. See 1984 *Pearls of Wisdom,* Book I, Introduction I, pp. *20, 57, 60–62, 64,* and *Pearls of Wisdom,* vol. 33, no. 1.
2. Western Shamballa. On April 18, 1981, Gautama Buddha announced "the arcing of the flame of Shamballa to the Inner Retreat as the Western abode of the Buddhas and the Bodhisattvas and the Bodhisattvas-to-be who are the devotees of the Mother Light." Shamballa is the ancient retreat of the Lord of the World. It was first established for Sanat Kumara when he came to earth from his home star Venus to keep the flame of Life for earth's evolutions. Shamballa was originally a physical retreat built on an island in the Gobi Sea. It is now in the etheric plane over what has become the Gobi Desert. The Western Shamballa is an extension of the Shamballa of the East and is located in the etheric plane over the Heart of the Inner Retreat at the Royal Teton Ranch. It is the Lord of the World's retreat in the West. The office of Lord of the World is currently held by Gautama Buddha. As Lord of the World, Gautama Buddha presides at both the Eastern and Western Shamballas. (See *Pearls of Wisdom,* vol. 24, no. 20, and vol. 32, no. 30.)
3. Jesus' ascension from Shamballa. See 1984 *Pearls of Wisdom,* Book I, Introduction I, p. *11.*
4. "No respecter of persons." Acts 10:34; Deut. 10:17; II Sam. 14:14; Rom. 2:11; Eph. 6:9; Col. 3:25; I Pet. 1:17.
5. Eph. 6:12.

CHAPTER 17 • To Restore the Christhood of America

1. Hymns, songs, mantras and decrees to the Holy Christ Self and threefold flame in the *Church Universal and Triumphant Book of Hymns and Songs* and *Prayers, Meditations and Dynamic Decrees for Personal and World Transformation:*

   hymn 29 "Introit to the Holy Christ Self"
   hymn 30 "Call to the Threefold Flame"
   hymn 31 "Christ, Light My Way!"
   hymn 32 "Light of the Threefold Flame"
   hymn 33 "O Mighty Threefold Flame of Life"
   song 34 "Balance the Threefold Flame in Me"
   hymn 35 "Holy Christ Flame"

hymn 36 "Keep My Flame Blazing"
song 37 "Deep in My Heart"
devotion 0.06 "O Mighty Threefold Flame of Life"
affirmation 0.07A "I AM the Light of the Heart"
decree 20.03 "Balance the Threefold Flame in Me"
mantra 30.01 "Keep My Flame Blazing"
invocation 30.02 "Introit to the Holy Christ Self"

2. See Gautama Buddha on "The Thoughtform of the Anchor," *Pearls of Wisdom,* vol. 35, no. 20.
3. As recorded in *The Forgotten Books of Eden,* the children of Jared were lured down the Holy Mountain of God by the sensual music of the children of Cain. Jared was a descendant of Seth, the son born to Adam and Eve after Cain slew Abel. See "Prologue on the Sons of Jared" (taken from the Second Book of Adam and Eve), in Elizabeth Clare Prophet, *Fallen Angels and the Origins of Evil.* A reading from the Second Book of Adam and Eve on the sons of Jared is included on the audio album *Enoch,* available from AscenedMasterLibrary.org.
4. I Kings 18:17–40.
5. Igor's vigil for Mother Russia. See Mark L. Prophet and Elizabeth Clare Prophet, *The Masters and Their Retreats,* s.v. "Igor."
6. "With God all things are possible." Matt. 19:26; Mark 10:27; Luke 18:27.
7. I John 4:1.
8. The fourth woe. See ch. 9.
9. Rev. 11:18.
10. Rev. 2:17.
11. *Siddhis* [Sanskrit, roughly translated as "perfect abilities"]: supernatural powers acquired through the practice of yoga. These include clairaudience, clairvoyance, the ability to read thoughts, knowledge of previous births, levitation, dominion over the elements, and the ability to make oneself invisible.
12. In Hindu tradition, Karttikeya is the god of war and commander-in-chief of the army of the gods. He is also known as Skanda, the son of Shiva—and as Kumara, "the holy youth." In the Chandogya Upanishad (7.26), Skanda is identified with the Vedic sage Sanat Kumara. According to Yogic teachings, he represents the power of chastity.

    Margaret and James Stutley write in *Harper's Dictionary of Hinduism* that he was born when Shiva, who, "having attained complete mastery of his instincts, applied his sexual energy to spiritual and intellectual ends." This is illustrated in the many legends that tell of Karttikeya being born motherless and from the seed of Shiva that fell into the Ganges.

Veronica Ions writes in *Hindu Mythology:* "There on the banks of the river arose a child as beautiful as the moon and as brilliant as the sun. This was Karttikeya. As he appeared on the bank of the Ganges the six Pleiades, daughters of six rajas, came to that spot to bathe. Each of them claimed the beautiful boy, and each wished to give him the breast; so Karttikeya acquired six mouths and was suckled by all of his foster-mothers."

Vasudeva Sarana Agravala explains this myth: "The power of the virile seed, preserved through penance and complete chastity, is called Skanda or Kumara. So long as, in the practice of yoga, complete control is not attained, Kumara is not born, and the mind is ever put in check by desires, that is, the gods are defeated by the demons."

Legends say that Karttikeya was born specifically to slay the demon Taraka, who symbolizes the lower mind, or ignorance. Karttikeya is often depicted holding a spear (which represents illumination) and riding on a peacock (which represents the ego). Karttikeya slays ignorance with his spear of illumination. According to one story, a demon whom Karttikeya defeated cried, "Your weapon has shattered my ego!" A. Parthasarathy writes in *Symbolism in Hinduism* that "the wielding of [his spear] of annihilation symbolizes the destruction of all negative tendencies which veil the Divine Self." In mystic tradition, Karttikeya is known as Guha (cave) because he lives in the cave of the heart.

(See Margaret and James Stutley, *Harper's Dictionary of Hinduism: Its Mythology, Folklore, Philosophy, Literature, and History* [New York: Harper and Row, 1977], p. 282 n. 3; Veronica Ions, *Indian Mythology* [London: Paul Hamlyn, 1967], p. 88; Vasudeva Śarana Agravala, *Kalyana,* Śiva anka, 1937, p. 501, quoted in Alain Daniélou, *The Gods of India: Hindu Polytheism* [New York: Inner Traditions International, 1985], p. 299; and A. Parthasarathy, "Subramanya-Karthikeya," in R. S. Nathan, comp., *Symbolism in Hinduism,* 2d. ed. [Bombay: Central Chinmaya Mission Trust, 1989], p. 151.)

CHAPTER 18 • The Crown Jewel of Peace

1. Rom. 7:15–25.
2. Matt. 11:28.
3. Matt. 8:12; 22:13; 25:30.

CHAPTER 19 • For the Victory!

1. Earthquakes. See *Pearls of Wisdom,* vol. 35, no. 28.
2. Portia stepping forth from the planes of nirvana. See the "Goddess of Justice's Discourse," April 9, 1939, in *The Voice of the I AM,* May 1939 (Los Angeles: Saint Germain Press), pp. 32–41. See also *The Masters and Their Retreats,* s.v. "Portia."
3. "Fight the good fight." I Tim. 6:12; II Tim. 4:7.

CHAPTER 20 • Play to Win!

1. Kali Yuga: Sanskrit term in Hindu philosophy for the "age of darkness." It is the last and worst of the four yugas, or world ages, comprising a cosmic cycle. It is characterized by strife, discord and moral deterioration. Most scholars agree that we are presently in a Kali Yuga that began in 3102 B.C. and that will have a duration of 432,000 years. Swami Sri Yukteswar, however, believes that this theory is based on an incorrect method of calculating the yugas. According to Sri Yukteswar, we are not presently in a Kali Yuga. In his book *The Holy Science,* he outlines an ancient method of calculation, based on astrological cycles, that makes the yugas much shorter. He says that scholars began miscalculating the yugas about 700 B.C. Sri Yukteswar sets the present age 292 years into the third yuga—the Dwapara Yuga, the age of rapid development in all departments of knowledge. See Swami Sri Yukteswar, *The Holy Science,* 7th ed. (Los Angeles: Self-Realization Fellowship, 1977), pp. x–xxi.
2. See ch. 2, n. 11.
3. The four seasons correspond to the four quadrants of the Cosmic Clock. In winter we receive the initiations of the etheric quadrant; in spring, the initiations of the mental quadrant; in summer, the initiations of the emotional quadrant; and in autumn, the initiations of the physical quadrant. See Elizabeth Clare Prophet, *Predict Your Future: Understand the Cycles of the Cosmic Clock.*
4. Ps. 24:1; I Cor. 10:26, 28.

CHAPTER 21 • "Meet Us Halfway!"

In conjunction with your study of this dictation, the Messenger recommends that you read the book *Vials of the Seven Last Plagues: Prophecies by the Seven Archangels.*

1. The following pieces are selected from the music played at *FREEDOM 1992.* (Album titles are in bold. Each album listed is recommended in its entirety.)

- Adagio from Concerto in A Minor, Op. 16, by Grieg. ***The Rubinstein Collection: Tchaikovsky, Concerto No. 1; Grieg, Concerto in A Minor,*** performed by Arthur Rubinstein, RCA.
- Poco sostenuto—Vivace from Symphony No. 7 in A Major by Beethoven. ***Beethoven: 9 Symphonien,*** performed by the Berliner Philharmoniker, conducted by Herbert von Karajan, Deutsche Grammophon.
- "Raga Jhinjhoti" (flute version). ***Yugal Bundi,*** performed by Shivkumar Sharma and Hariprasad Chaurasia, Ravi Shankar Music Circle.
- "Gat in Jhap Taal and Teen Taal" from *Raga Gorakh Kalyan.* ***Hypnotic Santoor,*** performed by Shivkumar Sharma, Chhanda Dhara.
- Toccata and Fugue in D Minor, BWV 565, by J. S. Bach. ***Bach: Great Organ Favorites,*** performed by E. Power Biggs, CBS Records Masterworks.
- "Sanctus" from *St. Cecilia Mass,* by Gounod. ***Gounod: Messe Solennelle de Sainte Cécile,*** EMI.
- "Worthy Is the Lamb That Was Slain" from the *Messiah,* by Handel. ***Handel: Messiah—A Sacred Oratorio: Highlights,*** performed by the Academy of Ancient Music, directed by Christopher Hogwood, Decca Record Company.

2. The fourth woe. See ch. 9.

3. As recorded by Matthew, in the hour of the crucifixion of Jesus "the veil of the temple was rent in twain from the top to the bottom; and the earth did quake, and the rocks rent; and the graves were opened" (Matt. 27:50–54). This is an example of the cataclysm that can result when there is a change in status of a Son of God in the earth.

4. The Sons the Solitude were an ancient Brotherhood of advanced adepts; the highest initiates on Atlantis, who were celibate, lived without families and often apart from civilization. The Sons of the Solitude attained their mastery through years of training in many lifetimes. Examples of the Sons of the Solitude include Abraham, Melchizedek, Jesus Christ, John the Baptist, and Rai Ernon of Suern. See *Pearls of Wisdom*, vol. 34 no. 60; and Phylos the Tibetan, *A Dweller on Two Planets*, pp. 80–81, 136–38, 157–62, 199–200 in paperback (Harper and Row, 1974); or pp. 83, 141–43, 162–67, 206 in hardbound (Borden Publishing Co., 1952).

5. Eph. 6:11–17.

6. Ps. 82:6; John 10:34.

CHAPTER 22 • "There Must Be a Commitment!"

1. Djwal Kul's Breathing Exercise, including the "Call to the Fire Breath," is printed as decree 40.09 in *Prayers, Meditations, and Dynamic Decrees for Personal and World Transformation.* See also Kuthumi and Djwal Kul, *The Human Aura,* pp. 33–34, 139–48. *Pranayama* [Sanskrit, literally "control of prana"] is the control of the vital energy through the practice of breathing exercises. Keepers of the Flame are protected under the sponsorship of Saint Germain when they practice these exercises for the purification, protection and strengthening of the chakras.
2. The judgment of the cigarette industry. See Archangel Jophiel, September 9, 1963, in *Pearls of Wisdom,* vol. 25 no. 46. As a result of Jophiel's dictation, cigarette smoking came under governmental scrutiny. On January 11, 1964, the Public Health Service released its report that linked cigarette smoking to cancer. This was followed by the U.S. Surgeon General Luther Terry's official statement that smoking is hazardous to human health. Federal legislation was passed in 1965 that required all cigarette packages sold after January 1, 1966, to carry the label "Warning: The Surgeon General Has Determined That Cigarette Smoking Is Dangerous to Your Health." Beginning January 1, 1971, tobacco ads were banned from television.

CHAPTER 23 • The Purging of the Blood

1. "A house divided against itself shall not stand." Matt. 12:25; Mark 3:24, 25; Luke 11:17.
2. This is a spiritual, not a physical, initiation.
3. "Without shedding of blood is no remission." Heb. 9:22; Matt. 26:28.

CHAPTER 24 • Let There Be the Assimilation

1. Serapis Bey, *Dossier on the Ascension.*

CHAPTER 25 • The Sword of the Fifth Ray Descends

At the request of Archangel Raphael and Mother Mary, the congregation sang hymn 303, "Beloved Raphael and Mary," in preparation for the dictation. The Messenger instructed the congregation to accept the Electronic Presence of Archangel Raphael and Mother Mary over them as they sang, "as a forcefield through which they could convey what they wished to convey." Following hymn 303, the congregation sang hymn 292, "Beloved Raphael," and hymn 91, "The Magnificat."

1. Healing Matrix and Healing Thoughtform. The dispensation of the Healing Thoughtform was announced by Archangel Raphael on March 28, 1964. This thoughtform is composed of three concentric spheres: white in the center, then sapphire-blue and emerald-green sacred fire. As described by Archangel Raphael, the white fire core is "surrounded . . . by a mighty, tangible blue sheath of light" which "denotes the will of God, . . . the manifest perfection for all mankind. The mighty sheath of green, vibrating and quivering around all, is the substance of the healing qualification for the earth and for the evolutions thereof."

    The thoughtform is scientifically formulated to bring spiritual and physical healing and to restore the soul's inner blueprint. It can be visualized over a specific organ or superimposed upon and penetrating every atom, cell and electron of the four lower bodies. The Messenger has taught that the white-fire center is for purification and restores the balance of Alpha and Omega; the blue sphere magnetizes and restores the inner blueprint; and the outer emerald sphere brings the continuous flow of healing and restores life. See Archangel Raphael, "The Healing Thoughtform: The Crystalline Star of Understanding," in *Pearls of Wisdom,* vol. 25, no. 49; Mark L. Prophet and Elizabeth Clare Prophet, "My Visualization for the Healing Thoughtform," in *The Science of the Spoken Word,* with color illustration, pp. 144–48; and "The Healing Thoughtform: The Perfect Picture of the Divine Design," decree 50.04A in *Prayers, Meditations and Dynamic Decrees for Personal and World Transformation.*

    On June 29, 1988, Archangel Raphael announced the dispensation of the Healing Matrix of the crystal electrode of the Fifth Ray of Elohim imbedded in the psyche of the planet. Archangel Raphael said: "The intensity and the depth of the positioning of this crystal, beloved, is truly for the creating of a spiral that does turn around the disintegration spirals that have affected the Lightbearers beyond their control. Thus, wherever hearts provide a correspondent spiral of intensity, there the action of this focus shall serve to multiply, to strengthen and to create within the individual that turning around whereby the spiral of wholeness can and shall displace spirals of disintegration." See Archangel Raphael, "A Healing Matrix: The Crystal of the Fifth Ray of Elohim," *Pearls of Wisdom,* vol. 31, no. 56.

2. The Mother as the Word in the Beginning. John 1:1 reads "In the beginning was the Word, and the Word was with God, and the Word was God." This verse parallels the Hindu teachings on the cosmic Principle and Person of *Vac* (pronounced Vwahk; meaning literally speech, word, voice, talk, or language) as recorded in the Vedas, the earliest scriptures of Hinduism, probably composed c. 1500–1000 B.C.

The Hindu text Taittirya Brahmaa (Brahmaas are commentaries on the Vedas) says that "the Word, imperishable, is the Firstborn of Truth, mother of the Veda and hub of immortality." Vac is called "the mother" of the Vedas because it is believed that Brahma revealed them through her power.

The Taya Maha Brahmaa teaches, "This, [in the beginning], was only the Lord of the universe. His Word was with him. This Word was his second. He contemplated. He said, 'I will deliver this Word so that she will produce and bring into being all this world'" (XX, 14, 2).

Scholar John Woodroffe (pen name, Arthur Avalon) quotes John 1:1 and says: "These are the very words of Veda. *Prajapatir vai idam ast:* In the beginning was Brahman. *Tasya vag dvitya ast;* with whom was Vak or the Word (She is spoken of as second to Him because She is first potentially in, and then as Shakti issues from Him); *Vag vai paramam Brahma;* and the word is Brahman. Vak is thus a Shakti or Power of the Brahman. . . . This Shakti which was in Him is at the creation with Him, and evolves into the form of the Universe whilst still remaining what It is—the Supreme Shakti" who is "one with Brahman" (*The Garland of Letters* [Pondicherry, India: Ganesh & Co., n.d.], pp. 4–5).

Brahman is the Creator—the ultimate Reality, the Absolute. *Shakti* is a Sanskrit term meaning energy, power, or force. The Shakti is that point of the Feminine Principle who releases the potential of God from Spirit to Matter. As Shakti, the Divine Mother is therefore the dynamic, creative force of the universe—the manifest power of her masculine counterpart.

Hindu texts refer to Vac as the wife or consort of the Creator "who contains within herself all worlds." Sarasvati, the consort of Brahma and goddess of language, speech, wisdom and art, is identified with Vac in the Mahabharata and later Hindu tradition. Quoting the Brahmaas, author Raimundo Panikkar writes that Vac "is truly 'the womb of the universe.' For 'by that Word of his, by that self, he created all this, whatever there is.'"

Panikkar also notes that "*Vac* was before all creation, preexisting before any being came to be. . . . *Vac* is the life-giving principle within all beings. . . . She has a feminine characteristic of complementarity, a mediatorial role, and a certain feminine docility and obedience. She needs always to be uttered, by men, by Gods, or by the Creator himself. . . . [The Vedic Word] is ultimately as important as Brahman and, in a way that has to be properly understood, it is Brahman itself" (*The Vedic Experience Mantramañjari* [Los Angeles: University of California Press, 1977], pp. 106, 96, 107, 89).

CHAPTER 26 • The Hour of Justice Is Come

1. Martian misqualifications. The Ascended Masters teach that Mars in its true state is the planet that represents the Divine Mother and the base-of-the-spine chakra *(mūlādhāra).* The Messenger has described Mars as "the white sphere of intense fiery energy of the Divine Mother." Long ago, the evolutions of Mars took that pure white light of the Mother and perverted it in war and misuses of the sacred fire. Through the misuse of free will and the base-of-the-spine chakra, they perverted the Mother Light in what we call the "Martian misqualifications." These misqualifications can manifest through any of the chakras but specifically relate to the misuse of the Mother Light in the base-of-the-spine chakra. They include: aggression, anger, arrogance, argumentation, accusation, agitation, apathy, atheism, annihilation, aggravation, aggressive mental suggestion; criticism, condemnation and judgment; malicious, ignorant, sympathetic and delicious animal magnetism; anti-Americanism, anti-Father, anti-Mother, anti-Christ and anti-Holy Spirit manifestations in the four quadrants of Matter. The fact that so many of these misqualifications begin with the letter *A* indicates that they are also a perversion of the Light of the Father, Alpha. The Messenger has explained that "family mesmerism" is another manifestation of Martian energies. It is human attachment based on blood ties rather than spiritual ties. War and other violent conflicts also come through the vibration and aura of Mars. The ultimate Martian misqualification is the creation of mechanization man, the godless creation (see the Great Divine Director, *The Mechanization Concept, Pearls of Wisdom,* vol. 8, nos. 3–26; also published as *The Soulless One*). Astrologers see Mars as the planet of action based on desire. The Messenger has explained: "Mars triggers energy that brings action, but whatever your desires are, that is where your energy will go and that is the type of action you will engage in." She teaches that by hitching our desires to the star of our Mighty I AM Presence, we can ride and subdue Mars—we can "ride the bull" and take advantage of the true creative fires of Mars, the pure white fire of the Divine Mother. She has counseled us that each time we see a Mars configuration in our own astrology, we must determine to have a "Martian victory" in order to not be overcome by the perversions. Through mastering the Martian energies, we can gain our victory in the white fire of the Mother.
2. "Withdraw the Light from the seed of the wicked." See: Alpha, April 17, 1981, in *Pearls of Wisdom,* vol. 24, no. 19; Helios, July 4, 1984, in vol. 27, no. 43B; "A Proclamation" by Alpha in Gautama Buddha, May

13, 1987, in vol. 30, no. 24; Alpha, July 5, 1987, in vol. 30, no. 38; Lady Master Venus, October 9, 1989, in vol. 32, no. 59; Gautama Buddha, May 9, 1990, in vol. 33, no. 17; Alpha, July 1, 1992, ch. 9 of this volume.

3. See decrees 63.00, 63.01, and 63.02 in *Prayers, Meditations and Dynamic Decrees for Personal and World Transformation.*

CHAPTER 28 • Defeat the Negatives

1. Lanello refers here to the Buddhist tale about the three men and the wall. As the story goes, the first man boosts the second one up to see what is going on on the other side of the wall. After surveying the scene, he goes into bliss and climbs over the wall. The third man is then boosted up and he too climbs over. The one remaining says to himself: "Well, I am going to find out what's going on on the other side of that wall!" He then climbs up and sees the souls of beings who are liberated. But instead of joining them, he forgoes his own liberation and climbs back down to tell the world of his discovery. See also Sanat Kumara and Lady Master Venus, *Pearls of Wisdom,* vol. 34, no. 7.
2. "Little piglets in the mud." In her lecture "The Inner Path of Hinduism," delivered June 29, 1992, the Messenger told the story of the God Indra embodying as a hog in order to better understand the dilemma of mortal creatures. He becomes enmeshed in the pleasures of his life with his piglet children. For the full story, see "When Indra Became a Hog," in Swami Jyotir Maya Nanda, *Yoga Stories and Parables* (Miami: Swami Lalitananda, 1976), pp. 108, 110.
3. John 12:32.
4. Matt. 4:9; Luke 4:6, 7.
5. Rev. 4; 5:11–14; 7:9–17; 14:1–5; 19:4–6; 20:11.

432 pp. ISBN 978-0-922729-27-2

Reincarnation

The Missing Link in Christianity

BY ELIZABETH CLARE PROPHET

"This is an extremely important book, a book providing profound insight and truth, a book which will open minds and remove fears."

—Brian Weiss, M.D., author of *Many Lives, Many Masters*

"Imaginative and provocative. . . . Elizabeth Clare Prophet's assertion that not only mystical Gnostics but also a Jewish wisdom teacher like Jesus taught reincarnation is sure to rattle your karmic chain."

—Marvin Meyer, author of *The Gospel of Thomas: The Hidden Sayings of Jesus*

This groundbreaking work makes the case that Jesus taught reincarnation and traces the history of reincarnation in Christianity—from Jesus and early Christians through Church councils and the persecution of so-called heretics. Using the latest scholarship and evidence from the Dead Sea Scrolls and Gnostic texts, it also argues persuasively that Jesus was a mystic who taught that our destiny is to unite with the God within. Your view of Jesus—and of Christianity—will never be the same.

312 pp ISBN 978-0-922729-35-7

Kabbalah

Key to Your Inner Power

BY ELIZABETH CLARE PROPHET

"A masterpiece. The rich tradition of the Kabbalah comes to life in a language that is accessible even to those unfamiliar with this ancient and classic tradition."

—Caroline Myss, Ph.D.,
New York Times bestselling author of *Anatomy of the Spirit*

"A clear and eloquent presentation of the Kabbalah, at once spiritual and practical."

—Daniel C. Matt, author of *The Essential Kabbalah*

Mystics are adventurers of the spirit who dare to push beyond the boundaries of orthodox tradition to pursue a common goal—the direct experience of God. *Kabbalah: Key to Your Inner Power* explores the once-secret Jewish mystical tradition known as Kabbalah.

With intriguing new perspectives, it shows how we can use Kabbalah's extraordinary revelations about the creation of the universe, our relationship to God and our purpose in life to unlock our own spiritual power. It brings to life the path of the Jewish mystics—their joys and ecstasies, their sacred visions, and their practical techniques for experiencing the sacred in everyday life.

160 pp ISBN 978-1-932890-16-7

The Buddhic Essence

Ten Stages to Becoming a Buddha

BY ELIZABETH CLARE PROPHET

We all have the seed or 'essence' of Buddha within us, and because we do we have the potential to become a Buddha. In *The Buddhic Essence: Ten Stages to Becoming a Buddha,* Elizabeth Clare Prophet gently traces upon the heart the pathway that can lead to Buddhahood. She does so in a way that we can relate to the different stages and also see them as steps that we can accomplish in our daily lives—we might recognize a stage as one we are passing through or one that a friend has recently passed through.

ABOUT THE SUMMIT LIGHTHOUSE

The Summit Lighthouse is an internationally recognized spiritual center for the advancement of inner awakening. Our international organization is a global family that is inspired, guided, and sponsored by those known as the ascended masters.

The ascended masters are the most beloved and trusted transcendent beings guiding our planet's material and spiritual evolution. Most of the world's religions are currently based on the revelations of one or more of these masters before their ascension. We openly embrace spiritual seekers from all paths of Light including the mystical traditions of the world's religions.

The ascended masters and their messengers have given us over fifteen thousand hours of invaluable inner wisdom and insightful instruction, and they have provided the means for our direct initiation into higher consciousness.

For the ascended masters . . . no subject is off limits! Their teachings contain amazing truths and awesome answers on spirituality, alchemy, astrology, sacred geometry, spiritual science, karma, reincarnation, ascension, archangels (and fallen angels), and even those issues that are considered taboo or "out of this world."

PRIMARY GOALS OF THE TEACHINGS OF THE ASCENDED MASTERS

The ascended masters challenge us daily to be bold, to dare to be who we truly are, and to face adversity with courage, patience, perseverance, honesty, integrity, inner love, discipline, and discernment—all for a greater sense of inner peace, fearlessness, stillness and silence, harmony, self-mastery, compassion, and wisdom.

These teachings help our souls get back to the origin of their individualized inner source of True Self Love—the Higher Self, or I AM Presence. Our point of contact with our Higher Self is the "Spark of Life" or "Sacred Fire of the Heart," the place where our consciousness expresses its true divine nature of unconditional love and happiness, universal oneness, and an authentic desire to serve others.

HOW OUR TEACHINGS CAME INTO BEING

Our teachings were all released through highly trained and trusted messengers, Mark L. Prophet and Elizabeth Clare Prophet. Mark was contacted by the Ascended Master El Morya at the age of eighteen and received training from him for many years before he was instructed to establish The Summit Lighthouse in 1958 in Washington, D.C.

With his ascension in 1973, Mark passed the torch for the mission to his gifted wife, Elizabeth Clare Prophet, who continued her service until her retirement in 1999.

The dictations of the ascended masters were regularly given in public. The ascended masters also inspired thousands of lectures delivered by the messengers. The content of the dictations are, by most human standards, beyond the mind's ability to construct in real time. They carry very powerful frequencies of light, awakening us to the highest truths we've ever experienced.

We leave it up to you to decide the value for yourself.

MOVING TOWARD YOUR VICTORY

No matter what path of light you are on, spiritual freedom is attained using tools that have been passed down in wisdom teachings through the millennia: meditation, selfless service, devotional music, prayer, mantra, and the science of the spoken Word. The masters bring an accelerated understanding of these principles, especially suited for the challenges of the modern world, including dynamic decree work and the use of the violet flame.

NEXT STEPS

We are genuinely excited to meet you on the path . . . and hope you are too. We extend a warm welcome from everyone at The Summit Lighthouse, and we invite you to explore the teachings of the ascended masters at our website. Check out our free online lessons and hundreds of articles on a wide range of spiritual subjects. Browse through our online bookstore. And if you would rather talk to someone in person, please feel free to contact us today!

Elizabeth Clare Prophet is a world-renowned author, spiritual teacher, and pioneer in practical spirituality. Her groundbreaking books have been published in more than thirty languages and over three million copies have been sold worldwide.

Among her best-selling titles are *The Human Aura; The Science of the Spoken Word; Your Seven Energy Centers; The Lost Years of Jesus; The Art of Practical Spirituality;* and her best-selling Pocket Guides to Practical Spirituality series.

The Summit Lighthouse®
63 Summit Way
Gardiner, Montana 59030 USA

1-800-245-5445 / 406-848-9500

Se habla español.

info@SummitUniversityPress.com
SummitLighthouse.org

Lightning Source UK Ltd.
Milton Keynes UK
UKHW022001051022
410007UK00019B/154

9 781609 884185